D1607687

THEOCRACY AND TOLERATION

CAMBRIDGE
UNIVERSITY PRESS
LONDON: BENTLEY HOUSE
NEW YORK · TORONTO
BOMBAY · CALCUTTA · MADRAS
Macmillan

TOKYO
Maruzen Company Ltd

THEOCRACY AND TOLERATION

A STUDY OF THE
DISPUTES IN DUTCH CALVINISM
FROM 1600 TO 1650

BY

DOUGLAS NOBBS, M.A.

*Lecturer in Political Science in
the University of Edinburgh; Sometime Scholar
and Fellow of St John's College
Cambridge*

CAMBRIDGE
AT THE UNIVERSITY PRESS

1938

PRINTED IN GREAT BRITAIN

CONTENTS

Chapter V. THE ERASTIAN CRITICISM   *page* 213

INTRODUCTION

ALTHOUGH the relation of church and state was debated throughout the seventeenth century in the Netherlands, the two controversies in the first half were the most significant, because both began as disputes in the Calvinist church itself. By the turn of the century, Calvinist theory had been clearly elaborated in favour of a church independent of political interference, while its critics adopted a more secular argument. These early controversies fell naturally into two groups in which there was a close relationship between the writings.

The first of these controversies arose out of the Arminian challenge in the Calvinist church, and lasted from 1609 to 1618, when the Synod of Dort expelled the Arminians from the church and Maurice the Stadholder drove the leaders out of the Netherlands. The first major writing was the *Waerschouwinghe* of Franciscus Gomarus, professor at Leiden and the enemy of Arminius. In 1610 there followed the *Tractaet* of Uytenbogaert, a work of great bitterness to the orthodox party, who replied to it through the works of Junius, Acronius and Walaeus. The Arminians were strongly supported by Grotius, but their attitude was considerably modified by Episcopius.

The second controversy began in 1637 when Vedelius, a foreigner but a zealous defender of the orthodox party against the Arminians, taught at Deventer a theory of the Christian magistracy which was alien to the Calvinist tradition since 1618. Therefore, he was answered by Triglandius and Apollonius. Voetius had already taught a doctrine of the church which was hostile to the position of Vedelius, though not directed against Vedelius himself, and this was collected in his greatest work published much later. Against Apollonius, there appeared a book by Salmasius, which ushered in a separate and worthless controversy fought out in many pamphlets of no originality. Voetius was attacked by Du Moulin who, though not directly connected with the Netherlands, was strongly influenced by the

Dutch controversy and was a self-constituted champion of Erastian theories against Dutch, Scottish and French Calvinism. The relations of church and state had been an acute problem in the Netherlands from the beginning of the Calvinist church,[1] partly because the Calvinists were a minority and many of the ruling classes were not Calvinists, partly because the church was organised before the States were free to control it, and partly because of doctrinal disputes which the States attempted to moderate. The very meaning of the Reformation was at issue; to the Calvinists it meant a rigid conformity to creeds, to others it meant hostility to sacramentalism and dogmatism. Calvinism had to combat a native and strongly humanistic movement, critical of Roman sacramentalism, hostile to dogmatic confessionalism, distrustful of any binding authority in the church save that of the Bible, evangelical and tolerant. The composition and character of the church was in doubt.

The rapid growth of the Calvinist church, identified with the national struggle against Spain, led to a development of its organisation and a consciousness of its unity and strength, marked by an increasing insistence upon the necessity of subscribing to a confession and submitting to the Presbyterian polity. Even before 1600, there were isolated rebels, and a conflict of church and state. It was, however, Arminius[2] who provoked the great struggle in the church against Calvinist confessionalism, and in consequence the greatest conflict between church and state in the Netherlands. There was a direct connection between the confessional dispute and the hostility of church and state, and it was that connection which made the Calvinist church defy the state. The claim of the church to impose a confession was a claim to independence at a time when national unity was most desirable.

The Arminians appealed to the States of Holland to protect them from this confessional demand. They claimed to recognise no authority but the Bible; they denied that the problem of predestination had been clearly answered in the Bible, and,

---

[1] See Knappert, *Geschiedenis der Nederlandsche Hervormde Kerk*; Reitsma, *Geschiedenis van de Hervorming, etc.*; Sepp, *Het Godgeleerd Onderwijs, etc.*; Visser, *Kerk en Staat*; and Rogge, *Johannes Wtenbogaert en zijn Tijd* (cited as *Joh. Uyt.*).

[2] See especially Harrison, *The Beginnings of Arminianism, passim.*

moreover, argued that it was not fundamental to salvation. The Calvinists rejected both contentions, and demanded a synod to decide the dispute. When the states insisted upon certain conditions for holding a synod, the Calvinists rejected them as incompatible with the power of the church to determine its own faith. The issue had become a question of freedom or authority in the church, and of freedom or authority in the relations of church and state.

The States attempted the part of mediation, and for that purpose forbade the church in 1611 to censure Arminians or to reject Arminian ordinands solely because of their adherence to Arminian principles. In 1614 the States decreed that the Arminian doctrine of predestination was sufficient for salvation, and that academic speculations were not to be pursued in the pulpits. It was this political oppression which was the strength of the orthodox party, particularly as a new generation had grown up during the war with Spain. Nevertheless, the orthodox themselves had adopted an extreme position, and from 1615 organised illegal churches. The threatened civil war was averted only by the unconstitutional action of the Stadholder, who dispossessed Arminian rulers in favour of the orthodox. He summoned and controlled the Synod of Dort which condemned the Arminians, and it was not until his death in 1625 that the Arminians were able to return, because his successor, Frederick Henry, refused to use the military to support orthodox aims, and because the constitution of the Netherlands enabled a few cities to thwart the will of the majority.

Although after 1625 the Arminians were allowed to establish a church upon principles of fraternity and toleration instead of authority and rigid creeds,[1] the Calvinist church became the nationally recognised, though not established, church of the Netherlands. It was reorganised upon the basis of doctrinal discipline;[2] the Bible was translated; social habits were reformed; and education stimulated and regulated. The church after 1618 had achieved much in its ideal of regulating society by Calvinist

[1] Cf. Tideman, *De Stichting der Remonstrantsche Broederschap.*
[2] Cf. Honders, *Andreas Rivetus,* chs. ii–v; Ter Haar, *Jacobus Trigland,* 97–121; Wijngaarden, *Antonius Walaeus,* 58–94.

principles, but by the middle of the century the supremacy of orthodoxy was challenged by Cartesian methods of thought and Coccejus' comparative study of the Bible. The church took to the defensive but failed to turn the secular stream.

The conflict between church and state was not limited to the orthodox church and too liberal governors, for even before 1618 there were disputes between the church and strongly Calvinist rulers, as in Zeeland, Friesland and Groningen.[1] The political control of the church in Zeeland reduced it to a more servile condition than in any other province. The constitution of the church was given to it by the ruler, few synods were sanctioned and political deputies had to be admitted. Moreover, ministers were appointed by a mixed commission representing the ecclesiastical council and the magistracy. In Groningen, the appointment of ministers had to be approved by the state. In Friesland, the political activities of the church were severely censured and its activity strictly controlled. The tendency to theocracy was resisted by even orthodox rulers. The Thirty-Sixth Article of the Confession gave to the ruler a duty to serve the church, and this was developed in the Groningen ordinance of 1601, intended to exclude all but Calvinists from the state and to disinherit all but Calvinist children as illegitimate.[2] A synod at Sneek in 1587 declared that only one religion was to be allowed and all heretics were to be expelled, since it was better to reduce the state to a desert than to suffer corruption with prosperity. But it may be admitted that these were exceptional and that in general the church showed a prudent respect for the limits of its own authority, and the independent sphere of the state.[3]

The Synod of Dort in 1618, the only national synod acknowledged by provinces and States, failed to settle the relationship of church and state upon Calvinist principles. Previous provincial and so-called national synods had formulated constitutions of the church which were not accepted by the ruling classes, which, in their turn, especially after Leicester's disastrous intrigue with the church in 1586 and the extreme ecclesiastical constitution formu-

---

[1] Rogge, *Joh. Uyt.* I, 194–197; Reitsma, 400, 406–410; Knappert, I, 69–70, 74–76.
[2] Visser, II, 132–139; Knappert, I, 56–57; Rogge, *Joh. Uyt.* I, 177, 180.
[3] Visser, II, 128.

lated by the synod at the Hague in that year, sought to impose upon the church a constitution framed to give an ultimate political power to the rulers. This attempt broke down in 1618, and the church tried to revive the constitution of 1586, which had modified the earlier independence by certain concessions to a "godly" ruler like Leicester, but which also vindicated the principle that the church was completely independent in deciding matters of doctrine.[1]

In 1618, the States allowed the synod to discuss the church-order only on condition that the rights of the different provinces were not attacked, and that patronage was not abolished. The States fixed the number of delegates to the synod, and sent deputies to keep doctrinal discussion within Scriptural limits. A compromise saved the communities from an abuse of patronage, but other appointments to the ministry were subject even more to the States. There was added to the Hague order the provision that all calls to the ministry were to be made after correspondence with the government of the locality, and omitted the limitation of the civil approbation to the civil conduct of the candidate. The civil power was acknowledged still further by the provision that the government might send two deputies to any church meeting so long as they were members of the church and sat only in an advisory capacity.

The answer of the Synod of Dort to the question whether the church was sovereign in its own sphere or whether the magistrates had a voice in the internal matters of the church was only an apparent solution. Utrecht, Gelderland and Overyssel accepted the Dort church-order after some modification; three of the quarters in Friesland rejected it and the church-order was abandoned, the Stadholder threatening to treat the frequent synods as disturbers of the peace. The attempt of Holland to revise the church-order in the interests of the government only led to the continuance of the customary usages, which left all but the direction of worship under the authority of the States. Zeeland adhered to its former order, seeing no need of a common order

---

[1] See, especially, Hooijer, *Oude Kerkordeningen*; Rogge, *Joh. Uyt.* I, 54–65, 111–125; Knappert, I, 59–70; Reitsma, 395–410; and Visser, II, ch. x.

when the churches were united in faith. The bid for a general constitution of the church had failed.

The policy of the governments toward the church after 1618 was in some ways even more oppressive than that of Oldenbarne-veldt.[1] They often acted arbitrarily to censure or dismiss hostile preachers, while their deputies in the classis threatened to turn it into a political bishopric. Events at Amsterdam, Gouda and in Holland showed quite clearly that the church was no more independent after 1618 than before, and that provided doctrine was not corrupted and that ecclesiastical forms were observed, the church accepted the inevitable. Political commissioners controlled church polity; the States of Holland interfered in doctrine, forbidding the South Holland synod to determine the Sabbath controversy, and determining the prayers and preaching upon the fast days which it commanded. Many consistories were so dependent that they did not allow sermons upon certain Biblical Books without political consent. While the doctrinal settlement of 1618 was not impugned, the church began to rely upon its own means to preserve the purity of its doctrine.

[1] Visser, II, ch. XI; cf. Ter Haar, 63–66, and Rogge, *Joh. Uyt.* III.

action of the church by his political power? Not only did the Contra-Remonstrants answer that the ruler was bound not to confirm such wrong decisions, but also insisted that the ruler was to bring the church back to the right way and to the right decision. His duty was to enforce the true faith of the Scriptures, and to prevent the possibility of false religions or the corruption of the true church. This duty was fulfilled only by accepting the responsibility of judging. But the Contra-Remonstrants also insisted that the ruler was not able to judge doctrinal disputes. His duty extended no further than providing that pure condition of the church by which the church itself was able to judge rightly. The ruler was to enforce this judgment. It was necessary for Contra-Remonstrant theory to secure the true interpretation of the Scriptures by a church which was fallible.

The second problem was the distinction between the church as a divine organisation and its human means. Not everything connected with the church was spiritual and determined in the Scriptures, for the church adapted itself to external circumstances and employed secular materials. By what principle was the function of the ministry to be separated from the merely human conditions of its execution? It was not enough to claim that the Scriptures and the Spirit of Christ present in His Church were the principles by which the two aspects of the church were distinguished, for, although this was true of the essential form of the church, neither distinguished the outward and local needs of the church from merely human means. The Scriptures did not determine the times, places and order of worship. How were these necessary conditions left to human discretion to be separated from such matters as finance which were undoubtedly secular? The same problem had another form. If it was necessary to separate spiritual and temporal in a way which destroyed the Roman interpretation of spiritual, upon what grounds were the Contra-Remonstrants to separate the outward organisation of the church from political organisation, and at the same time justify the regulation of the first by the church, and of the second by the state?

The final problem was the one most evident to the Contra-Remonstrants and the one which they undertook to solve. The accusation which Uytenbogaert had made against their theory was that it established the collaterality of church and state, and reverted to the papal theory of two societies, each with a supreme power over its members. The Contra-Remonstrants denied that theirs was a theory of collaterality and rejected the Roman system of collaterality as unchristian. If the issue was whether to obey God or the ruler, no sincere Contra-Remonstrant doubted the answer; but few Calvinists wanted the state to regard Calvinism as an anti-social movement which undermined established order and political sovereignty. Willingness to obey God was not to be interpreted as a principle of anarchy, which left problems of political obedience to the individual conscience. Still less did any Contra-Remonstrant desire to revive Catholic ecclesiasticism, and thereby to confuse once more the spiritual and the temporal.

The Contra-Remonstrants denied that the issue in a Christian state was whether to obey God or the ruler; it was whether the ruler who professed the true faith was to obey God or not. The affirmative answer ended the conflict between church and state; the negative answer simply renewed the problem of the relation between the true church and an unchristian ruler. Contra-Remonstrant theory was not a theory of church and state, but of church and ruler, and the problem which it met was very different from the problem of church and state. It was possible to consider church and state as distinct institutions, and the state as the supreme institution. The Christian ruler, however, was a member of the church and subject to its authority. Between the Christian ruler and the church, there was an intimate relation, which served in Contra-Remonstrant theory to set the state within the divine order and therefore in co-operation with the church. The Calvinists hated the consequences of and not the principle of cujus regio, ejus religio; for they did believe that the subjects were to accept the religion of their ruler, provided that he was a member of the true church.

The problem of collaterality raised the question of sovereignty, and the way by which the administrative autonomy of the church was to be reconciled with it. In denying the accusation, the Contra-Remonstrants had to deny that their theory limited or undermined political sovereignty. At the same time, they had to prevent any concession to the ruler which threatened ecclesiastical independence. To some extent, their answer rested upon the definition of collaterality; for they defined it as the equality of two powers of the same kind in the same sphere. Therefore they denied that theirs was a collateral system, since they set up two independent powers of totally different kinds and in two different spheres. The authority of the church was in religion and was a spiritual power; the sovereignty of the ruler governed external life by that coercion which was effective only upon the body. So long as each was active in its own sphere and faithfully observed the limits of its own function, there was no collateral authority and no possibility of conflict. The two powers were thus able to work for the same end and to supplement each other's means, without interfering in each other's function and office.

The Contra-Remonstrant theory[1] was developed in four major writings, although there were a large number of mediocre and partisan pamphlets without more than an immediate and passing value. Every instance of political oppression stimulated some new statement of ecclesiastical resentment, designed to win public support against the official policy of the States rather than to clarify the relations of church and state by expounding the principles underlying those relations. The argument of the four major writings was so much above the level of these pamphlets that it was obviously much more sympathetic to the principles of Uytenbogaert than the practice and manifestoes of the Contra-Remonstrant party suggested. The theoretical exposition of the orthodox case was much less uncompromising than the actual opposition to the government.

The first of these writings was the *Waerschouwinghe* of Franciscus Gomarus, the hotheaded and impetuous opponent of Arminius in the Leiden theological faculty. Gomarus had already expressed his own attitude and had acted upon his principles during his opposition to Arminius. But in 1609, Gomarus attacked the argument of a speech of Uytenbogaert before the States, by the publication of the *Waerschouwinghe*. Uytenbogaert

[1] See Rogge, *Johannes Uytenbogaert in zijn gevoelen aangaande de Magt der Overheden in Kerkelijke zaken* (cited as *Jaarboek*), I, 364–374, II, 76–79; and Visser, *Kerk en Staat*, II, ch. xv.

attempted to persuade Oldenbarneveldt to prevent its publication, having obtained some pages of it and realising the controversy which would follow. The appearance of the *Waerschouwinghe*
was followed in 1610 by Uytenbogaert's *Tractaet*, which roused
the orthodox because its argument destroyed the supremacy of
the church in matters of faith and offered a chance of toleration
to the Arminian party.

In the same year, two writings were published against the
Tractaet. In the first, the opinions of the great French Professor
at Leiden, Franciscus Junius, were drawn from his work against
Rome, the *Ecclesiasti*, published in 1581, and presented as the
Verclaringhe van twee vraghen, as if he had knowledge of the
events likely to occur after his death. The first question was "of
the agreement and difference of political and ecclesiastical
offices"; the second, "of the right of Magistrates in the visible
church". Uytenbogaert refused to reply to this book on the
ground that its argument in no way conflicted with his, and,
indeed, it has been pointed out[1] that the distinction of church and
state was developed least effectively by Junius.

The other writing was the *Nootwendich Vertooch* of Acronius,
which was welcomed by Uytenbogaert because it accepted so
much of his own principles. Nevertheless, there were fundamental differences which were the very points upon which
Uytenbogaert was most insistent. It may be questioned whether
Acronius' argument was very consistent. In no other writing
was there so much strain in reconciling two divergent lines of
argument.

In 1611, Uytenbogaert already knew that Walaeus was busy
upon a work dealing with the relation of the ruler and the ministry,
but this was not published until 1615. The *De Munere Pastorum*
gave to Contra-Remonstrant theory its classic expression, re-
vealing a moderation of tone and a judicious estimate of argument.
It acknowledged that Uytenbogaert had not been answered, but
instead of a formal refutation, Walaeus set out his own ideas,
which were somewhat different. It is worth noting that
Apollonius[2] doubted whether Walaeus represented the purer

---

[1] Visser, II, 348.
[2] Apollonius, *Jus Majestatis circa sacra*, I, 12, 17.

stream of Calvinist thought, and turned to the Scottish Calvinists as more orthodox.

Between these four writers there were some differences, arising, in most cases, from a different method of approach; but the essential principles were of the same character, and the ultimate solution was shared by all. Acronius and Walaeus alone attempted a more than partial treatment. The small size of the pamphlets by Gomarus and Junius prevented more than a superficial study, stating but not demonstrating the true theory. In Acronius and Walaeus, demonstration was emphasised particularly, but it tended to become a theological discussion of textual interpretations. Indeed, to these theologians, the true theory was a matter of Scriptural study, and, unlike the later Calvinist controversialists, primarily of the Old Testament.

The conditions which Contra-Remonstrant theory had to satisfy were reconciled largely by the conception of a fixed constitution ordained by God for the government of mankind,[1] and determining the means and methods of making that constitution effective among men of different times and places. This conception was the natural conclusion of the belief in one absolute body of truth, universally valid inasmuch as it expressed the ideal of God for the entire span of time. The object of this constitution was the absolute determination of the earthly means by which the Kingdom of God was to be achieved among men, and the collaboration of the different agencies sanctioned by God. The Calvinist had to discover within the Bible the eternal plan which established the organs and functions necessary for the fulfilment of God's Will, giving the one form proper to church and state, and the one relation between them compatible with the divine purpose controlling both. This conviction of a divine purpose underlying human life and revealed in the Scriptures prescribed the constitution as the divinely ordained arrangement of offices and functions, and, therefore, as the means of harmonising social relations under the sovereignty of God's Will. Not only was it impossible to consider that that constitution sanctioned the antagonism of church and state, but it was also obvious that God's

[1] Rogge, *Jaarboek*, II, 77; Visser, II, 352, 354, 360; *Noot. Vert.* ch. 5, and Junius, Question 1.

purpose demanded the co-ordination of means for the regulation of society according to His eternal plan.

Within this divine constitution, the spheres of church and state were allotted with precise respect for the Will of God. Individual and social aspects of life were both subject to the rule of law, embodying the one truth, and thereby subordinated to that co-ordinating force by which the means were made to work for the ultimate end. In admitting the supremacy of that law, the state ceased to be a humanly manufactured institution of human life because it was a necessary part of that order for which that law was prescribed. It was, therefore, set by its recognition of that law within a framework of duties and responsibilities which limited its discretion, directed its power and regulated its function.

The members of the state entered into a new capacity demanding willing acceptance of their appointed services to God's community on earth. The ruler, as head of the state, enjoyed the authority and power of a divine agent, and lost all moral, if not legal, claim to command if he contravened the laws of this divine agency. Loyalty to the ruler was loyalty to God so long as the sovereign power followed the divine will. But there was a difference between the duty of the ruler toward the state and toward the church. In civil matters, the architectonic power was granted a considerable discretion by God, and for the use and abuse of that discretion the ruler was responsible to God alone. In relation to the church, the ruler had no discretion, because his actions were defined by the Scriptures. Gomarus[1] had insisted that the ruler's power was always under God's Law, and therefore not unlimited and absolute; neither was his pleasure a fundamental rule, nor his will the law. He insisted, however, that subjects were to obey an oppressive and unjust ruler so long as they did not sin against God. In general, the Contra-Remonstrants were willing to acknowledge that sovereignty in secular matters was not defined so minutely and exactly as was the ruler's part in religion. The Scriptures were not a political code, although therein was the norm by which the end of the state was to be understood and its part in human life allotted.

[1] *Waerschouwinghe*, 14.

The Scriptures left no discretion to the church: its organisation, function and administration were narrowly defined. Its offices and institutions were sanctioned and created by God through His Law. Its ministers were the legates of God who stated in terms intelligible to mankind the divine commands. So long as they followed His Will they were endowed with the authority of God Himself, and directly empowered to undertake their function without human authority. It was not possible, therefore, for any human authority to violate this constitution without denying the legitimacy of that authority which it itself possessed and exercised.

The true sovereignty was with God, and under Him and on earth it was vested in this constitution. Neither the state nor the ruler, neither the church nor the ministers, nor even the Holy Community, held the sovereign power, but God in them. The great architectonic function which shaped the means to achieve the end of life, an end appointed by itself, was a supernatural force of which man was the instrument. The constitution embodied God's Will in an impersonal and practical formulary, and was the only means available to men of directing and co-ordinating their lives according to one purposive and final end. Thus, the powers of this world knew their allotted tasks and held to their own functions, in the faith that in obeying the law of God they served the divine end.

The collaterality of church and state ceased where and when this constitutional conception was accepted. It was no longer a question of reconciling the equal status and powers of two institutions within the same social framework, for society was united by the supremacy of the divine constitution. Church and state were no longer rivals for the direction of society, but co-ordinated parts of a whole which transcended both. The state's power was not undermined by the authority of the church, nor the spiritual function of the church corrupted by the action of the state so long as each adhered to the divine ordinance. Independence yielded to interdependence, and the unity of society was produced by the collaboration of two complementary functions working for the same purpose by a power peculiar to each in its own function and without effect in the function of the other. Neither the ministers nor the ruler were controlled by the other; nor were they independent of each other. Both were partners in the divine scheme.

Important as was the sanction and form of this constitution, it was still necessary to build up a content which should establish the independent authority of the church in spiritual matters. The conception of a divine order which gave a religious function to the ruler was used by Uytenbogaert, and to meet his argument it was necessary to interpret God's Will as giving to the church adequate powers to govern itself.

The first dictate of the constitution was the differentiation of institutions and specialisation of functions. Without denying the duty of the ruler to foster religion or his sole responsibility in purely political matters, the Contra-Remonstrants were deter-͟ed to prove the divine responsibility of the ministers for the government of the church and the regulation of religion. It was argued that God had instituted two types of protectors, inspectors and administrators of the church, the one armed with corporal power and the other with spiritual authority. It was concluded that the judgment of each type was distinct and supreme. The rulers of the spiritual realm were the ministers who sat in judgment, even over magistrates.

The differentiation of church and state was formulated in the vigorous antitheses made by Junius[1] and Acronius. First, Junius contrasted the authority in political matters which God had entrusted to men, and the "bare service and simple command" left to them in religious matters. God had never conceded to men the authority and power to determine those by their own judgments. Secondly, he contrasted the secular matter of the state and the sacred matter of the church. Thirdly, he argued that the political office existed to preserve "the civil fellowship of human things", while the clerical office was instituted for "the Holy community of Holy things". The civil office established no more than a sociability of a civil nature, whereas the clerical office created the greatest and wholly just community, holy in itself.

Acronius[2] was even more emphatic. The government of the church was by the spirit; that of the state by a civil law which only affected the motives of human conduct in so far as it encouraged

---

[1] Junius, 5–10 (unnumbered).   [2] *Noot. Vert.* 32.

men to please the government by their behaviour. The one was ruled by the moral law and the law of the Gospels, the other by a human law according to the customs and morals of each land, in themselves often ungodly. The one led its members to a union with God, the other to the preservation of civil life by prudence and discretion. The one was the kingdom of those reborn and obedient to Christ; the other was the kingdom of obedience to human government. The one strove for a righteousness which counted with God, the other for civil justice. The object of the first was a spiritual peace and well-being; of the second, peace and prosperity upon earth. In the one were spiritual, in the other bodily, punishments. Church and state were essentially distinct.

The principle of specialisation was held by all four writers and implied the differentiation of church and state. Gomarus[1] admitted that many rulers possessed gifts useful and necessary to divine worship, and that many ministers were fitted to sit in the councils of state. But God demanded that each should serve Him according to the utmost in that office to which he had been called and for which He had granted fitting gifts. To the ministers were entrusted the things of the Lord; to the rulers, the things of the world. From God, who demanded order and hated confusion, there issued the command that each was to devote himself to his own calling and not to trespass upon that of the other. Junius distinguished between the ecclesiastical function to teach, and the political function to rule. The ruler had no right to interfere with the teaching function nor to modify the instruments and means which God had established for that function. He was limited to the bodies of his subjects and had no power over their souls.

It was this point which Acronius[2] and Walaeus[3] developed as the basis for the distinction between the two offices, so that the holders of the one were unable to control the other. True obedience was that of a sincere heart, and not that won by threats. Only by the grace of God did men truly repent and reform, for the secular arm was able only to dictate external conduct. The magistrate was not the minister of Christ because his resources

[1] *Waerschouwinghe*, 19.   [2] *Noot. Vert.* 32.
[3] *De Munere*, 11.

were insufficient to save men through faith in Christ, so that he had no share in the work of salvation and no right to regulate spiritual matters through which grace was given to men.

Walaeus[1] pointed out that the ruler punished men innocent before God, and failed to punish sins which were not crimes. Vices like avarice were neglected by the ruler. Since ecclesiastical discipline and political justice differed in their purpose, means and subject, the ministry was not subject to the ruler as if the ministers were his deputies. Moreover, the ruler in virtue of his office alone had no right to the ministry itself, for thus it would permit a woman to teach in the church contrary to divine law, and even minors to conduct God's worship. Never did Christ or the Apostles hold that the political office included the ministerial. Walaeus appealed to the Old Testament and denied that the kings had ever acted in religious matters except from an extraordinary call. If it was granted that the ruler had no power to preach or to administer the sacraments, Walaeus still rejected the claim that the ruler ought to control the operation of ecclesiastical discipline. The Bible clearly showed that among the Jews the priests directed the moral life of the community, refusing to open the temple to the unreconciled. The Law gave jurisdiction in religious matters to the priests. The Gospels gave to the minister all spiritual jurisdiction on earth, and the Apostles exercised it as belonging to the successors of Christ. Nowhere was there a single instance to justify the argument that that right to discipline ceased when the ruler was converted. Lastly, Walaeus denied that there was any appeal from an ecclesiastical sentence to the ruler, and he was careful to prove that the appeal of St Paul to Caesar was upon civil and not upon religious grounds.

In its final form, specialisation meant self-government, and the direct communication of the church with God. The church was in no way dependent upon the ruler in its own function, but was guided by its ministers according to their knowledge of the Law and of Christ. It followed that the church was empowered by God to choose its own ministers, to hold its own meetings and to regulate those activities by which the church realised the order of worship commanded by God. Whatever share was conceded

---

[1] *De Munere*, Part I. Cf. Wijngaarden, *Antonius Walaeus*, ch. III.

to the ruler, it was always subordinate to the authority of the community, of which he was but a part and the interests of which he had to serve.

Gomarus insisted that the first duty of the ministers was to God, but that they were to obey the ruler in everything which did not cause them to sin against God. The ministers, he pleaded, neither desired power nor to rival the government. "But they only sought, as true servants of God, to undertake and fulfil their heavy responsibility for the salvation of souls, to the Glory of God, to the foundation of His community and to their own salvation."[1] God's Truth was above all, and according to His Will the ministry was His instrument to save men. Therefore, it was responsible to God alone and was not to deviate from His Will, observing faithfully His commands to punish unbelief as well as to teach the true doctrine. The means necessary for both ends were given by God in the "godly order" of the church, of which the ministerial office was the chief. In order to undertake that office, the ministers had to meet two demands; godliness of life and faithfulness to the obligations of their office. Those obligations were to serve the community by the pure teaching of the Word, by the faithful administration of the sacraments, and by the preservation of orderly government in the church, particularly by the god-fearing examination and appointment of ministers, and by the pious use of the keys and disciplinary authority.

Junius[2] was the most moderate in defending the claim of the church to direct itself according to God's Will without political interference; but even he insisted that neither ruler nor church was able to modify the church government given by God and therefore that the ministers as instruments of Christ were alone entitled to govern the church. The community of saints was ruled by Christ alone, who spoke through the witness of the visible community whenever He used visible and human means.

The idea that the community was the mediatory organ between Christ and His worshippers was stressed by Acronius, to whom ecclesiastical self-government was the absolute condition for fulfilling the revelation of the Gospels. His book began with a definition of the community which guaranteed its independence

---

[1] *Waerschouwinghe*, 21–24.　　　　[2] Question 2.

from all human powers.[1] Originally, he admitted, the word
signified any gathering of men for good or ill, but he understood
it to be "a visible meeting of men confessing the doctrine of the
Gospels; in which the doctrine of the Holy Gospels was purely
preached by Ministers lawfully called thereto, and the sacraments
administered strictly according to Christ's injunction; in which
also God was powerful by the ministry of His Word, and many
came to everlasting life".[2] God had promised to men a holy
community on earth, distinguished from all other communities
by its observance of that faith and worship ordained by God
Himself. Since this visible community included insincere
Christians not of the Elect, it had need of a certain form of
government and supervision, especially to control the wicked.
All social bodies, Acronius believed, had need of laws and forms
to regulate the means by the end they were to serve. Those members who pursued their own will and their interests at the expense
of the order of which they were a part were the faithless. The need
of man's corrupt nature was government, and discipline was
essential in the church.

God did not allow any human will to rule the community but
bound all members, whatever their position or office, by a Law
necessary for their co-ordination and planted in their hearts by
the Holy Ghost.[3] All who belonged to the community had submitted to this Law, and accepted the direction of the church by
the preachers, elders, and deacons who corresponded in the
church of the New Testament to the Priests, Levites and Elders
who ruled the church of the Old Testament. The governors of
the community were the pastors and elders governing "according
to a fundamental and immutable law, contained in the Bible".

The appointment of these governors was by the community
according to the way commanded by God. "In order that the
call be lawful, it is necessary for it to take place with the un-
checked, spontaneous and sincere agreement of that community
which he who is called shall serve. Thus the community preserves
the freedom permitted by God, thus can the chosen pastor enter
on his office with a better conscience, and thus also can the
community submit with greater confidence to him." Although

[1] *Noot. Vert.* chs. 1–10.   [2] *Ib.* 1.   [3] *Ib.* 11.

the ministers were the leaders of the community and therefore important agents in the call of ministers, yet they formed but a part of the community and had no exclusive right to determine a matter in which all shared. The call was by divine right in the whole community and in no part; so that the ruler had no exclusive right. Indeed he had no share, for the ministry was of Christ's Kingdom, in relation to which the ruler was no more than a foster-father.

This method of calling ministers observed the "fixed foundation" in God's Word, whereby those properly called were granted the gifts necessary for their office. Thus, God raised up in His community the normal means and instruments to do His Will. Not only was the call the right of the community, but the government of the church was entrusted to the lesser and greater church meetings, according to the local or more general interests of the churches. The lesser meetings, or the consistory, supervised the faith and conduct of church members, including the officers of the church. The greater meetings, or the classes and synods, decided upon common measures for preserving the many churches from corruption or disorder. By these councils, Acronius established a wholly ecclesiastical means of deciding whatever disputes about life or doctrine troubled the church. If the dispute was local, it was settled by the consistory; if it was more important, a provincial or even national synod was to decide. The final decision rested with a general council. The church possessed a definitive judgment in all matters of conduct and belief.

If the ruler had no part in the call of ministers, he was granted a part in the holding of synods, for they were to be summoned by a Christian ruler and not by the ministers. Moreover, he was allowed to send deputies to sit beside the representatives chosen by the communities, provided that they participated not as authoritative officers of the ruler but as members of the communities and of the synod. Both the lay and the ecclesiastical members were held to act according to the rule of God's Word, and the ecclesiastical members were further bound by the instructions of their churches. The business of the synod was to be regulated by two presidents—the political to preserve order, moderate quarrels, provide for fair debate and ensure that a decision by a majority was accepted by the whole synod; and the ecclesiastical to conduct the actual business of the synod. Finally, no synod was lawful unless it followed the authority of the Holy Ghost. Acronius had allowed to the ruler no effective part in deciding religious matters, for "neither God can preserve entire for long His Honour, nor His Word its light, nor the members their freedom, if the full government in church-matters is put absolutely or wholly into the hands of the ruler". History showed the evil consequences of the ruler's power in religion. Acronius pointed to the number of Christian emperors who had used their office to foster heresy.

Walaeus[1] also believed that the church ought to be free to order its own affairs and that the ruler had no part in church government by which he was able to control ecclesiastical interests. In particular, he discussed the extent to which the ruler shared in the call to the ministry, in the holding of synods and in the determination of disputes. In these matters, the regulation of which meant the regulation of the whole church, Walaeus granted a minor share to the ruler.

Walaeus distinguished three separate stages in the call to the ministry: the examination of the candidate's fitness to be a minister of God, the appointment to a particular community, and the induction itself. Only in the second stage had the ruler any claim; for the examination was in general a matter for the whole community, and in particular for the ministers, although customarily in the presence of lay deputies, while the induction had always been the duty of the ministers with the agreement of the community. But Walaeus denied even in the second stage that the ruler or local magistrate was authorised by God to appoint according to his pleasure. God had determined in His Law the way in which a minister was to be appointed to a particular church. Christ had chosen His own disciples, and the Apostles had called the prophets and evangelists. The teachers were called in the presence of the community by the Apostles, prophets and evangelists. Wherever the true order was politically accepted, the Christian ruler left to the church and its officers the power to appoint to a particular church. Walaeus only granted

[1] *De Munere*, Part III.

that the subordinate magistrate as the foremost member of each community was to be consulted, but not to appoint to the ministry as he appointed to civil offices, and that the ruler as the guardian of divine law was to see that the appointment was made in his presence. It was his duty to supervise the choice and to add his authority. Therefore, he was to interfere only to prevent a disorderly or irregular call, and to preserve the church from the evils of a disputed call. But even in these abnormal cases, the ruler acted with the consent of the ministers.

In the same way, the synod was to be composed of representatives of the churches, chosen by the communities or by their officers, and approved by the ruler, who was to be present in person or by his deputy, together with his own pious advisers. His office and duty were the preservation of order according to God's Law, but only to enable the synod to determine ecclesiastical problems by its own judgment. In the ministry were that special knowledge and supernatural gifts by which the revelation of God became the measure of all judgment in the church. The Holy Spirit speaking in and through the Scriptures was the supreme judge, and secondarily the ministers in so far as they were the instruments of the Holy Spirit. The true church was directed by God, and, therefore, in subjection to Him, was independent of all human authority.

It seemed that Contra-Remonstrant theory had no place for the secular ruler and his secular power. Ecclesiastical self-sufficiency was complete and inherent in the church; but the ruler was treated as the divinely ordained collaborator of the church, with religious obligations and an ecclesiastical mission. The corpus christianum was still the objective of Contra-Remonstrant theory, and no Christian society was possible wherever church and state were opposed. The individual was both a citizen and a church-member, with duties in both capacities and obedience to two different powers. Because of the connection between those two capacities in the same man, Junius and Acronius both held that the ruler was not to be removed from the community.[1]

It was evident that the Contra-Remonstrants had virtually

---

[1] Visser, II, 347, 354.

claimed independence for the church on the ground that it was voluntary; for the authority of the church was without that absolute and human sanction which characterised the power of the ruler. The independent activity of the church rested upon the willing obedience and ready acceptance of its decisions on the part of its members, since the spiritual discipline of the church was effective only in so far as it convinced members of their error, and persuaded them to obey God in the church. But the missionary character of Dutch Calvinism—the successful and aggressive assertion of sect principles—was not the work of a truly voluntary church. A sect was unable to convert a nation unless it was transformed into the national church; the force of the state had to be yoked to the teaching authority of the church, so that ecclesiastical discipline rested upon the ultimate and understood co-operation of the state. Then, self-government became practicable because the decision of the majority became a political reality.

To Gomarus,[1] "the sovereign authority must remain with the States both in ecclesiastical and in political matters", but it was a sovereignty defined by God's Word. The ruler was to do the Will of God in the same way as the kings of Israel had served the Lord; by preventing heresy and punishing idolatry.

Junius[2] held that the ruler, because he was a Christian but not because he was a ruler, was both in and of the church, and obedient to God, the creator of human power and institutions. The church promoted the welfare of the inner, the state of the outer, man; but both were concerned with the same individual, and both claimed his loyalty. Junius thought it wrong to contemplate the possibility of a Christian ruler refusing his protection to the church, but even so the ruler was only able to undertake certain duties, and not the whole function of the ministry. He gave to external man a Law, and ruled everything belonging to that external life. The church, however, did not only direct and teach the inward man, but also used the aids and services of the outward man in so far as the external signs of the community of saints were necessary for the development of the internal community. To that extent, the ruler had some authority in church matters,

---

[1] *Waerschouwinghe*, 12.   [2] Question 2.

but never so as to control the inward man. It was for him, as a true member of the church, to accept the laws ordained by God as the means and instruments instituted for the nurture of the inner man; and as a ruler thereto divinely appointed, it was his duty to preserve those laws and protect the ecclesiastical and political order framed according to them. His function was not to teach the inner man but to curb the outer. He had to protect those things necessary for the communion of saints, given by God alone and regulated by Christ alone, either through the church or directly by His Spirit. In matters unnecessary to that community Junius was not prepared to dispute the claim of either ecclesiastical or political officials to determine them. That was needless controversy when the church was free to decide everything necessary to the progress of the communion of saints.

In spite of his zeal for ecclesiastical self-government, Acronius[1] was equally convinced that the ruler was necessary to the church, which would not long survive without his helping hand. The ruler was not to withdraw his power from church government, for he, as much as the minister, was ordained of God to promote His Glory, and men's bliss and welfare, not only in temporal but also in everlasting life, as the ultimate end to be regarded by men. The ruler was not merely the guardian of the body but of the two Tables of the Law, and was bound by his office to strive for the salvation of the soul and not merely for the security of the body. Acronius illustrated this duty by examples of pious kings of the Old Testament, and of the Christian emperors. That piety and Christianity were proved by the fact that these rulers did nothing in religion by their own will, but consulted the communities and did their duty with the advice, consent and through the medium of the ministers, according to God's Law. God demanded from ministers and rulers a mutual communication, deliberation, agreement and co-operation in the furtherance of ecclesiastical interests. Therefore both were to work for the same end in their own ways without interfering with the other.

These common labours and mutual help never conflicted, for God had instituted both offices and their mutual relations. Both were necessary in human life; the civil power extended over those

---

[1] *Noot. Vert.* chs. 16, 17.

who were not of the church and refused to bow to its authority. The ministers' mission led to proper obedience and to law-abiding habits; the ruler's work enabled the ministers to fulfil their mission in peace and lead the people in the fear of God without the obstruction of wicked men.

Acronius did not fear to state in greater detail the nature of the service which the ruler was to extend to the church. He had to study the condition of the whole church, to examine doctrine and conduct, and to know how to distinguish the good from the bad, and the true from the false. He was to ensure that the communities living under his government and protection like other subjects were not oppressed nor ruined by external force or other evil practices, provided that their doctrine was pure, and that their conduct was not punishable. He was to see that they were lawfully protected against all molestation and interference. With the advice of pious and learned men, skilled in religious matters, the ruler was to provide for the preaching of the Word, for the strict observance of their duties by the ministers, for the right worship of God, for the removal of all corruption and heresies, and all obstacles to the fulfilment of the church's mission, and finally to confirm and guarantee the church as instituted by Christ, so that not only did it govern itself but had its proper decisions and actions ratified legally and politically by the ruler.

Walaeus[1] advocated the same duties of the ruler to the church and used very similar arguments. He was committed to that position by his distinction between the two functions, the one spiritual and the other corporal.[2] Both functions were necessary to realise God's purpose, and therefore both ministry and magistracy were united by that purpose. Their powers were complementary and were only in conflict when abused. The Christian ruler was not only a member of the church, but also its foster-father and protector, for Christ had established over His church two kinds of inspectors and leaders, the one armed with corporal and political authority, and the other with spiritual authority. Each was intended to strengthen the other in its duty not by interfering in the office, but by seeing that each ordered its

---

[1] *De Munere*, Part II.   [2] *Ib.* 40.

function according to Christ's Will. So that the ruler was bound
to prevent the ministers from neglecting, exceeding or abusing
their authority, while the ministry was equally commanded to
use its spiritual weapons against a ruler who failed in his proper
duty. He had, therefore, more than the negative task of protecting
the church from external interference; he had the positive mission
of using his coercive power to promote the work of the church by
ensuring that it was rightly, and self-, governed, by removing all
impediments, and by providing adequate resources.

The final form of Contra-Remonstrant theory established
first a differentiation of church and state, secondly their interdependence, and thirdly reciprocal obedience. Both were instituted by God, and both were directly responsible to Him; but
both had separate spheres and separate powers, to be co-ordinated
for a common end. The ruler was supreme in all political matters,
and the ministers were supreme in all spiritual matters.[1] The
ministry itself was never subject to the ruler, but the ministers
as citizens were subject to the ruler in political matters. They
were like any other citizen subject to political laws and liable to
political punishment. Moreover, they were subject also as officers
of the church because the ruler had to compel them, if necessary,
to observe their functions as commanded by Christ, although the
ruler himself had to act in this matter according to that same law.
Likewise, the ruler was subject to the ministers in all spiritual
matters, not only as any other member of the church, but also as
a ruler bound by God's Law. The ministers could only use their
spiritual weapons, but although the ruler was to be excommunicated if necessary, his political power was in no way subject. An
excommunicated ruler was still to be obeyed in political matters.
Therefore, each was supreme in its own sphere, and each was
subject to the other in the opposite sphere. The church governed
all matters of the conscience by its teaching power: the state
governed all matters in which the conscience was not concerned
by its coercive power. If each observed those limits, there was
no opportunity to conflict but there was instead a condition of
co-operation.

[1] *Waerschouwinghe*, 14, 18; *Two Questions*, 17; *Noot. Vert.* 44; *De Munere*,
17–24.

The Contra-Remonstrants denied that this theory was a collaterality of church and state. Collaterality was properly that Catholic theory in which church and state were separated to such a degree that there were two distinct powers not subordinate one to the other, and without rights and duties in relation to the other.[1] Bellarmine had rejected such collaterality as weakening the spiritual power; the Contra-Remonstrants as depriving the Christian ruler of that power in relation to the church which he had received from God.

The ideal relation of church and state was the relation of the soul and the body, each dependent upon the other but superior in its own function.[2] In that relation neither was independent nor isolated nor wholly dependent, but interdependent. Thus did the Contra-Remonstrants reconcile sovereignty and ecclesiastical self-government in a common loyalty to the Christian revelation.

It was possible that this analogy proved more than was intended; for it suggested that the sovereign state was guided by the church, and that the ruler was instructed by the ministers. It is true that the ruler was supreme in civil matters, but who was to say which were ecclesiastical and not civil? It is, again, true that the ruler was bound to use his power in church-matters according to the divine law, but who was to determine the precise form of that constitution and who was to judge when the ruler had violated its terms? Lastly, while the ruler alone had the power to coerce, was he free to decide how, when and where he exercised it? The Contra-Remonstrants held that the church, led by its officers, determined these questions; the interpretation of the Word was by the Holy Spirit working in the church. Acronius stated explicitly what was in fact assumed by all: "that the judgment of the communities in religious questions is greater than the judgment of the political magistrate, and therefore that the communities ultimately have in religious questions the supreme judgment above which no greater judgment of men can be given on earth".[3]

The ruler had a claim to obedience only in civil matters, but

[1] *Waerschouwinghe*, 13; *De Munere*, 16; cf. Wijngaarden, 158.
[2] *Noot. Vert.* 54; *Two Questions*, Question II.
[3] Quoted Rogge, *Jaarboek*, I, 326.

that was due to all magistrates. The difference between a truly Christian ruler and other rulers was his duty to act in ecclesiastical matters according to the judgment of the church. He was less independent than they were. Moreover, the Christian ruler had duties which were in fact religious. He had no power but to help and confirm the true church; but he also had a power to eliminate all other churches, a power, that is, which was essentially respecting the conscience. In this, he was acting according to the Word, and the interpretations of the Word made by the orthodox church, and therefore Contra-Remonstrant theory gave to the church the use of the ruler's power which it could not claim outright. The church had no longer reason to fear that power, but to use it to realise that national church for which its own teaching power was inadequate. Even in political matters, the ruler was subject to ecclesiastical discipline, although his political power was thereby in no way threatened.

Finally, the Contra-Remonstrants evaded rather than answered the objections of Uytenbogaert to their theory. He did not want the ruler to decide matters of faith, although he wanted to prevent a tyrannous misuse of this power by the church.[1] He did not challenge the right of the church, but insisted that the question was whether a Christian ruler had the highest command over that right after God's Word.[2] The issue was really whether the ruler was to be obeyed when his commands did not conflict with God's Word.[3] Uytenbogaert argued that the Christian ruler had by and under the Word the right of supervision, and that the ruler was to be obeyed so long as he did not act contrary to the Word.[4]

There was no dispute about the function of the church nor that the ruler was to act according to the Word, but there was disagreement about the content of the law governing church and state. To Uytenbogaert much in the church apart from the function had not been prescribed by God, but left to the decision of men. These matters were regulated in the interests of order and not of salvation, and there was no reason why the Christian ruler should not have the final power in their regulation.

[1] *Ib.* II, 85, n. I. [2] *Ib.* I, 374.
[3] *Ib.* II, 81. [4] *Ib.* I, 362.

The Contra-Remonstrants did not give a real answer to this point of Uytenbogaert. They admitted that the church had power only in matters laid down in the Bible, and only as the instrument of the Holy Spirit. They denied that the ministers had any discretion. They accepted the necessity of further regulations for the sake of order, for as Acronius said every society had need of laws and organisation, but these regulations were not given by God, unless it was argued that they were the consequences of what God had given. Moreover, God had not prescribed an immutable form of the church which was not to be adjusted to circumstances and locality. In essence, the church was of God; in circumstances, the church was regulated by men. The church was in fact to be self-governing, for it determined matters not laid down by God; and, it was asserted, the ruler had no final power in those matters. But the argument by which the Contra-Remonstrants protected the pastoral function—the teaching power granted by God—was not an argument against the claim that the administrative and governing power of the church was under the final supervision of the ruler.

Not only did the Contra-Remonstrants fail to answer the claim that the ruler's orders not conflicting with the Word were to be obeyed, but they had in fact accepted it as a principle of their theory. The ruler was to command within the limits of the Bible and Christians were to obey; but it was understood that the ruler could only command thus (except in purely civil matters) when he ratified what the church determined. The fundamental distinction between Uytenbogaert and his opponents was his claim that the ruler had a real judgment in the use of his power in religious matters, for the Contra-Remonstrants had left to the ruler no effective judgment in meeting his obligations to the church.

CHAPTER II

ARMINIANISM AND ERASTIANISM

§ I

THE ARMINIAN theory of church and state, which like that of Erastus was chiefly a denial of any independent ecclesiastical jurisdiction, was formulated by four writers and from four points of view. In its earliest form, it was a theological conception: Uytenbogaert relied upon revelation. In the thought of Vossius, this developed into a doctrine of divine right of the ruler. To Grotius the legalistic theory of sovereignty was more important. Finally, Episcopius was influenced by a theory of toleration which demanded the toleration of private churches alongside the state church. The decade 1610–1620, during which the essential ideas of these writers were formed, saw the struggle of the Arminian party to remain within the Reformed church and their ultimate failure.[1]

In general, all of these writers were struggling with the problem of minority rights. From the Calvinist point of view, their position in the church was untenable, and their appeal to the secular arm was sacrilegious. But, it was not decided until 1618 in what form Calvinism was to be accepted in the Netherlands. To have left the church would have invited not only the reproach of schism but also denied their claim to be true parts of the Reformed church.

The real difficulty which the Calvinists found in the Arminian theory was the fact that a truly Christian ruler was not guaranteed. One of the orthodox party was prepared to accept Uytenbogaert's thesis provided that the ruler was Christian.[2] But this was one of his assumptions. The other three Arminians also held that

---

[1] See Rogge, *Johannes Wtenbogaert en zijn Tijd*; Harrison, *The Beginnings of Arminianism*; Knappert, *Geschiedenis der Nederlandsche Hervormde Kerk*; Reitsma, *Geschiedenis van de Hervorming en de Hervormde Kerk der Nederlanden*; Maronier, *Jacobus Arminius*; Haentjens, *Simon Episcopius*; and Itterzon, *Franciscus Gomarus*.

[2] Rogge, *Jaarboek*, 1, 316.

only a Christian ruler would be willing to undertake his duty toward the church. The difference between the parties was their interpretation of the Christian ruler. To the Calvinist, it meant political ratification of decisions taken by the properly instituted organs of the church. Only in that sense had the ruler a final judgment. Thus, that same Calvinist who was prepared to accept Uytenbogaert's thesis demanded that the ruler should prove his Christianity by banishing all who would not conform. To the Arminian, however, comprehension, and even toleration, were the true aims of the ruler: he was therefore a moderator between the divine revelation and political realities.

Arminianism continued in large part the ideal of the national evangelical church, distrustful of any binding authority in the church save that of the Bible, hostile to dogmatic confessionalism, and tolerant of other creeds and of unorthodoxy among its own members. The state had a negative rather than a positive function toward the church: it was to protect and cherish the church in so far as it was loyal to the Bible, but the state was not to act in any controversial matter at the will of the majority. This implied the distinction between fundamentals and non-fundamentals which the Calvinists could not accept in regard to the points claimed by the Arminians to be non-fundamental. Biblical teaching was always clear because the church was able to make a decision.

Arminian theory attempted to protect both the function of the church, and the duty of the ruler, by distinguishing the acts of religion from the organisation of the church. Its ideal was state control, but not state operation.[1] It was not government of the church by the state; but political inspection and supervision of government of the church by the church. While the state had a share in controlling the institution of the church, it had neither power nor right to usurp the spiritual function, to override the divine mandate or to violate the individual conscience.

The difficulty in this theory was that a political control of the constitution of the church was at least liable to lead to control of the function, and therefore of religion. It may be pointed out, however, that Calvinist theory had its own logical difficulties—how to reconcile the definitive power of the ruler with the pro-

---

[1] Rogge, *Jaarboek*, I, 344, n. 2.

vision that he was only to ratify the decisions of the church—and the same practical difficulty of preventing an abuse of that ecclesiastical power which the ruler was granted by the Calvinists themselves. Their method was to put pressure upon the ruler as a member of the church, and if that failed they had no remedy but to suffer or to abandon the public church. Now, it was here that the Arminians differed fundamentally, for they recognised only the latter means of dealing with a ruler who abused his power and office. They rejected the Calvinist attempt to dictate to the ruler as a member of the church. This was the crux of the controversy, and in different ways it exposed both Calvinist and Arminian theorists to great theoretical and practical difficulties.

§ II[1]

Uytenbogaert's theory was simple and straightforward: certainly it had none of the pretensions or ingenious arguments of the Contra-Remonstrants, largely because it defined the problem in a simple manner and answered it equally directly. The problem which the *Tractaet* formulated and solved was this, "viz: What Authority, Command, Power and Jurisdiction a chief sovereigne Magistrate (be it Emperor, King, Prince or States) hath according to God's word, in matters concerning religion: within the Lands and Dominions, over the which those magistrates are supreme governours."[2] The power of the church was a matter of incidental discussion consequent upon an independent settlement of the sovereign's power in religion; it was defined negatively by defining what the sovereign might and might not command. Uytenbogaert confined his attention to one front, and not two: his thesis was more coherent and organic than the Contra-Remonstrants' because it determined one issue, and had not to be related to a second, which was decided with equal precision upon different principles and had to be consistent with the first. Therefore, his theory was able to ignore the complex border-line cases which forced the Contra-Remonstrants to claim more for

[1] The quotations in this section are from the MS. translation (British Museum Reg. 17, B. XLIV.) referred to as MS. Reference should also be made to the 3rd edition (in Dutch), including Uytenbogaert's replies to Acronius, Walaeus, Voetius, Revius and Vedelius, and referred to as *Tractaet*.

[2] MS. 18; *Tractaet*, 7.

the church than their ostensible theory warranted. This simpli-
fication of the problem was coupled with a particularly straightforward application of the Contra-Remonstrants' own principles,
which were pressed with great logic to meet Remonstrant ends.
Starting from few and simple assumptions, Uytenbogaert preserved a simplicity of design which gave great plausibility, consistency and integrity to his particular interpretation of divine right.

He agreed with his opponents that human life was governed
according to a divine teleology which exercised a constant and
creative influence upon the means to attain the end. Life was
regulated by the Will of God embodied in objective and impersonal
formularies of human conduct, which determined the divine
organisation and allotment of spheres for each human association.
Within the Bible there was outlined a social system which ought
to meet the needs of any Christian people. God had prescribed
there the forms of human association and their relations, and all
authority over human beings was of divine ordination, for either
it was tacitly recognised or deliberately sanctioned by God. The
Bible, therefore, was the written constitution for church and state,
for minister and magistrate: both were established by the divine
creation, both received a divine authority, both were related by
the divine purpose.

The divergence between the two parties only became apparent
when the clauses of this constitution were formulated, and the
constitution as a whole interpreted according to political or
ecclesiastical interests. Uytenbogaert discovered within the
Scriptures an authorisation of the ruler's ecclesiastical power;
the Contra-Remonstrants sought and found a divine basis for a
pastoral authority which was independent of and ultimately
superior to that of the state. Uytenbogaert enlarged the divine
right of the ruler to exercise his power within the church as well
as in the state; the Contra-Remonstrants claimed for the church
and the ministers a divine right to govern almost all ecclesiastical
business independently of the state and even to force its
decisions upon the state in so far as it was part of the church or
possessed a religious capacity.

Uytenbogaert swept away all such ecclesiastical claims by his
emphasis upon the divine right of sovereignty which was as valid

and effective in ecclesiastical as in political matters, and was the peculiar responsibility of one sovereign body. The church was not invested by God with this sovereignty and therefore the church was under it. Uytenbogaert formulated this proposition "that God hath given the supreame superintendency, the chiefest command and authority, over all cases and persons, both spirituall and temporall, and consequently the religion, or forme, and manner of the publiq worship of God, unto the highest magistrate of every land: over the which he is soveraigne, Yet verily alwayes under God, and according to his Word: as thus,

God : & his word

The Soveraigne Magistrate

The Clergie

Here we see a superiority of the Soveraigne Magistrate, under God, & his word, above the Clergie."[1] He stated the same thesis in a negative form. "I say that God hath never appointed amongst his people, two sorts of Soveraigne Magistrates, the one Spirituall, & th' other Temporall, being of equall high authority and standing in one degree syde by syde, to governe the one sort of busynesse, to witt, that which is Spirituall by the one; and the other sorte, to witt, that which is Temporall by the other. But that he hath given the highest authority & power of the outward, visible government, over both th' one and th' other sorte of affayres unto one only soveraigne magistrate......because it is He that is bound in duty to have a care generally of the wellfare of all the people, both in soule and body, both in things naturall and supernaturall."[2] Of the two ways by which this principle, which in its positive and negative form constituted the theory of Uytenbogaert, was demonstrated, the negative was the more important. The greater part of the *Tractaet* was devoted to an analysis of the possible solutions of the relations of church and state, and to the rejection of all but the one formulated in favour of the ruler. In his dedication to the "Estates" of Holland, Uytenbogaert frankly stated that "this is the proper Subject that I handle in this Treatise, and labour to prouve by refuting the papall Superioritie and that Collateralitie which some dream of:

---

[1] MS. 22 *seq.*; *Tractaet*, 10.   [2] MS. Part 3, 176; *Tractaet*, 70.

That to your U (being the soveraigne christian Magistrates over these lands) belongeth the highest superintendency & chiefest command in matters ecclesiasticall yet under God and according to His word." The refutation of that collaterality was his primary object, even though it was directly intended to prove the intermediary status of the magistrate between God and the clergy in virtue of his office, which was the only human power directly responsible to God. All other authorities and institutions were properly subordinated by God's Will to the final responsibility of the ruler, who alone was to be credited with the divine right of sovereignty. His office was the apex of a divine hierarchy of divinely ordained associations with their own peculiar and divinely determined functions, and his own unique function was the supervision of all these other offices so that each operated according to the divine purpose and was properly related to the others in order to fulfil its allotted share. This final responsibility to God required a sovereignty which governed the entire range of corporate life and allowed no institution to escape from its co-ordinating authority. Human associations might be differentiated but all ought to be subordinate to the final judgment of the sovereign, which should govern their relations according to its insight into the divine purpose.

"Let the soveraigne Magistrate in God's name freely and clearly distinguish the inferior offices: Let him freely appoynt on the one syde, honest and godly men of good Experience, as overseers for matters ecclesiastical, to this end and purpose, that all scandalls and stumbling blocks, may with good order and Christianlike discretion, be taken out of the waye: & that everything be done in the house of God, so as may best serve to edification: and on the othersyde, for the good of the Country & administration of Justice, let him in God's name see it be performed, by men of worth, wise and substantial, men well qualified thereunto. Let him freely limit both their Offices, to the end that each of both, containe himselfe within the Circuit of his owne element: all this (I say) is very good, very praysworthy, very profitable, yea necessary. But for all this they must both of them remaine in their proper places, under the overruling eye of Jehosophat: both must be alike subject, to his soveraigne authority: so that when they shall be sent for by Jehosophat, that is by the soveraigne magistrate to come to court, & render a reckoning of their proceedings to him; they must not any of them give for answer, that such matters are ecclesiasticall:......neither is it lawful for any of them, to appeale unto any other Principall;......as likewise, they must not come with a spetiall Charge, for to doe nothing prejudiciall to the privileges of the Church & the Libertyes thereof: for that belongs chiefly unto Jehosophat to looke unto, that the Church suffer no prejudice; for wrong the Church, wrong him, he being appoynted of God, as the principall Protectour of the same: he is, ex officio, the chiefest defendour of the Churches Right: they may exhort, & intreat him, that it would please him to defend the same; but that there should be any other Defendours of the Right, there where the Magistrates are Christian, unless it be under Jehosophat, in Jehosophat's name, & by Jehosophat his direction, that it should be any otherwise, I saye it were a great abuse and horrible irregularity."[1]

Uytenbogaert was evidently prepared to accept the argument of the Contra-Remonstrants that ecclesiastical and civil were to be differentiated for the purposes of administration, and even that the specialised function of each was to be exercised within separated spheres by different officials, since church and state were distinct institutions; but he would not accept the conclusion drawn by his opponents that each institution was directly responsible to God and that sovereignty was different in civil and in ecclesiastical matters. Instead, he denied that there were two sovereigns and asserted that God had instituted one sovereign to which all differentiated functions and their administrative offices were subject and responsible. The government of church and state was to be conducted according to the discretion of the sovereign, which was to appoint the high officials in both, to call them to account, and to determine the policy they were to pursue. The church, no more than the state or the family, could not limit the sovereign by setting up its own officers as interpreters of the divine constitution so far as it applied to ecclesiastical interests. The sovereign was the official interpreter; and therefore was the

---

[1] MS. 99; *Tractaet*, 39.

official protector of the church and its Christian services. The church, indeed, was not complete until the sovereign assumed this divine commission to use its sovereign powers on behalf of the church but according to its own judgment.

Such a conception of sovereignty might well have justified the Contra-Remonstrants' fear of a new Caesaro-papism, in which the ruler assumed the position and prerogatives of the pope, uniting in his person an absolute power over religion as well as society. In this way, a change of ruler might involve a change of religion on the part of the subjects, when faith was governed by the oath of allegiance and the divine revelation fashioned by the law of the land. Sacred rites and the absolute Truth would depend upon the favour of a human power; Christianity might be denied by a hostile ruler, or made a matter of expediency and treaties as in France. The fundamental truth of Calvinism that Christ's spirit and church were not to be moulded by human circumstances would have lost all substance, and Hobbism would have been a fact before it was a theory, since Christ would have been deposed in favour of a human monarch.

Needless to say Uytenbogaert would have cut off his right hand rather than pen a theory which made religion the pensioner of an absolute king, and never would he willingly have advocated a Caesaro-papist ideal. The *Tractaet* expounded a doctrine of sovereignty in, of and over the church which depended upon a series of axioms, and its argument was only applicable to human sovereigns in so far as they fulfilled these preliminary and essential conditions. His opponents made much of a divine right which sanctioned Caesaro-papism, but usually only by ignoring the significance of the qualifications with which he limited and defined his sovereignty. The simplicity of his diagrammatic table—God and His Word, the sovereign, the clergy—lent colour to the arguments of his critics, and was inadequate as a representation of his theory; it needed, to do it justice, a number of defining clauses which removed from sovereignty most of its offending attributes. The charge of Erastianism was then much more difficult to prove than at first sight seemed likely. These qualifications were, in consequence, the most critical and important part of the *Tractaet*, and yet Uytenbogaert did not attempt to prove them but laid them down as self-evident truths possessing political reality.

Throughout the Treatise the sovereignty referred to was that of a Christian magistracy, and none other. "For I confesse, that the Magistrate wch is no Christian, cannot use this kind of authority, whereof I doe here speake: not for lacke of power but, because such magistrates not being Christians, will not trouble themselves with any care for the Christian religion, nor the appendancies thereof."[1] Only when the magistrate was enlightened as to the true religion would he use the powers which properly belonged to him to further the work of God by assuming his responsibilities for the welfare of the church. When a ruler was converted to Christianity, he did not receive from God a wholly new authority to govern the church but "having the same Authority in matters of religion, and the worship of God in generall, which he had before, being simply considered as a magistrate; doeth then beginne, rightly to know the proper dutyes of his Charge and to apply himself accordingly thereunto, when being illuminated, with the true knowledge of God, & of Christ Jesus, and being brought to the true acknowledgeing and embracing of true religion: he doeth beginne, rightly to use the office which God hath layed upon him; which before in these cases, either he used not at all or did abuse". Once the magistrate had been enlightened by the church and brought into religious contact with God, he ought to be received as a religious agent of God in the same way as ministers were. Conscious then of his duty to God, he would use his power for the advancement of the church, but was in no way made responsible to it for the use he made of his office. Only as a Christian could he realise the true nature of his function and the manner in which it should operate, and if he was truly Christian, the church had nothing to fear; if he was not truly Christian but hostile to the church, he would not enter into his divine function but would exercise a power according to political dictates which was not to be resisted by force although not obeyed. Granted that the magistrate was Christian, he filled a function which must be accepted by the church as part of the divine scheme.

[1] MS. 19; *Tractaet*, 7–10.

A Christian magistrate was not any ruler baptised in the name of Christ and making a general profession of Christianity but "such a magistrate as doeth embrace that exercise of christian religion which is most sincere, upright, and agreable to God's word: (the wch I doe take to be for the most fundamentall points which are called by that name of the Protestants, or those of the Reformation) embrace it I say, and professe it openly within their Dominions: whether the government be chiefly in one man's person as in a Monarchy or else in a Colledge or body pollitiq where the soveraignty of government, is in the many; whoe declare themselves, in the view of the whole world, to be defendours and maintainers, of that only one religion, and no other publiqly".[1] Such public profession of the Protestant religion was not to make the magistracy intolerant advocates of an exclusive religion:[2] "howsoever such magistrates, beside that religion, which they hold to be the only true religion, and maintaine as that, wch they have made choise of to be theirs: doe permitt and tollerate in their Dominions, other kinds of Religion, by waye of connivencye; looking upon them, as it were, through the fingers".

This sovereignty was the prerogative of the supreme power in the state, and belonged in their own right to no subordinate officers of state. In so far as these acted in ecclesiastical matters, it was upon the instructions and by virtue of the command of the sovereign.

A still more important qualification defined the scope of sovereignty in ecclesiastical matters. "We doe understand hereby, those matters which concerne the religion and divine service: first, such points as concerne the external worship of God, as preaching of the word, the administration of the sacraments, the exercising of discipline (as it is called,) and care of the poor: then such points as serve for the maintaining of good order, in the publiq worship of God, according to the convenient custome of severall laws: as the particuler consistoryes, the classicall, & synodicall assemblies, with all thereunto pertaining. Thirdly, the Ecclesiasticall persons, or spirituall officebearers, in the house of God: the ministers of that divine service, wch

---

[1] MS. 20. Cf. Rogge, *Jaarboek*, i, 343.
[2] Cf. also Rogge, *Jaarboek*, ii, 117.

according to the custome of these lands, and manner of our churches, are called Preachers, Elders, & Deacons: and that not only, in so far as they be citizens, inhabitants, and subiects of the magistrate, but also in that they doe performe th' aforesayd offices, in Christian Congregations. I speake this peculiarly of the externall worship of God; for as touching the internall worship of God, I doe referre that wholy, unto God himselfe: whoe is the only king of the conscience, & the searcher of the heart, & minds."[1]

The only[2] distinction which Uytenbogaert would recognise was between the internal and external worship of God, that is between the profound and inward reverence for and consciousness of God's sovereignty, and the outward emanations of that spirit in human and corporate activity. Over this latter, sovereignty by its nature had legitimate authority. The activity of the church was not separated into internal and external sections, the one governed by the church, the other by the sovereign. In so far as the church required government, it was the duty of the Christian sovereign to undertake it. The distinction of spiritual and temporal, interpreted as ecclesiastical and civil, was equally futile: it divided what was essentially and organically one, and therefore offered no valid barrier to the natural flow of sovereign authority over society and social activities. Uytenbogaert had indeed taken the wind out of the Contra-Remonstrant sails. Accepting the argument that the spiritual was beyond coercion, religion became a matter of conviction and of the mind over which God ruled, and not of external action which had need of human government. Admitting that law and government were the attributes of sovereignty, the Contra-Remonstrants could not deny Uytenbogaert's conclusion that sovereignty extended over the administration, organisation and institution of the church; and in so far as they believed that spiritual and temporal were matters of the authority used, the Contra-Remonstrants again found it hard to resist the argument that the final human decision was with the sovereign,

---

[1] MS. 22. The distinction between "Religie" and "Godtsdienst" was fundamental: by the first he meant spiritual as opposed to worldly; by the second clerical as opposed to political. See Rogge, *Jaarboek*, I, 345, n. I.

[2] Cf. Rogge, *Jaarboek*, I, 344, n. I.

even in ecclesiastical matters. Holding that God ruled in the church and not the ministers, his opponents found it difficult to relate this rule to anything but the conscience, or the internal worship of God, as Uytenbogaert called it. He simply pursued their own argument that God ruled the internal and the sovereign the external.

The danger from this wide interpretation of external worship was the possibility that the essential stimuli of grace might be usurped by the Christian magistrate. Uytenbogaert had no wish to destroy the objectivity of the Word and the sacraments as the means of salvation, nor to permit them to fall into the hands of those to whom God had not given the gifts requisite for their dispensation. He avoided this danger and guarded against it by distinguishing the pastoral function from the power of sovereignty. "Whence I speake of Authority, Command, Power and Jurisdiction, then I doe not understand, the exercising of the office of preaching, with the appertinents thereof; but the soveraigne, superintendent care, & (as the very words do emport) authority and command, as well over the persons that doe the office, as over the manner of administration, & exercise itselfe." The ruler could not invade the sanctuary of the pastoral function but neither could he surrender the obligations of his own function, which gave him the supreme and ultimate responsibility for the way in which that pastoral function was conducted.

His last qualification was drawn from the Contra-Remonstrants' own theory, and was as valid in his hands as in theirs. "I doe add hereunto that phrase, according to God's word, whereby I give to understand, that wee must not only learn out of God's word, what authority and power belongeth to the magistrate in these cases: but also that the authority & power wch is given to the magistrate in God's word, over such matters, must remaine perpetually confined within the limitts and bounds of the same word: in such sorte, that it may not be any otherwise employed but according to the same word." The supreme authority of the Word of God was as real to Uytenbogaert as to the Contra-Remonstrants, and just as legitimate a part of his theory as of theirs. The difference was not a denial of that

authority or of its reality, but whether that authority was delegated to the magistrates or to the ministers.

The *Tractaet* attempted to prove that this conception of
sovereignty was the divine ideal when the church was properly
established and therefore under that sovereignty, and the only
possible relation for a church which required the co-operation of
the state. The corpus christianum implied this relationship and
depended upon it for its creation and preservation; otherwise the
Christian society was unrealisable, and the only alternative was
a self-sufficient church in an indifferent state, to which Calvinism
was inherently opposed. It was, in short, committed to the corpus
christianum, and so to the sovereignty of the magistrate even over
the church. Uytenbogaert was right: until Calvinism adopted
the most hated tenet of the Anabaptists—the total separation and
incompatibility of church and state—it was inconsistent and
illogical to establish a theory of church and state upon any other
basis than that of subordination to Uytenbogaert's sovereignty.
His own method of proving the necessity of this relationship was
to consider what were to him the only other possibilities; for he
refused to discuss the ideas of those "whoe make the whole
worship of God, to be so spirituall, that the Civil magistrate ought
not in the least point, to meddle with it". The two which he
discussed and rejected were "that God will have all things whatsoever, spirituall and temporall, espetially religion, and the
worship of God, governed by spirituall and ecclesiastical persons:
having appointed over the same, one supreame, ecclesiasticall
head: to the which, he to this end, hath given the chiefe, supreame
command"; and the second, "that God hath ordained two great
powers, which are Collateralls, both standing in one degree of
height: the one spirituall, and ecclesiasticall to have a care of the
religion, of the worship of God, and only in such spirituall cases
to have jurisdiction, namly the Church, or Prelates, as providers
for the spiritualty, in all points concerning the soule, and Life
Aeternall: the other, for to looke into affaires pollitiq, civill, and
temporall, and over such cases only, to have the chiefest power,
and authority: namly the civill magistrate, as some call them, as
providers only for that, wch concerneth carnall, bodily and temporall things".

Of these two the first was of little importance, for no Calvinist ever made so bold as to erect theocracy into the ideal form of government. So that Uytenbogaert rapidly passed to the second, which was a collaterality of powers to which the Contra-Remonstrants approximated according to his argument.[1] His definition of collaterality was "a power of government standing in the very like degree of equall authority"[2]. His interpretation of the argument for collaterality was that all men were subject to the magistrate in civil and political parts of temporal existence, but religion and the service of God being ecclesiastical were reserved to ecclesiastical assemblies in which the magistrate might sit and hear, and even have a voice if he was a member of the church. As a magistrate his authority extended no further in ecclesiastical matters than to open the public buildings to the church, to make provision for public worship and to use his coercive power to execute clerical decrees. This he was to undertake "upon the declaration and judgement of those ecclesiasticall persons and their Assemblies without enforming themselves of the matter or takeing on them the judgement or iudicatura, as being matters that are only ecclesiasticall and therefore by God almighty committed only to ecclesiastical persons".

This collaterality seemed to be denied by three things. First, the clergy and members of the church did not withdraw from the coercive power of the ruler. Secondly, the magistrate as a member of the church had a voice in its government. Thirdly, the magistrate executed the will of the church, and alone possessed the coercive jurisdiction necessary for execution. But in spite of these three qualifications, the collaterality remained, for "the one hath the chiefe authority in temporall affayres; and the other the highest voice in matters ecclesiasticall". This "highest voice" was on a parity with the "chiefe authority", as was to be seen from two facts. First, the magistrate was bound in virtue of his office to use his coercive power to execute the decrees of the church, and as a member of the church could not refuse or withdraw his service from the church; "for then he would deserve,

[1] MS. 44 *seq.* He held that Gomarus only called the Roman system collateral in order to reject the name but not the fact, MS. 36.
[2] *Ib.* 15; cf. 49.

for the neglect of duty ecclesiasticall censure & punishment". Secondly, the church exercised a "compulsive power" similar to that of the state, and by its use of ecclesiastical judicature it vindicated its claim to be as absolute a sovereign in ecclesiastical affairs as the state in political. Indeed those very qualifications illustrated the completeness of this collaterality which established two supreme authorities under God, one over temporal, and the other over ecclesiastical matters; the clergy being subject as citizens to the magistrate, and the magistrates as "sheep" to the clergy.[1] In order to complete the collaterality the clergy wanted to exclude the magistrates from ecclesiastical office as they were from civil, and so to deny that God had appointed the magistrate as one of His agents to realise His Kingdom.

Uytenbogaert then pointed out that since Gomarus had rejected papal collaterality, he must admit that ministers were subject to the magistrate as "Politiq Pastours and Foster-fathers of the Church"; that is, as a sovereign over all matters of the church with the supreme authority peculiar to sovereignty, but not as ministers with the spiritual power of the keys which consisted "in the opening of Heaven to the penitent and believing" and "in the shutting of the same to the impenitent and unbelieving, by the publishing of God's word in general termes". The ministers were responsible even for their function to the magistrate's power in his capacity of sovereign. Gomarus certainly agreed with this: but he also used "politiq pastours and foster-fathers" to indicate authority in political matters only, which were external, temporal and civil, thus setting "the politiq pastours over against the spirituall pastours, and the politiq feeding over against the spiritual feeding". This led direct to an "equal high authority"—to collaterality. Gomarus was wrong,[2] Uytenbogaert concluded, in

---

[1] MS. 91; *Tractaet*, 37:

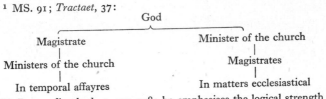

God

Magistrate	Minister of the church
Ministers of the church	Magistrates
In temporal affayres	In matters ecclesiastical

[2] Cf. Rogge, *Jaarboek*, I, 353–358; he emphasises the logical strength of Uytenbogaert's argument contrasted to that of Gomarus.

pretending that this was not collaterality, "for, if that Collateralitie be such a good and godly order, wherefore should wee
not call it by the owne proper name of it". The reason why
Gomarus retained the fact but rejected the name was that
collaterality meant that "disobedience against the Soveraigne
Magistrat is procured: Confusion is hatched; and the true
Ordinance of God is troden under foot".

The Bible,[1] according to Uytenbogaert, did not provide
examples of ecclesiastical behaviour which sanctioned the conclusion that "ecclesiasticall persons had the like authority in
ecclesiasticall matters, as the kings had in politiq matters, which
is here the principal question in hand". The action of prophets,
priests and apostles revealed quite the contrary, although they
did not fall into an abject submission: "whereas the Magistrate
shall bring in anything, or shall institute or command anything,
be it unto ecclesiastical persons, or to any other whomsoever,
which is contrary to God & his Word:......that then in such
cases, the faythful servants of God may not shrinke nor give way
to wickednesse; but are bound in Conscience, manfully to resist
such wicked Magistrates, with the Word of God: (I say with the
word of God) as it becometh the faythful servants of God: yea,
though it were with the hazard and losse of their lives". Their
godly examples of how ministers of the Word ought to conduct
themselves "never made any question about Jurisdiction, and
Intrusion into an other man's office:......their laudable and
godly resistance, was founded upon this ground: that these kings
and Rulers did abuse their office, theire owne office, the office
that God hath committed unto them, the office which properly
belonged unto them, whereas they instead of serving the true
God, and setting forward the true worship of God, by their
authority, did directly to the contrary worship idols: did further
the false worship of God: and did labour by their injunctions,
either to hinder their Subjects in the true worship of God, or else
by violence to force them to doe contrary to the commandment
of God. This was not founded then, upon any power or Jurisdiction, which these men of God would challenge, to appertayne

[1] MS. 103 seq.; Tractaet, 41. The Gospel did not abolish the powers of
the ruler under the Old Testament, MS. 173.

unto themselves, in matters ecclesiasticall, which the magistrate would wrongfully bereave them of: but it was founded hereupon; that those Magistrates, who were placed under God & his Word to submitt themselves to God and his Word, did sett up themselves as opposites, against God and his Word: that earthly kings did rebel against the heavenly king: instituting such a worship of God, as they thought good themselves:......commanding moreover, that their subjects should yield and applaud thereunto, yea without speaking so much as one word to the contrary; and should blindly followe, which way so ever they were ledde."

Here then was the authority of the ministers: it did not require that the sovereign should be excluded from his proper place over discipline, synods and ecclesiastical constitutions, nor did the one conflict with the other. Unless this was granted, there would exist two coercive and independent powers in the same state, when ecclesiastical censure in public congregations would affect more than merely ecclesiastical.[1] Such independent jurisdiction involved worldly prosperity as well as moral discipline; while it was not always limited to expulsion from the church but extended to the subsequent regulation of conduct and action of those who were expelled. A preacher might be expelled; but the church often expected that he should be forbidden to preach any more, and it would compel the ruler to prevent him under penalty of censure. In the matter of synods how could a magistrate execute their decrees with a good conscience unless "he first understand the matter, and that in his own judgement...he is thoroughly persuaded"? If this was denied, it would create the absurd situation that "a Christian Magistrate shall pronounce punishment upon a fact he understands not, only upon other men's reports". In the same way, the sovereign must possess supreme power in the formulation and authorisation of ecclesiastical constitutions. Uytenbogaert readily admitted that God's Word prescribed adequately "in that which we must believe for the salvation of our soules; and to that end, what we must doe and leave undone", but he questioned whether it was sufficient in "such poynts as concerne the externall policy or outward government of the church".[2] The early church had not been agreed

[1] MS. 143 *seq.*; *Tractaet*, 58. [2] MS. 162.

upon the form of its government, which had often changed and was capable of change. God had laid down only general principles "which must be fitted into the present State of the church". What was universally applicable in time and place must be differentiated from what was prescribed for one particular time and place, and this properly was the work of the sovereign who alone possessed the power to enforce and adapt the constitution.

Although Uytenbogaert admitted that church and state were different associations concerned with different subjects, and therefore to be governed separately, he denied that both were so sovereign that one was not subordinate to the other. In this way the ruler retained his sovereignty over the church, its jurisdiction, its synods and its constitutions, without usurping its function or overriding the distinction between ecclesiastical and civil interests. "For there be many matters to be governed in the world, and every sorte have the owne proper administration and execution, so that of necessity there must be severall persons appointed for that purpose: yet nevertheless, the highest soveraigne government & supreame Jurisdiction can admitt no partners....... But to all these severall purposes there are not required severall lawgivers: for one & the selfsame soveraigne magistrate must not just in his own person neither play the Mechaniq part in them: but he is to direct & correctly, guide and governe, command and overrule all, using unto each one such able ministering Spirits & qualified Under officers, as shall be found best furnished for that work."[1]

This sovereignty was not to be exercised according to the ruler's humour, "for since that he in the administration of Justice and temporal affayres which concern this present life, may not exceed the limits of equity, righteousness, moderation, neither may disannul the Lawes & ordinances of that Republiq: how much less shall it be granted unto him, to ordayne or command in any one poynt touching the Religion & worship of God, any thing that is without the limitts of God's word or contrary thereunto: God's word is the Rule which the Magistrate must followe in all things, from which, he hath no warrant to straye neither to the right hand nor to the left, no not a hairebreadth".

[1] MS. 166; *Tractaet*, 66.

The ideas expressed in his *Predicatie* were not wholly contradictory to the *Tractaet*, but were inspired by the difficulties of an
earlier period.[1] In 1590 the church was faced by internal disruption arising from the independent action of ministers like
Herbertsz, Wiggertsz and Sybrandts, and by the absolute claims
of the magistrates of Leiden. Uytenbogaert, therefore, attacked
the action of a government which forced ministers on a community and abused its powers by arbitrary appointments and
depositions. In 1610, the church was united and was determined
to use its power to crush Arminianism, adopting a policy which
Uytenbogaert regarded as an abuse of its legitimate authority,
particularly when the Contra-Remonstrants tried to interpret
the idea of a church in a way contrary to the principles of
the Reformation. In the *Predicatie* Uytenbogaert attacked the
absolute power of the government; in the *Tractaet* he resisted
the denial of its supreme authority under God's Word in clerical
matters. Although he declared in the *Predicatie* that the choice
and ordination of ministers was a matter peculiarly competent to
the ministers, he added in the same context that the government
in virtue of its office should restore and preserve the forms of
worship according to God's Word, and that the church owed a duty
to the government to see that no one should be admitted into the
service of the church without the government's express authority,
will and consent. In the *Voorlooper*[2] he defended himself against
the charge of inconsistency with this familiar distinction: that to
the government was due the right of supreme supervision, to the
ministers the right of service, both according to God's Word. If
the government was Christian it assumed this right of supervision
and its obligations without denying the church's right to serve
and the community's right to share in the choice of its ministers;
indeed both were then established in their rights by the authority
of the government.

In precisely the same spirit, he answered the gibes of the
Jesuits who, when he was in exile at Antwerp after 1618, challenged him with the penalty of giving too much power to the
government. His exile ought to teach him the evils of such a

---

[1] Cf. Rogge, *Jaarboek*, I, 327, 361; *Tractaet*, 145–180.
[2] Rogge, *Jaarboek*, I, 362.

theory. But his faith was unshakable. The attitude of the government after 1618 to the Remonstrants was inexcusable, and was
not sanctioned by his theory in spite of the Jesuits' gibes, since
they did not take sufficient notice of his distinction "between the
lawful use and unlawful abuse of lawful authority".[1] The
government exceeded its powers in limiting the godly right to
expound God's Word, and, in becoming the chief supporter of
a church which had shown itself to be no longer founded upon
the Reformation, it was acting in the way Uytenbogaert had been
most careful to denounce.

In general, the validity of Uytenbogaert's theory rested upon
the validity of its innate principles and upon the justice of his
criticisms of the Contra-Remonstrant theory—two very different
things. The fact that his own principles may not be acceptable
to this century does not necessarily detract from their validity
for his own time. It is sufficient if he disproved the Contra-
Remonstrant argument and substituted a more consistent theory.
Although both must be subjected to the test of subsequent
thought, and although both would be rejected by that thought,
his claims as a political theorist rest upon the soundness of his
thought as judged by the thought of his contemporaries. Now,
the leading ideas of Calvinist thought and its primary assumptions
were: the objective authority of an absolute truth embodied in
the Scriptures and self-evident to any open-minded and pious
reader; the objective and miraculous dispensation of grace
through the preaching of the Word, participation in the sacraments, and a moral discipline; that this grace worked through the
conscience and through conviction, and therefore in a spiritual
way to which force was wholly alien; that the authority of the
church depended upon its identification with the Will of God, and
that in so far as it deviated from that Will its authority lapsed; that
the church could err, and then it had no authority to enforce its
decisions, which ought not to be made by a majority vote but by
a study of the Bible; that no formularies could take the place of
the Bible; that the church was not a sovereign or law-making
body, nor did it have jurisdiction save the spiritual formulation
of God's own decisions; that human authority was only needed

[1] Quoted Rogge, *Jaarboek*, i, 340.

in indifferent matters or adiaphora, where God had not given any rule, or where His rules had to be adjusted to circumstances or where man had been left to work out the details of any general principle; that the church had no final authority in these adiaphora: that these belonged to the state as the seat of final human decision, of human discretion, and of all coercion; that sovereignty belonged to the supreme ruler of the state as the only law-maker, the essence of law being the force to compel obedience; that this sovereignty was of God whether its holder was Christian or not; that a Christian ruler must dedicate his sovereignty to God and His church, using it to support the church; that the combination of sovereignty and revelation produced the corpus christianum, the unitary ideal of society, in which the Christian ideal of the church was compulsorily applied to the whole state; that society was one, and not dual; that the real distinction was between spiritual and temporal, and not between ecclesiastical and civil.

These principles demanded a theory in which church and state were most intimately related upon the basis of the fullest recognition of the sovereignty of the state by the church and of the highest reverence for the revelation of the church on the part of the state. The church must not act in any way which challenged the sovereignty of the state; the state must not use its sovereign power in any way which was contrary to the divine revelation and the dispensation of grace through the church. Both church and state must be subject to the sovereignty of God divinely revealed in the Word: this was the basic condition for any Calvinist theory upon church and state. According to this theory, therefore, the church was to enlighten, the state to command; the church to uphold the Will of God and to operate that machinery through which grace was conveyed to the Elect, and the state to legalise and enforce. The supernatural monopoly of the church was to be realised in a natural life by the power of the state. But just as Calvinism had found that if its ideal of a sect-church was to be a reality the state must use its sovereignty on behalf of the church, so Calvinism found that if its ideal was to retain its characteristics as a sect, the sovereignty of the state must be limited by an independent organisation which should act independently of the state, and the decisions of which should be regarded as authoritative interpretations of the divine will. This implied the moral sovereignty of the church—the "blind obedience" with which the critics of Calvinism charged it, and which it denied by qualifications leading to contradiction and inconsistency. The cause of this fundamental and besetting weakness of Calvinist theory was its failure to acknowledge what its modified theory implied—that there was no objective standard interpretation of the Word. In its formal theory, the dictates of the Word were so obvious that the Christian sovereign knew what was his divinely ordained duty, and the church was free to perform its own task and to indicate to the ruler when he deviated from the divine standard, censuring him if he persisted. But in practice the sovereign had no absolute standard of the Word to follow, and when he followed his own judgmer ⸱ ~~ that of a minority, he was censured by the church; the church had to claim that it was the divinely con- stituted interpreter and expounder of the Word which the ruler was to obey.

Uytenbogaert's reaction to these principles and the theory evolved from them was threefold. First, his own theory was obviously akin to the primitive theory of Geneva, before there dawned upon Calvinist theory the necessity of strengthening the independent operation of the church. On this account, there was singular agreement between his theory and that of the moderate Contra-Remonstrants in those parts of their treatises where the corpus christianum was an active ideal. Both emphasised the unity of society, the existence of one sovereignty in society, the flow of that sovereignty over all society in the form of co- ordinating coercion, its extension over clerical matters and its use on behalf of the church, its exercise under the divine revelation and so by a Christian sovereign. Both emphasised the church as a source of grace, its spiritual authority, the exercise of that authority as the outcome of its function, the unique character of that function, the exercise of that authority by its appeal to the conscience and by causing a change of heart, the duty of the church to exercise its authority and function by spiritual means and methods over all members and under all conditions, the dependence of this authority upon identity with God's Will, the duty of the ruler to keep the church to this identity, the impossibility of his sovereignty interfering in the spiritual because force cannot create conviction, and its limitation to external activities of the church. Therefore, both Uytenbogaert and the Contra-Remonstrants approximated to the same theory, in which the sovereign had a distinct share in the activities of the church but did not deny its initiative and its right to share in its own adminis-tration. To some extent they differed concerning the importance of their respective shares, but Uytenbogaert's limitations mini-mised the difference even here.

His second reaction was very important. He was able to prove in respect of the church's claim to be the authorised interpreter of the constitution, of its independent and compulsive jurisdiction and of its classification of all clerical matters as spiritual and internal, that the Contra-Remonstrants had erected behind the ideal of the corpus christianum a system of collaterality which diverged considerably from Calvin's teaching and which con-tradicted the doctrine of sovereignty adopted by Calvinism as an essential part of its theory. Uytenbogaert was closer to the Reformation and to Calvin; the Contra-Remonstrants were turning back to medieval dualism. Uytenbogaert had certainly modified his Calvinist inheritance by accepting Erastus' ideas upon excommunication, but he had not contradicted Calvinist principles as the Contra-Remonstrants had done.

His third reaction was to formulate his own theory upon the same essential ideas, and it was as consistent a version of Calvinist theory as Calvin's paradoxes would allow. His conception of sovereignty was real; nothing was to escape it, nothing to defy its absolute power, where force could act. That sovereignty was the sovereignty of the state, and not necessarily of an individual. The members of the church shared in that sovereignty if they were also members of a constitutional state. No other institution could share this sovereignty—the church possessed no sove-reignty. It could not compel but convince, not command but persuade. It might control the conscience, but it could not command the body. But he admitted also that the church had its own function which the sovereign could regulate but not usurp, and it remained master of the conscience in so far as it possessed the spirit of God. Sovereignty meant, therefore, the final and supreme regulation of a function which it did not exercise. His theory left religion to the judgment of the minister and to the conviction of the faithful, and ecclesiastical administration to clerical officials under the supervision of the sovereign. Normally that supervision was a formal authorisation of clerical decisions; but the final sovereign power must rest with the ruler for use in any crisis. Each acted then within the sphere allotted to it by its own natural powers, the one convincing by the truth of its message, the other commanding by its force and co-ordinating by its supreme power in accordance with that message. Christianised sovereignty would know its own limits; a truly Christian church would know its own limits. There was no greater demand made upon the operative authority of the divine revelation in Uytenbogaert's theory than in the Genevan or Contra-Remonstrant. Upon the principles of Calvinism it was hard to adopt any other theory and at the same time preserve the consistency of its argument. Particularly is this evident in the light of two important considerations. First, the Calvinist church rose from the stunted form of church sub cruce through the favour of a Christian sovereign; it became the one established church through the coercion of that sovereignty. If the Calvinist church was degraded by this superintendent care of the sovereign, its logical duty was to return to the status of church sub cruce, or to the position of a sect connived at by the tolerant state of Uytenbogaert's ideal. In so far as it enjoyed an authority and privileges greater than these, it derived them from and through the sovereign. Secondly, the sect-church possessed a voluntary within an involuntary character: but the involuntary was derived from the power of sovereignty, to which it ought to be responsible for its use. Even the Calvinists admitted that the church could not enforce this involuntary character without the co-operation of the state.

Quite evidently there was no means of reconciling political sovereignty and ecclesiastical autonomy without danger to both, until the ideal of toleration was generally accepted; and curiously enough, it was the cause and motive of the *Tractaet*, but was incompatible with Contra-Remonstrant theory. The ideas of sovereignty and function were more valid than collaterality until the idea of liberty became an integral and essential part of

political thought and practice. The *Tractaet* was the theory of a
preliminary stage; Contra-Remonstrant thought had not even
advanced thus far. Calvinism opposed the state on behalf of
corporate liberty: Uytenbogaert set up the state to limit this
corporate tyranny of the church on behalf of individual liberty.
The difference between the two arose from this fundamental
difference in attitude, and Uytenbogaert was a greater champion
of liberty than the Contra-Remonstrants although his theory was
so Erastian.

§ III

The first half of Vossius' letter to Grotius was a general argument
in favour of the ruler's authority in the church, largely demonstrated by the progress of the Reformation and by the witness of
a great number of classical and medieval rulers and philosophers.
The more rational arguments were not very profound. He argued,
first, that history showed the disastrous consequences following
the ruler's neglect of religion, and, secondly, that his function
was concerned as much with eternal as temporal salvation.
Lastly, as parens patriae, the ruler was responsible for the welfare
of each of his subjects. Vossius endorsed the principle that the
state existed for the good life, although this natural goodness,
arising from the common rationality of humanity, was enhanced
by the Christian revelation. In Vossius' thought, the natural
political society and the kingdom of God were not opposed
conceptions, nor was his idea of the good life purely theological.
The state existed for more than material necessities and its
function was more than to provide the social environment for the
church. His thought was more liberal in its estimation of the
purpose of the state than was that of the orthodox party.

He was, however, no radical thinker, and was reluctant to
abandon the traditional line of thought. While he welcomed the
natural state with its conception of the good life and insisted also
that the magistrate was directly concerned with the advancement
of religion, he none the less recognised the exceptional revelation
of the Christian religion. He never meant that the state could
ever find that revelation by itself, but that, when enlightened by

the church, the state's native power received a greater aptitude for the creation of the Kingdom of God.

So that he was not inconsistent when, dividing public authority into civil and ecclesiastical, he stated that the civil power sought the human good, and the ecclesiastical the spiritual felicity of men. In a sense, he had not discarded the conventional dualism which dominated the life of man as a social animal and as a citizen of salvation. But he had interpreted civil good so as to include the noblest purposes of the mind and body, and spiritual felicity as the Protestant revelation. There was no opposition between them, for in a Christian society they were united as God's peculiar blessing of His work in nature. This society,[1] governed by Christian principles, was the state so long as its object was human good, but became the church when its effort was directed toward the spiritual good. The one stable body was the territorial group in its collective organisation, and church and state appeared as the manifestations of its purposes. The difference between the two institutions and the powers each wielded was only caused by their different ends; whether the society sought a worldly or an other-worldly good. Of these two aspects of the same society, the political was the more important in human life. The purpose of the church was more specialised than the state's. From the state arose the imperium of the ruler to fulfil this general purpose. In virtue of that, the ruler was the constituted co-ordinating power, determining the contribution of each part to the whole and securing the interest of the whole. Force, without which human society was but a figment of the mind, was the product of the state, which was in consequence the most powerful human organisation. It was the one coercive organisation of society. The church as a public body was within that organisation.[2] Through the organisation of the state, the ruler might alone transform the vision of the church into the Kingdom of God on earth.

Any seeming contradiction with his previous position is reduced, at least, by noting his distinctions. He never asserted that the Christian state could promote the invisible Kingdom of God, which was beyond the possibility of political powers, but

---

[1] *Dissertatio Epistolica*, 27.   [2] *Ib.* 24, 44, 53.

only implied that the fulfilment of God's Will on earth was within its resources. The visible kingdom was a human good, but the more specialised salvation of revelation upon which the invisible kingdom was established was a spiritual good. Above all, his deliberate emphasis upon society as the ultimate form of corporate life prevented its organised expressions—the state and church—from being conceived as two kingdoms, the secular and sacred, in antagonism, but they were co-ordinate and mutually dependent activities of the same body with a common good, which in the one case was interpreted according to the limitations of its human environment, and in the other according to the spiritual standards of the divine revelation. God expected His faithful to achieve the communion of saints, but He also expected them as men to express that communion in a human system in which that ideal was adjusted to the restrictions of human nature, of natural resources and of external and visible contracts and organisation.

Society as a church, therefore, had a double character and a double power. It was to be understood as a spiritual body, its members having all the virtues of true Christians intimately associated with and guided by the will and grace of God, who had endowed this body of the faithful with a power and with a commission directly under Him. But the heavenly city had an earthly form, since its members were citizens of the state, and it used external, non-spiritual forms of organisation and methods of self-determination. The church was in the state, was endowed with material forms through that, and used them to attain its purpose. It required such things as time and place, form and mode. These were accidental attributes indeed of the divine legation—but they were essential to its earthly operation. Under whose mandate did they fall? Were they Caesar's or God's?

It was here that Vossius' refutation of Walaeus emerged in the one constructive principle of his letter. His solution rested upon the divine right of the ruler. That in itself was neither very original nor very profound, but in his hands it became the means of a shrewd division of the function of the church and the power of the ruler. Divine right was an absolute. If only the disputed point could be shown to be of divine right to a particular authority the dispute was at an end. But it was also rather obvious. No

Calvinist in the seventeenth century would have denied that the church and its ministers possessed of divine right the miraculous gifts of Christ's Spirit and the forms divinely ordained to communicate His Spirit to men. Nor would he have denied that these forms were unchangeable by man; nor that the ministry was directly responsible to Christ for their proper use. The church, therefore, possessed a divine mandate which was in no way subject to the state or the ruler. The divine right of the ruler was never framed so that the ruler had the final judgment or discretion over the terms of the mandate, which found an objective charter in the Scriptures. Vossius himself fully respected this divine right of the church. He defined the four fundamental principles of the Christian church as preaching and ordination, the administration of the sacraments and the exercise of the keys. These were operations defined by God and divinely ordained for His Glory and the edification of the Elect. Doctrine, discipline and communion remained established behind these operations, and preserved the Christian church as the civitas dei, the mystical body with Christ at its head. Accordingly, the church had full control of these great spiritual forces, since it must defend its integrity as the instrument of God's saving grace.

Just as it seemed obvious that the ministry was of divine right, so it seemed obvious to many that the magistracy was of divine right. It was perfectly obvious when the state was a Christian state and the ruler a Christian: the monarchomachi were only hostile to a corrupt state the ruler of which acted tyrannically toward the true religion. The Dutch States were Christian rulers to the protected Calvinists, and there was no denial of the ruler's divine right. This was admitted in civil matters, for it was most evident there that God had conferred a mandate upon the ruler analogous to that of the ministry. The church had no right to interfere in civil life, for God had given to the ruler the full responsibility for the use of the imperium.

Vossius approved of Walaeus' recognition of these two distinct divine rights directly derived from God, so that the ministry did not depend upon the magistracy in its mandate, nor the magistracy upon the ministry in civil matters. But he censured Walaeus because he verged upon papal theory in thinking that power in

ecclesiastical matters was from God to the church and was given
to the magistracy by the church; for then it was used according to
the judgment of the church, which was responsible directly to
God for its use. In that case, the magistracy was accountable to
the church for its use. Whereas Walaeus advocated the divine
right of the church for the imperium in sacra, Vossius established
the divine right of the magistracy instead.

This thesis was the crux of the controversy. Its validity depended upon two distinctions according to Vossius, and Walaeus'
error arose from ignoring both. The first[1] was the difference
between the interior and exterior ecclesiastical power. The interior sprang from the divine mandate and was concerned with
the essence of Christianity; but in addition to the pastoral legation
and its inherent power, there was that exterior power which
consisted in the government of the church, through which religion
gained a public sanction and the organisation necessary for a
public religion. Goldast interpreted this exterior power as the
defence of the church; the custody of ecclesiastical discipline;
the holding of ecclesiastical meetings; ecclesiastical legislation;
modification of ritual and worship; and so on. Vossius[2] described
the exterior as the circumstances of time and place, of numbers
and methods, undefined in the Word of God; and again as all
actions related to the polity of the church. The exterior power was
not in itself spiritual but human facilities for the efficient organisation and operation of the church, through which the spiritual
mandate might be realised more easily, more widely and more
fully. The essential principles of Christianity were fundamentally
distinct from these external agencies and medium, which though
ecclesiastical were not attributable to the church because they
constituted no element of the mandate. The second distinction
was between that of the spiritual function and of the human
organisation of the public church; the one was divine, the other
was not. The emphasis in this distinction was upon the word
"public".

In the exterior ecclesiastical power, the magistracy possessed
the imperium directly from God, so that the church and the
ministry were subject in this primarily to the magistracy, and

---

[1] *Dissertatio Epistolica*, 27.   [2] *Ib*. 40.

only through it to God. Therefore, the ruler was responsible for the use of the exterior power and determined how it should be employed in the interests of the church. The ministers, on their side, had no right to resist its use and control by the ruler and none to usurp it in defiance of the ruler; the one limitation was that in the event of abuse the ministers were to be passively disobedient. Power in the public church was equally given by God directly to the magistracy. For this reason, Vossius would not allow the suggestion that if the magistrate had abused his proper power in the election of a minister, the minister should be re-elected by the church. Re-election[1] would be proper in the church as such, but it would be needless in the church as a public institution, since the re-elected minister, though a minister of the church, would not be a minister of the public church. In the same way, the public exercise of the keys was controlled by the ruler, since church discipline was partly divine and partly human, and therefore as a positive human penalty was not to be exercised independently by the church. Marsilius, Vossius added, had refuted the exclusive claim of the church to ecclesiastical discipline. This emphasis upon the public above the simple nature of the institution illustrates the importance of society, and of the church as an aspect of society, in Vossius' theory, and of the intimate regulation of the church by the ruler, as governor by divine right of all that is public, including the public church.

Vossius was not content with gaining this addition to the jus divinum of the magistracy. He was not prepared to leave the interior power wholly to the church and beyond all earthly regulation, for the Reformation implied the supervision and protection by the magistracy even of the ministerial mandate. It was necessary for Vossius to encroach in some way upon the jus divinum of the interior ecclesiastical power, and to reserve some control by jus divinum to the ruler. The method Vossius adopted was a further analysis of his conception of interior ecclesiastical power according to its source, communication and superintendence. It was derived immediately from Christ, whose legates were the ministers of the church. The power of the magistrate shared with that of the minister this common source, since

---

[1] *Dissertatio Epistolica*, 45.

the right of teaching in the church was not less from God than the right of governing in the state. These powers were communicated to them by the same channels. As the power of governing with the plenary imperium was directly from God, in spite of its communication to its official holder by the human constitution of the state, so was the right of preaching and of administering the sacraments, of ordination and of discipline directly from God although conferred upon the pastors through the agency of men. But,[1] and here he intruded his magisterial inspector, the two powers differed when the primary care of the public exercise of religion, which was in itself a Christian obligation, was regarded. This public care of the essence of religion was necessarily part of the magistrate's imperium. It was for him to rule all public things, and in this respect the interior ecclesiastical power was subject to the public supervision of the public authority, which extended beyond the public necessities of the church to include the restoration of true religion and its preservation from corruption.

The divergence between the offices and powers of magistracy and ministry was now evident. Not only had the one imperium and the other merely ministry, but also ecclesiastical matters in so far as there was a public religion[2] were subject not to God immediately but to the magistrate directly in the exterior ecclesiastical, in which he had proprium imperium, and indirectly in the interior ecclesiastical, in which he had only an improprium imperium designed to ensure whatever God commanded. In all that was of human institution, the ruler had the divine right of imperium directly; in matters of divine institution only indirectly, because he was bound to use it to enforce and publicly to sanction the mandate given to the church by Christ. That mandate was immutable, and never subject to human authority. The ruler was excluded from its operation. But if the church and the ministers neglected, falsified or exceeded their mandate, they did injury to God's Glory and trespassed into the human realm of the ruler, who was in either case divinely authorised to act. Whatever was beyond the mandate was subject to him; whatever was ill-done or partially omitted ought to be corrected by his supreme

---

[1] *Dissertatio Epistolica*, 36; cf. 42. [2] *Ib.* 41.

authority. This did not mean that the ruler assumed the function of the ministry; that was impossible. But it meant that he was responsible to God for the constant exercise of that function according to the mandate. Thus he had power over ecclesiastical persons to compel them to fulfil that function, and not over the function itself. The magistrate could not undertake functions which sprang from God or nature, such as a doctor's, a husband's or a minister's, but in each he could ensure that the inherent power of that function was not abused but used according to the divine purpose. This was an outcome of the imperium and did not require a medical, conjugal or sacerdotal power.

Therefore, Vossius decided that the magistrate's power was by divine right and used upon his direct responsibility to God, when he commanded whatever God Himself had commanded, and when he commanded whatsoever was consonant to God's commands, not being divinely defined and yet necessary to the church. Beza, Vossius said, went so far as to grant an indirect power over the essentials of the church to the magistrate while he enforced God's commands; surely Beza would have granted a direct power to the ruler in matters not specially commanded by the Word, but useful and edifying to the church.

The operation of this ecclesiastical power, whether internal or external, depended upon judgment. The acts of preaching or of administering the sacraments or of discipline were effected by human volition, and so by human discretion, as much as were acts of the government of the church. It was true that acts of internal power were determined by the Will of God, but even the ministers, who were His legates in these matters, received His commands through their own judgments and distinguished God's Will from men's by His guidance of their judgment. The ministers voiced the judgment of God against sins committed in these interior matters of faith, but their action was persuasive or directive. The ministers could only explain to the sinner the nature of his sin and the possibility of a divine penalty, and so to direct him by persuasion to return to the way God desired. The ministers, therefore, only exercised their power by convincing the conscience. But this was very different from the rulers' judgment which was imperative and compulsory, though confined to the external regulation of the church.[1] This judgment was final, and must be obeyed as an order, since its validity depended entirely upon the ability of the ruler to enforce it. The distinction between the judgment of authority and that of power was very precious, because its observance obviated all possibility of a mutual encroachment, as the moral judgment of the ministers was left unimpaired while the imperium of the ruler was not denied. It enabled the minister to preserve the highest moral standards and the magistrate to order what he deemed necessary for the administration of the institution. But he himself must decide who were the true ministers, whose judgment in matters of faith he would adopt.

Therefore, since the decisions of a synod must be approved by the individual conscience, the magistrate as parens patriae had an even more important share in judging their value, especially since canons only became law through his assent. It was for him to call a synod and to contribute his opinion, and because synods were as fallible as magistrates, he must exercise his own discretion. "Their function [of synods] is to guide the intellect to a recognition of truth: the magistrate should command rather what is right and safe."[2] But the Will of God must always be obeyed, although the magistrate had the right to command anything which was not repugnant to God's Will, and to command whatever God Himself ordered. He had his share, therefore, in promulgating ecclesiastical laws.

Finally, Vossius argued that this power was an inalienable prerogative, given by divine right to the ruler alone, or at least to the office he held. This was admitted of his civil power: if he renounced the summum imperium in civil government he ceased to be the supreme power in the state. With far more reason should the ecclesiastical power of the ruler be deemed inalienable; for the end of political society was eternal as well as temporal felicity, and since the ruler existed for the good of the state, he should govern ecclesiastical as much as civil life. To surrender this power was to abandon the primary part of the imperium, and to cease to be the supreme power.

A fortunate illustration of this theory was given by Vossius

---

[1] *Dissertatio Epistolica*, 31.   [2] *Ib.* 48.

himself, and served to answer many questions arising out of an
abstract discussion. The example to which he applied his principles was the communion.[1] In its essential and divinely ordained
form, the ministers had no right to omit or to change any element,
while the magistrate as the supreme governor of the church had
only the power of ensuring that its divine institution was faithfully
observed by the ministers; so that if the ministers offered to the
communicant merely the cup or the bread, the magistrate ought
to prevent this abuse. In its external and accessory attributes,
the church, and therefore he who as magistrate ruled the church,
had the power of instituting whatever was required on account
of time, place, numbers and methods: to determine in what church
buildings the communion should be celebrated; what times were
most suited for pious devotion; how often in the year, and whether
on weekdays or on Sundays; and with what prayers, hymns and
ceremonies. In these matters the church had the right to define,
and to issue canons; and in these same matters the magistrate was
granted the direct and proper imperium.

Convinced of the validity of this distinction between ecclesiastically essential and accidental, the direct and indirect
imperium, Vossius claimed that his theory reconciled the divine
right of the ministry with the divine right of the magistracy. He
vindicated to the magistracy that external and corporal power
which Walaeus recognised, and denied that any pious ruler
claimed any more. Finally, it is obvious that most of these ideas
were incorporated into Grotius' *De Imperio summarum potestatum
circa sacra.*

The foundations of Vossius' thought were the system of divine
rights and the dual organisation of a unitary society as church and
state, which had some resemblance to Hooker's thought. The
first testified to the influence of the Reformation which made
divine right fashionable; the second to the reaction of Renaissance
politics upon thought, and to the growing consciousness of the
fundamental meaning of the Greek and Roman thinkers. Protestantism tended to rely upon divine right; but in England and
the Netherlands, the Renaissance-Classical concepts expressed
the national ideals which dominated the period of transition. The

[1] *Dissertatio Epistolica,* 42.

nation seemed a living and corporate entity, which included the personalities of its members, and was, therefore, the one social unity. The state became the organ of sovereignty, the national and state church the organ of national salvation. The intimate relation of the two made the sovereign responsible for the moral, religious and spiritual welfare of the nation as well as for its material convenience; but he undertook this by his imperium, and where that could have no effect, his duty ceased. By the seventeenth century, these ideas were blended with divine right, partly in order to limit the jus divinum of the Calvinist church, partly because a Christian humanism was the spiritual synthesis of the century and that was easily expressed in the divine ordination of the national society, state and church. This type of divine right was triumphant over all others in the seventeenth century, and rose to intellectual priority upon the practical policy of the Calvinists, which discredited their own conception of divine right. In this way divine right was used in the hands of liberal "high state" thinkers to express, expound and preserve the organic conception of society and the liberal function of the state, and to develop the theory of sovereignty without destroying the unique character of revelation and function. Vossius' Erastianism was thus a product of his Christian humanism. It was as natural that he should apply political principles derived from the ancient city states to Renaissance national states as it was for Calvinists to apply Genevan ideals to national states. To the Renaissance, the ideal of the city state was the ideal of the nation state; but the Reformation left an indelible principle, the religious origins and ends of the state. Vossius, bred in the Reformation and student of antiquity, humanised the corpus christianum by Classical ideals, and used divine right to vindicate a theory produced by the interaction of Renaissance and Reformed principles.

§ IV

Grotius had little sympathy with the Calvinist ideal, and his life conspired to make him a champion of the humanistic and evangelical aspects of the Reformation rather than of the doctrines and creeds of the Reformed Church. To him the value of the Reformation was in reform, and not in the revolutionary interpretation of the Apostolic Church which Calvinist theology stressed so much. In spite of Oldenbarneveldt's attempt to avoid internal conflict and dissension, the politicians found themselves drawn into the great struggle between the Remonstrants and Contra-Remonstrants. Grotius, the publicist of his party, was reluctantly forced to take up his pen against the orthodox clergy and in defence of the States of Holland.

The pamphlets and apologies which he composed in the period from 1612 to 1622 were ephemeral, topical and controversial. In none of them did he escape from the immediate issues which had become not only confused but partisan. Misrepresentation and intrigue were current on both sides: hotheaded and unwise publications falsified the real issue. Ignorance and party passion allowed no time for the production of serious and moderate expositions, save that of Walaeus, unfortunately not the model for either party. Grotius did not, and probably could not, adopt a dispassionate treatment of the political problems which were so acute in that period.

He was a leading official in Holland and wrote at the command of the States, partly in order to influence the burghers of Amsterdam and the political and civil leaders of the other States, partly in order to defend the policy of Oldenbarneveldt to the outside world. His reputation gained at least a hearing for his party, but his publications had little influence upon either the leaders of the other provinces, or upon rulers such as James I of England.

In these topical and controversial apologies for the States of Holland, Grotius appealed primarily to the facts and precedents which recent history afforded. He tried to meet an obviously novel issue by an appeal to the past, particularly to the development of the Reformation under the leadership of William the Silent. He sought to vindicate the policy of the States largely by the argument that the claims of the Contra-Remonstrants were contrary to the practice and policy of the Fathers of the War of Independence, to whom the danger of Calvinism as another tyranny over the conscience was very real and to whom provincial sovereignty was the very basis of their union against Spain.

Grotius, therefore, opposed divine right by appealing to the historical and the practical, and met the claims of theological absolutism by the experience and customs of the period. It was, perhaps, a tactical error to try to stem the passions, let loose by the challenge to the old order, by pleading the sanction of that order. It was an appeal to the governing class to remember their traditions at a time when that class itself was doubting their value under the strain of new needs. Grotius hardly appreciated the political realities of the time, and failed to convince his own countrymen that custom justified the policy of Holland.

Grotius took his stand upon two main principles. The first was the sovereignty of the provinces, a point which was in fact at issue. However strong might be his position as a student of constitutional law, it was not adequate to meet a crisis which was greater than any one province could solve. The preponderance of Holland in the federation accounted for its desire to avoid any system in which it might be outvoted, since the other provinces tended, through their relative weakness, to accept the leadership of Holland. Grotius attempted to establish this strong claim in matters of religion. He accepted the current view that the rulers were responsible for establishing one public church, in which nothing conflicting with the Word of God was to be permitted. Apart from that condition, the rulers were free to order the church in the interests of the whole land. This was for him one of the foremost principles of the Dutch Reformation against the ecclesiastical supremacy of Rome. He appealed to the example and warnings of William I, to the attitude of the States in 1586, and to the proposals of the ecclesiastical constitution of 1591. He appealed, also, to the rights of the Counts of Holland which had passed to the States, and pointed out that even Zeeland had asserted such rights against the orthodox party in the church. He argued from the evolution of church-government during the first centuries of Christianity that much of church organisation was relative and human. Arguments of this kind were not, however, likely to convince genuine Calvinists at a time when bitter controversy made principle of supreme importance. Moreover, the application of these arguments meant for the church a state control which denied the freedom essential for its spiritual progress. Provincial sovereignty in matters of religion thwarted a national and authoritative synod since any one province might veto its meeting and its actions. Provincial synods would have been tools of the provincial governments, and the claim of the politicians to exercise more than a formal approval of pastoral appointments was equally suggestive of the subordination of religion to a church, in itself merely an organ of the provinces.

It is difficult to estimate the extent of the tyranny with which the States of Holland afflicted the orthodox party, and there would be little need to consider such a question but for the tendency in Dutch history to adopt contrary conclusions. Thus, Visser assumes that Grotius' argument for provincial sovereignty in religious matters would have destroyed the church by squeezing it into a system of political uniformity. On the other hand, critics of Calvinist ideals in that period, 1610–1620, tend to emphasise the intolerant and exclusive character of the Contra-Remonstrant church, and to argue that the policy of the States was moderate and liberal, in intention at least. The issue was between fundamentally divergent ideals linked by the principle that the state was to allow only one public church. Tyranny was the accusation of the party whose ideals were in danger, and the course of history showed that neither ecclesiastical nor political claims were to be admitted in full. Neither Calvinism nor the States of Holland was the advocate of genuine toleration; but toleration was gradually conceived in the struggles between them.

The posthumous *De Imperio summarum potestatum circa sacra* was a philosophical defence of Erastianism as a principle of church-government, and was not limited by circumstances of Dutch history. Grotius did, indeed, make great use of the history of the early church, but the real principles upon which he based the *De Imperio* were borrowed from political theorists. His standpoint was an academic and dispassionate examination of the relation of the church to the sovereign state. He did not try to meet jus divinum by historical precedents and constitutional rights, but by examining the implications of sovereignty.

The *De Imperio* was published in 1647, but there is evidence in his letters to G. J. Vossius and other scholars that he had planned and in some measure executed a similar work between

1613 and 1617.[1] In the latter year,[2] two letters to Grotius acknowledged the receipt of a treatise *de Imperio*. In a letter[3] of the August or September of 1614 he referred to a writing *de jure magistratuum*, and in a letter[4] to Grotius dated 27 October 1614, Vossius expressed his thanks for copies of the *Edictum Ordinum* and *Bona Fides*, but added: "utinam vero simul emisisses scriptum tuum, de summi Magistratus jure circa Ecclesiastica". Grotius[5] referred to his "dissertatiuncula de imperio circa sacra". After receiving Vossius' *Dissertatio Epistolica*, Grotius[6] excused himself in several letters for retaining it, pleading that it was useful to him in compiling the "diatribe de Imperio", which he sent to Vossius toward the end of 1616. He asked Vossius to delete anything which might cause ill-feeling.[7] He asked Overall, Bishop of Coventry, to show it to the Bishop of Ely and to win the approval of the king himself.[8]

The *De Imperio* was intended to be Grotius' authoritative work upon the relations of church and state, but his argument seems inadequate in form, logic and substance. In part, this was due, first, to his clear grasp of the fact that the central issue was the nature of sovereignty, and secondly to his wholly superficial treatment of that issue; for his proofs were without validity, at least to all who had given a fair hearing to the Calvinist case. Although the significance of the *De Imperio* rested chiefly upon its investigation of the implications of sovereignty when it was applied to matters of faith and of conscience, and therefore upon its treatment of the relations of church and state as the relations of a sovereign body to a social group within it, Grotius attempted no analysis of sovereignty. He assumed that there was no opposition of law and theology, for law was a social necessity for which grace was no substitute. Grace did not destroy nature, but enlightened the mind as to the way of salvation. So that Grotius rejected the view that the Christian revelation was even a partial substitute for or encroachment upon the existing divine provision, which, while equally necessary for the work of revelation, was not

[1] Cf. Thomasius, Chr., *Historia Contentionis inter imperium et sacerdotium*, Halle, 1722, 348.
[2] *Epist. Praest. Vir.* 484.
[3] *Grotii Epistolae*, Amst. 1687, 14.
[4] *Epist. Praest. Vir.* 392.
[5] *Grotii Epistolae*, 16.
[6] *Ib.* 32, 33.
[7] *Ib.* 41.
[8] *Ib.* 44.

governed by that revelation. Indeed, it seemed that Grotius assumed that anything threatening the nature of sovereignty was not of the Christian revelation, and consequently had no claim to human obedience. If the state was truly sovereign, the church was subordinate; if it was not sovereign, it had to be proved that sovereignty had been destroyed by the Christian revelation, thereby freeing the church.

The subordination of the church threatened the Christian revelation, and it was the object of Grotius' legal argument to define the legal conception of sovereignty so that the moral mission of the church might not be impaired. His task was to find the natural limits by which a legal conception was confined.

In the terms of his thought, this sovereignty was identified with the imperium, invested in the supreme power, by which "I understand a Person, or a Company, that hath Empire, or Authority over the people subject to the Empire of God alone".[1] As the imperium was not inherent in the jus but in the body administering the jus, and as the supreme power was a unity, if not of person yet of convention, it is evident that the idea of a divine right, which it was the duty of the ruler to apply to human circumstances, was accepted by Grotius, but with the qualification that divine law had no legal obligation until it was ratified by the human sovereign. The imperium was more positive than the enunciation of jus; therefore, to Grotius, jurisdiction was part of the general and imperative obligation to enforce right, and was an attribute of sovereignty. The possessor of imperium was responsible alone for the measures by which right was vindicated in human society, and was entitled to decide how far subjects were to be compelled, to be permitted, and to be forbidden to obey divine right. Right was transformed into law only when the sanction of force was added to its promulgation. Behind Grotius' argument was the conviction that the use of force to determine social relations was only moral in so far as it was concentrated at one known centre in the state. All force other than that proper to the official possessor of the imperium was immoral because it was antisocial. In short, there was one system of law in the state, one legislator, and one authority to coerce.

[1] Transl. Barksdale (1651), 1.

The *De Imperio* assumed that this was the nature of the imperium and defended it only by appeal to Bodin, the Dominican Victoria, and the Jesuit Suarez. But Grotius was immediately concerned with its implications when he passed to the main problem of the first chapter—whether the imperium was operative around religious and ecclesiastical organisation. It was not enough to quote Bodin or Suarez without enlarging upon their argument, nor was the issue to be evaded. Therefore, Grotius had to prove that "sacra" were not outside the imperium, and to indicate the manner in which and the extent to which sovereignty and absolute power might be finally responsible to God for the conduct of ecclesiastical affairs. In conceding to the supreme power this same discretionary and coercive authority in sacred as in civil matters, he had to plead with more than his usual eloquence to meet papal and presbyterian prejudice, and with more than his usual ingenuity to avoid pagan emperor worship.

This thesis rested upon three primary principles: the unity of matter, the operation of the imperium, and the universality of end corresponding to the universality of matter.

The unity of society was reflected in the unity of social matter, and in defending this principle Grotius had set himself against any concession to the medieval ideal of independent and self-sufficing societies. He saw a revival of the old dualism of church and state in Contra-Remonstrant theory, defended on the ground that the ecclesiastical society was constructed of materials in themselves sacred, whereas the civil society was built of secular materials. Grotius denied that church and state were two societies because he was convinced that the material underlying both social groups was of the same nature. His conception of social matter was obscure, but it seems that he was distinguishing between the purpose and the structure of different societies. He admitted elsewhere that social bodies differed in their specialised purposes but he seems to have denied that they differed in their structure. He seems to have understood by society those ordered external relations of men without which any group existed only in the gregarious sympathies of its individual members. Such external relations were necessary and common to all communities, and, within the limits of any given territory, were most developed in the state. There was, as it were, a common stock of social materials regulated by the most comprehensive society, but drawn upon by all lesser associations of men. Social matter was, therefore, those forms of administration and organisation which every association as such, whatever its purpose, had to adopt. The church, as an association of men, was organised and governed in the same way as any group in society, and used the same social means and external organisation. The church as a society used means not intrinsically different from those of civil society; they differed only in so far as the social structure common to both was used for a sacred or civil purpose in a sacred or civil way. Matter was of one kind which could not be artificially subdivided and intrinsically differentiated. Ecclesiastics and citizens employed as men a common inheritance of matter. It was not possible to separate sacred and secular matter, and in consequence it was not possible to limit the imperium merely to civil matter. The imperium operated within the sphere of matter, of external action and of force, and was not to be turned from its legitimate and natural activities because sacred matter was considered as something fundamentally distinct from civil. Wherever there was matter, the imperium was the architectonic authority and power because its superior force, moralised by its corporate origin, was final wherever force was capable of determining human life—in matter, external, physical and visible. The Apostle Paul accepted this principle. The supreme power was a ministry of God appointed to punish by the exercise of coercion all who do wrong; so that misdeeds, whether ecclesiastical or civil, were to be punished coercively by the supreme power alone. Its imperium extended over sacred as much as over secular matter: for its coercion was effective in both. There was no ground on which to claim an immunity from the imperium. God, the author of unity, disposed all things moral and natural in due order, and grouped society under the final compulsory authority of the imperium. That body which would exempt itself from the imperium defied the intention of God and so was not authorised by Him: "for if that which is excepted be subject to no Authority at all (which who can prove?) there will follow confusion among the things exempted, whereof God is not the Author: or if it be subject to some other Authority, not under the Highest Power, there must then bee two Highest Powers distinct: which is a contradiction; for the Highest hath no equal".[1] As there is one will in man, Grotius concluded with a somewhat trite anthropomorphic analogy, so there must be one will in the body of society, since Art always imitated Nature.[2]

The effects of the imperium demonstrated the same idea— that sacred and civil were both subject to it—and denied that sacred things might be exempt from its definitive judgment. These effects were "obligation" and "co-action". If there were many powers in any territorial unity, there would be a corresponding number of effects which would be opposed and would produce a contrariety which was incompatible with obligation and co-action. On the one hand, where two laws commanded contradictory duties, "the obligation of the one ceaseth"; on the other, where there is a multitude of powers and so a division of authority, the citizen "is bound to obey them all at once, which is impossible: or, if not to obey all, then there must be some order among them, and the inferiour yeeld to the Superiour, and then 'twill not be true that the highest Authority is divided among them". Therefore, the supreme power cannot be divided according to the diversity of functions, as military or judicial or ecclesiastical, without sacrificing the essential order of society and without destroying the peculiar attributes of the imperium, obligation and co-action. The unitary character of man and society demanded a unitary conception of the imperium: for if there were several imperia with obligation and co-action, the individual citizen would be placed in the awkward situation of obeying some and disobeying others. To permit more than one depository of ultimate coercion would disintegrate society and invalidate the conditions of its existence. Such supreme regulation was required to prevent the collision of the various members of the state and the resultant destruction of civilised life, but such

[1] Transl. Barksdale (1651), 3.
[2] Cf. *ib.* 53, where Grotius held that the ruler was superior not only to all the people severally, but also the whole people altogether.

power and potential direction could not be exercised over the Supreme Power itself because it was the final coercive authority, from which there was no appeal save to God. Although He laid down the general principles governing human conduct and social life, He required the supreme power as His agent to apply these principles to social necessities and to adapt them to particular cases, but above all to preserve the harmony and co-ordination of the elements of society by the use of its supreme coercive power. If the imperium, as the heart of the social organism, was supreme, and if it possessed the final word in all cases where obligation and co-action were feasible, then sacred or ecclesiastical affairs were not outside its scope. There must be some institutional embodiment of that corporate coercion which must be supreme throughout society, as much in ecclesiastical as in civil administration: if not, there could be no imperium, for it was manifested in obligation and co-action which could no longer exist where there was more than one such institution recognised in society. Coercion was naturally destined to concentrate at a few centres, and, the more organised society became, in the one supreme power. The church did not claim the power to coerce its members, indeed it expressly discarded such pretensions. In so far as sacred matters needed the services of the imperium—obligation and co-action—it was the function, duty and right of the state to act, and not of the church to usurp a power which it was never granted and could not possess without being sovereign. Since the state possessed the monopoly of coercion, all activities of the church which were derived from its character as a human association using visible means, and dependent upon the sanction of the corporate power of the community, were subject to the supervision of the state in consequence of its responsibility for the use of that coercion. There was, Grotius concluded, only one supreme power in the state with an imperium which extended over ecclesiastical and civil matters alike in so far as force was necessary and possible: the church was in the last resort subject to the sovereignty of the state in so far as the church fell within that medium in which sovereignty was operative.

Finally, Grotius proved his contention that the imperium included ecclesiastical activities within its range of action by an appeal to the end of the state and to its function in the service of mankind. "The Universality of the End is correspondent to the universality of the matter." Just as matter was unitary, so was the purpose of life: just as church and state employed the same materials of human existence and intercourse, so both directed their efforts to the same objective—the ultimate divine intention of life. God created man with many interests but for one end, and He created the state and the church to meet those interests and to achieve that end by their different means and methods. The individual was essentially a unity, and so God did not propose that he should serve and be served by different institutions which sought distinct and peculiar ends. Man's life on earth was, therefore, of one piece which state and church together directed to its conclusion upon the earthly stage. The church did not hold before his eyes a supernatural end which was wholly unrelated to the natural end of human life: both were integral parts of an end which included and transcended such distinctions. The state served God's Will by using its power in its own prescribed way to promote that end of human life which existed in God's mind: the church brought to the same task the miraculous offices with which it was endowed by and through the Word of God. Grotius, however, had a more liberal conception of the end of life and of God's purpose than had the theologians: it was here that he really deviated from Calvinist thought and betrayed humanist and pagan sympathies. He held it false to contrast spiritual and civil good because human felicity contained both as inseparable complements. Not only had man as a Christian to seek personal salvation, but also as a citizen to contribute his utmost to the advancement of the happiness of society. Happiness and goodness became synonymous to Grotius, the Christian life meaning the good life in society and not an anti-social devotion to a particular end, since the universality of end corresponded to the universality of matter. Just as it would falsify God's Will to oppose spiritual and temporal, as destructive of the harmony of life, so it would render His purpose unnatural to oppose the unitary nature of the subject-matter of life and the end to which life was directed. The end and material of life being joined in the divine plan, to correlate both in human society there must be one final authority concerned as much with ecclesiastical as with civil matters. It was the duty of the supreme power to promote that eternal blessedness which sprang from the vision of God, and because that vision was the most perfect good, the supreme power was responsible for its achievement by all the citizens. So said the author of the *De Regimine Principum*. Ammianus looked the same way when he stated that the imperium was the responsibility for the subject's salvation. Aristotle was yoked to these medieval authorities. His ideal of a state was that in which every member could act best and live most blessedly; it was more than external peace, it was the fruition of the "virtus" inherent in every citizen. Paul emphasised the same responsibility of the state for the tranquil life in piety as well as honesty, according to the inward springs of revealed religion as much as the accepted commonsense of morality, and according to the life-changing force of faith as much as the social wisdom governing external conduct. If it is granted that the supreme power ought to dedicate its activity to the creation of a citizenship animated by the most inspiring religious faith and principles, then the imperium must be understood as the only means and methods available to the supreme power. As Grotius so succinctly stated: "if this be true, that the end proposed to the Highest Powers is not only external Peace but that their People may be most Religious; and the things conducing to that end are called Sacred; it followes, that these things are all included within the Command and Authority of the same Power; for the End being granted, a Right is granted to all that, without which the End cannot be obtained." As the imperium was the bond between ruler and subject, the instrument of official capacity, and the expression of will endowed with an amplitude of authority, it was the one legitimate method of government. Since, also, everything relating to the religious life of the subject was contained within the purpose of the state and was collectively described as "sacra", Grotius concluded that the supreme power was not debarred from applying the imperium in sacred matters.

These doctrines were elaborately illustrated from the Old Testament and the Protestant Confessions: while approving reference was made to the eminent political philosophers to whom the imperium in "sacra" was not only a part of the supreme power's prerogative, but the most potent and distinguished part. From Suarez, Grotius quoted the opinion of Aquinas that the human state using its natural power had the primary care of divine worship and religion, and added the comment of Cajetanus that this was true not only of states in which false gods were worshipped but also of those in which the true God was reverenced from the light of nature, and not of revelation. It only remained to conclude with the Basel Confession that, as this office was enjoined upon the gentile magistrate, how much more so upon the Christian magistrate as the true Vicar of God. With Plato and Cicero, Grotius exploited God as a social asset: piety was the truest safeguard of peace and concord, not only in the life to come but also in the life on earth. Dogmas and rites were less important than social customs and public felicity, and therefore were subordinate to the wisdom of the supreme power. Finally Grotius made the most of the danger of priestly rivals to the rulers, and of the reactions of religious changes upon the state. The spectre of theocratic tyranny, direct or indirect, was laid only by taking refuge in the charity of the supreme power.

Grotius had clearly indicated his thesis in the first chapter: that the imperium could not be restricted to purely temporal matters, and that it ought to function equally in sacred activities. But this was no absolute claim, for his Erastianism was not that of Hobbes but of the liberal protestants of the early Reformation to which Arminianism was deeply indebted. Sovereignty was no tyranny, no unconditional authority, and not universally applicable or operative. Grotius had to make a closer analysis in order to denote the limits of that power, and the nature and scope of sovereignty: so that the remaining chapters of the De Imperio constituted a qualification of his opening thesis.

His first distinction was simple. The holy function was fundamentally different from the exercise of the imperium in the sacred medium of that function, since the pastoral office did not draw its inspiration nor its essential factors from the magistrate but from the divine ordination. This difference between the function and the imperium was further justified by the axiomatic fact that "it is the Ruler's office not to do the things commanded but to command them to be done".[1] All functions were, therefore, subject to the imperium, but not in the same way: "some are subject both by nature and order, as effects proceeding from their cause; some only by order". In other words, some functions were derived from the nature of the imperium, others from God or nature, but all were subject to the imperium in consequence of the necessity of order, which was the outcome of the imperium. To the first type belonged "the offices that hath in them Authority and Jurisdiction", to the second the function of a physician or philosopher. The pastoral function was of this second type. It had its own rules for the administration of its office and for the realisation of its purpose, as befitting a skilled craft in which the province of the expert was inviolate because its specialised training could not be usurped but had to be learnt. Since doctors determined the principles of medicine, and sailors the method of navigation, pastors also had the right to regulate the science of salvation within the bounds of their divine commission and natural conditions. It was for them to prescribe the conduct of the spiritual life and to sanction the methods by which it should be cultivated. Yet as doctors and sailors were subject to the magistrate in all things outside the innately natural principles of their function, so should pastors accept the architectonic supremacy. In so far as they possessed any imperium or jurisdiction which was not attached to the pastoral function they were the vicars of the magistrate: so that when judicial or coercive authority was exercised by them, so far the overlordship of the supreme power was legitimate. In no case could pastors be superior to the supreme power, for their authority was that of counsellors whose advice might be taken or rejected, and who while controlling their own function were without the power to force the supreme power to accept their decisions.

In theory it was possible for both the imperium and the function to belong to the same person or body: the diversity between them was no reason why both should not be competent to the same authority, as a doctor might be a singer, and yet would not sing as a doctor nor practise his profession in virtue of his singing. In order to unravel this theoretical combination it was essential

[1] Transl. Barksdale (1651), 16.

to distinguish between natural law and positive divine law. Natural law instituted no barrier to this conjunction, since the two need not conflict although vested in the same entity. A king might be a doctor or a priest. But the positive divine law did ordain the separation of the imperium and the holy function. Each required a specialised and trained official class, which could not interfere with the other without mutual detriment. In spite of this differentiation, the two remained intimately related, since the unique task of the pastors was the chief but not the only responsibility of the supreme power: that the divine will should be properly sanctioned in society. Grotius concluded that it was not surprising nor improper to attribute to the supreme power, in virtue of the connection of matter and end, a name strictly applicable to the holy function. The imperium might be called spiritual in so far as it dealt with religion which was spiritual. It was spiritual, therefore, in subject-matter but not in the way of operation. So that it did not in the least usurp or invade the function.

By his second distinction, Grotius denied that the government left to the pastors could nullify the imperium, since the method by which the church and its members were ruled was radically different from the method of political government.[1] Any analysis of the nature of government laid bare certain fundamental distinctions which must always be valid in any society. One broad division arose out of the extent to which the liberty of the subject was respected or ignored, and was dependent upon government by persuasion or command. The demagogue who, though without any constitutional status, ruled the mob by the magic of his personality, was as much a ruler of men as the properly appointed magistrate, and that rule might be even more powerful. All government was ultimately embedded in public opinion, although that form which relied wholly upon the response of the individual's free will to its appeal was exceedingly precarious. So long as government was by the authority of persuasion, it was powerless to withdraw from the subject any freedom of action or judgment which he was not willing to surrender spontaneously; in this way the doctor and lawyer ruled their clients. Their control over men

[1] Transl. Barksdale (1651), 59.

was more rational but no less impotent apart from the readiness of the ruled to adopt the offered advice. Such also was the rule of a society through the representations of experts, who though nominally the servants of the public were often its real rulers. Their advice need not be accepted because it was the opinion of a counsellor but it possessed a certain weight in consequence of the experience it embodied.[1]

The other form of government denied all right of the subject to withhold a ready allegiance because the element of persuasion had given place to that of compulsion. There was a power above and apart from the individual which bound his rational will to a wholehearted loyalty to the dictates of this superior, even when his will was perverted by passion and had to be forced to conform. In this category there were the absolute authority given by the declaration of an immutable law, and the absolute power granted to the legitimate constitutor of the law: government "Declarative of Law", and government "constitutive". The distinction arose from the different method by which the obligation to obey was imposed upon the subject. Declarative government did not compel at its own discretion but occasionally as when a man was informed of any obligation to which he was liable. Its power was the result of a simple statement of inevitable consequences, and thus a doctor ruled his patient and the philosopher regulated the moral and civil life, when each uttered his expert judgment not as the opinion of counsellors but as the verdict of inexorable circumstances. Obedience to them, in short, was acquiescence in the facts of nature. Once the subject had been shown the proper conduct of his life or business for his own good, as when a doctor prescribed, then he was bound to act accordingly "not by any Right which the Physician hath over him but by a Law of Nature which commands everyone to have a care of his own life and safety". Both the "declarative" and "suasory" types of government were aptly included in the more general title of "Directive Regiment".

Constitutive government was distinguished from the directive by added powers of compulsion and therefore by the increased obligation to obey. It arose either from consent or from command.

[1] Transl. Barksdale (1651), 59.

That from consent was derived from the obligation imposed upon the covenanters by the law of nature to keep the covenant, provided that it was within their right and power to make it. This government, however, was not that of a body created by an irrevocable and unlimited contract. The parties consenting were bound only so long as that consent was tacitly renewed, and not in perpetuity by that first consent. Dissentients were not directly bound, but indirectly if three conditions were present at the same time: provided that they were part of the whole, that the major part of the whole had consented, and that the matter in hand was necessary for the preservation of the whole. Grotius was so summary in his development of this point that it is difficult to be satisfied with his argument. Apparently the members of a group which dissent cannot be coerced, while those which consent may be compelled to obey. Apparently also the consent or dissent is more or less specifically related to the individual activities of the constitutive government by consent. A member may dissent on one matter, not be compelled to conform, and remain a member; he may consent on another matter, fail to fulfil his agreement, and so be subjected to the obligatory action of the constitutive government sanctioned by natural law. Membership of these groups is not the consequence of agreeing to some general contract but of a general agreement which does not bind the free will of the individual to dissent, in which case constitutive rule by consent is powerless. When dissentients were subject to coercion, the highest form of government had been achieved—the imperative which "obligeth by the intrinsecall force of its own supereminence". Where the jus obligandi resided there was the imperium: this therefore was vested in the supreme power alone.

The importance of this analysis of the different kinds of government was evident when Grotius applied it to pastoral government. The Scriptures, he triumphantly showed, had withdrawn all force and so all imperium from the ministry which held no sword but the Word of God and purely spiritual influences. The church, as its champions only too freely asserted, existed in heaven and was exalted by its spiritual nature beyond the world of matter; so that it acted on earth not as a citizen, but as a mere resident whose privileges depended upon the grace of the ruler and the tolerance of the citizens.[1] The church as the heavenly city had no legal claims in the earthly state, and the laws, institutions and chattels of its human manifestation depended upon the favour of the ruler as truly his. The invisible church was an alien without any status; it was the visible church, instituted as a society of men with certain beliefs and not as a mystic communion of saints, which was a citizen of the state, and therefore under the corporate authority. The difference was of the church as a natural and supernatural organism, the one being within the state and the other without because by its own nature it could not share in the life of the state. In either instance, the church was dependent upon the civil ruler for human and earthly activities.

Grotius' argument is clear. The invisible, spiritual and heavenly church was beyond the scope of sovereignty and therefore was not subject to it, unless it was localised in human beings and in a terrestrial form. In that case, when it adopted human characteristics it descended to an earthly condition which existed through the consent of the ruler. The visible church was a human association which was formed within the confines and out of the material of the state. In neither case was the church the legitimate possessor of the imperium; as invisible and spiritual, the church and the imperium were incompatible; as visible and external, the church was subject to the imperium.

"Yet since the Church is a company, not permitted only but instituted by Divine Law (I speak of the Church Visible) it follows that all those things which do naturally agree to lawful companies doe agree to the church also......among those things is the *Constitutive Government* which we called by consent."[2] The church was thus empowered by natural law to bind all who consented to its policy but not to compel those who dissented in greater or less degree. As a spontaneous human society to which voluntary allegiance was given by its members, it possessed the power of government from which there was no escape so long as conviction gained consent. The real government of the church, therefore, was the "directive regiment": in its train followed constitutive rule by consent, which was not by any means absolute even when accepted voluntarily. It[3] was always subject to the

---

[1] Transl. Barksdale (1651), 65.   [2] *Ib.* 65.   [3] *Ib.* 67.

imperative rule of the supreme power because no member of the state could transfer by his consent rights and powers which he did not possess to a minor corporation within the state: but no member of the state retained his right or power to resist the supreme power, and therefore he could not transfer such rights and powers of resistance. Government by consent was subject to the imperium because all social groups within the state were subject as parts to a whole.

According to this analysis of government, Grotius had divested the church of any rule which might conflict with the imperium, so that no rivalry was possible: for within the truly pastoral government there existed no imperative method of enforcement. It had to rely upon persuasion by emotional or rational appeal, upon the declaration of an infallible revelation, and upon that government devolved by consent. It depended upon the voluntary co-operation of the individual, overawed and overwhelmed by the weight of supernatural revelation. It was possible and consistent for Grotius to claim that the authority conceded to the church was not incompatible with the imperium. Through the justice of this claim, he was able to respect, acknowledge and provide for the genuine, natural and divine authority of the church without invalidating the fundamental premise of his theory that the supreme power alone possessed the imperium. In so far as the church and ecclesiastical society sought and employed the imperium, it was as a favour from the state.[1] The ruler alone controlled the imperium in sacred as in civil matters: whenever this ultimate sanction was necessary, the state acted upon its responsibility to God alone. The church, devoid of imperium, retained its own effective authority which could not challenge nor clash with the imperium. Each, therefore, acted in its way without mutual hindrance or hostility. Sovereignty was vindicated without the degradation or enslavement of the church; for the imperative government could not eliminate the directive or the constitutive government by consent, so long as the church fulfilled its function and gained the conviction and loyal obedience of its members. In the formulation and development of this principle, Grotius had become the prophet of a sound Erastianism, and

[1] Transl. Barksdale (1651), 66.

fused the contributions of lawyers and theologians into an equitable synthesis.

"Whatsoever we have given to Pastors, derogates nothing from the authority of the Highest Powers over Sacred things: for the *Directive Regiment*, consisting in the giving of counsell and declaring of the divine command, is quite of another kind. And 'tis no marvel if the same person do govern and is govern'd, in a divers kind of government; for the Counsellour governs the King by persuading; he that is skilled in Naturall right, by declaring divine Law; the Physician and Pastor both wayes; yet hath the King command over them all and that the Highest. The Government by consent, although Constitutive, is also subject to the Empire of the Highest Powers; because no man by consenting, can confer upon another more right, than he had himself. For this obligation, arising from the Liberty of everyone is not larger than that liberty; but they have not liberty, being single, to do anything against the command of the Highest Power (except the things which God commands:) therefore they have no right to bind themselves so farre."[1]

His third distinction undertook still more to make just division between the things of Caesar and of God. It depended upon what actions were controllable by sovereign authority and what were beyond that control. He took as his standard the capacity to command an action, which was the only way in which sovereignty could exercise its authority; and where an action could not be subjected to command, sovereignty was evidently inoperative or non-existent. The church might find some security in this.

All human power in his view[2] centred primarily round external matter, since the very nature of power demanded some positive material which might fall to the notice of the commanding authority, whose business was with manifest actions related to external changes. But the mind was beyond the range of the legislator and possessed its own laws. God alone might search the human heart, and to Him alone was the imperium over the mind and its activities possible. The internal acts of any man by their very nature were unknown to his neighbour and unknowable by the ruler; "and therefore, about the internall, which are wholly

---

[1] Transl. Barksdale (1651), 67.   [2] *Ib.* 28.

separated from the externall, and respect them not humane
commands are not given". Internal acts could not be accurately
ascertained, and could not be affected by those forces which
governed external acts: true sovereignty was concerned, therefore, with external and not internal action; but in so far as internal
affected external, there was a secondary authority over internal.
The two were intrinsically separate, but conjunction precipitated
a medium within the cognisance of the imperium, not on account
of internal but of its effect upon external. If the supreme power
saw that certain internal processes emerged into certain external
acts which were undesirable, it could only force the external to
conform to its will, but in so doing it warned every subject to
regulate his internal acts by the necessity of external conformity.
Internal acts were subject to command secondarily in two ways:
"either by the intention of the Ruler, or by a kind of repercussion:
in the first manner where the inward act is joyned with the outward, and hath influence upon it (for the mind is esteemed in
offences, either perfected or begun;) in the latter, when, because
any act is made unlawfull by the interdiction of the Ruler......
by thought to intend that action, is unlawful: not as if humane
Law were properly made for the thought: but because no man
can honestly will that, which is dishonest to be done". Sovereignty
could only affect the internal working of the mind, its convictions
and its motives, indirectly through direct regulation of external
conduct. Beyond its power there stretched whole worlds of inward
experience and spiritual intercourse which drew none of their
vital existence from external and visible forms but contributed
to those forms a control and guidance which were outside and
above the imperium, and therefore beyond the range and subject-
matter of sovereignty. The keys of these kingdoms were faith and
conviction; the way, persuasion. Force was incompatible with
their existence, and sovereignty was by its nature and their
constitution a meaningless conception. By defining sovereignty,
Grotius had released the mind and personality from the tyranny
of alien legal principles. The supreme power could not invade the
sanctuary of the soul nor despoil the treasury of the spirit.

The seeming value of this distinction was considerably reduced
by further development. Not only were actions divided into

internal and external, but also into those defined by morality and
those left undefined and consequently amoral. Action defined
by morality must be performed or eschewed; and its sanction
was drawn either from its own nature or from the positive
divine law. Natural law gave obligation not only to actions
"which flow from principles known by nature; but those also
which come from natural principles, certainly and deter-
minately". Natural actions were not merely those of nature
but of rational and equitable principles of ordered life. In this
sense, natural was opposed not to supernatural but to arbitrary
action. Actions defined by the law of nature were not only those
of non-human nature but also those of a rational human nature
regulating its life by principles as universal and as absolute as
those of nature. The impersonality of nature was balanced by that
of reason. Actions defined by the positive divine law were those
prescribed by God.

The immediate presumption from this argument was that only
those actions which were in no way defined remained to the human
sovereign. This Grotius admitted where it was a matter of the
defining authority. God alone could change the intrinsic character
of an action by giving it a moral sanction which raised it above the
power of the human ruler. The ruler could not treat as undefined
what God had defined, nor as prescribed what God had left free.
In this sense, the ruler was allowed discretion only in those actions
which God had not determined. But "when the things that ought
to be done, and those that ought not, are capable of a change
extrinsecall, and may receive it from humane Authority, it is
manifest, they are subject to the same Authority, unless they be
Actions meerely internall".[1] If the divine commands were
abstract generalisations requiring for their human operation
concrete forms which caused external reactions, the supreme
power was the legitimate means by which this process of adaptation to environment, and adjustment to time and place, might be
accomplished. "Hither it pertains to assign the time, place,
manner and persons, for performing of due actions, so far as the
circumstances are undefined by the nature of the thing, and the
Law of God; also to take away impediments......and to re-

---

[1] Transl. Barksdale (1651), 31.

straine unlawful actions, by such punishments as are in the Rulers power." Whenever these prescribed actions depended for their complete fulfilment in human society upon local external facilities, and would suffer transformation or deformation otherwise, these actions fell to that extent to the control of the supreme power. When these prescribed actions were defined down to the smallest detail, the supreme power had no right to authority over them.

All actions except such as were "repugnant either to the Naturall or to any other Divine Law" were the subject-matter of sovereignty. Internal actions and those completely and absolutely prescribed were excluded: but for the rest "there are two acts of Empire which belong not to the Right of him that Ruleth; to command what God forbids: To forbid what God commands". With that proviso, even external actions which were morally defined but not determined in every detail were subject to the imperium: it was a power complementary to that of God. The ruler could not intervene in internal actions; nor in external actions determined by God or nature could he defy the principles laid down prior to his own power; but so long as the supreme power respected the will of God and nature it was free to use its power round all external actions to advance that will, although in fully prescribed actions it was merely enforcing or facilitating the instructions of God.

Ecclesiastical and civil actions in relation to the imperium followed this general relation of actions to command. Ecclesiastical actions as such were no more immune than civil: they escaped human and imperative regulation only in so far as all actions did. The issue was not whether ecclesiastical actions were sacred, but whether they were internal or external, morally determined or undetermined. In so far as they were internal, the imperium possessed only indirect control: thoughts were not to be ruled so easily as words, while inward acts in themselves were not the subject-matter of human power, but of divine and supernatural authority. Although God used His bishops "to move the minds of men with voices and signs", by ministering not by commanding, yet the grace which brought these ministering attentions to fruition was with God Himself. But Grotius added "notwithstanding, inward acts of all sorts, taken joyntly with the outward, fall under Humane Authority".[1] As soon as these spiritual services were linked with external and visible activities, they were subject to imperative control. It is difficult to think that Grotius believed that inward life save in the rarest and most rigid souls could resist the pressure of imperative government.

The vague and doctrinaire character of this argument about internal and external actions, formulating a theoretical distinction of small practical significance, was somewhat corrected by the application of his other contention, that the supreme power was limited by the divine will. It was as true in ecclesiastical as in other matters that the ruler could not command what God forbade, or forbid what God commanded. So long as he respected the positive assertions of divine authority, the ruler was not debarred from promoting ecclesiastical actions by the imperium. In this sense, the ruler might use his power around the Gospel, the ministry and the sacraments, for their advantage, and yet not subject them to his power, for he must not change that which God had instituted. Obviously, "the Preaching of the Word of Salvation and the exhibition of the Sacraments, being commanded by God, cannot effectually be forbidden by men". Moreover, since God had prescribed the forms of the ministry of the Word and sacraments, these could not be altered by human action; nor was such transforming action proper in sacred matters. It followed likewise that "it belongs not unto Humane Power to make new Articles of Faith".

It was not true, according to Grotius, to deny that the supreme power could regulate such actions, for it was its duty to use the imperium to facilitate their proper and complete realisation so long as it respected their divinely or materially ordained form and content. Accepting their fixed character, the imperium was serviceable to their advancement in human and imperfect conditions. "Yet to speak accurately, these things which we have rehearsed, Sacred and others, may be rather said to have something in them of immutable right, than simply and altogether exempted from the Rule of the Highest Powers; seeing that there be very many and very great acts of Authority concerning them."[2]

[1] Transl. Barksdale (1651), 40.   [2] *Ib.* 43.

Subjects had the right to expect from the supreme power even in such immutable matters "liberty and convenience to doe the things which God commandeth, being freed from impediments, and supplyed with helps". Secondly, by commanding what God commanded the supreme power added to their sanction the human obligation of the imperium. Thirdly, the supreme power provided ordained actions with prescribed circumstances of place, time and manner in the interests of efficient operation. Fourthly, the supreme power removed all temptations to commit what God had forbidden. Fifthly, by its punishments, the supreme power led its subjects to do what God ordered and to avoid what He forbade. These five duties constituted the function of the ruler as "the preservative of the Divine Lawes", a function which preserved by the exercise of its independent legislation.

God had not, however, determined every action: for the formulae of life were not all "written in the hearts of men, or in the Holy Bible", but left to human invention and discovery. Actions in this category were the matter of sovereignty, and were judged to be sacred or secular as the supreme power decided. Thus the ruler determined such ecclesiastical offices as existed "more for convenience and ornament than for necessity",[1] and such ecclesiastical business as the building of churches, the method of electing ministers, the occasions for the holding of synods, and the alienation of ecclesiastical property.

Supposing that the ruler abused his power and exceeded his proper limits by authorising anything contrary to the rules of faith and religion which were prescribed by God; then the subject must disobey and suffer the consequences of attempted coercion without resistance.[2] In this he was acting as he should when the ruler violated the perpetual rule of equity in civil matters. Therefore, Grotius[3] rejected the Calvinist doctrine of official resistance by the minor magistrates, unless this was strictly constitutional in consequence of contracts or positive laws of the State.

There remain certain actions called "intermediate"[4] by Grotius and some of these were "about the inward, some about the outward man". Those about the inward man were partly in

---

[1] Transl. Barksdale (1651), 45.
[2] Ib. 45.
[3] Ib. 36, 38.
[4] Ib. 56.

the man and partly concerning him, but all exceeded the power
of mere men, being peculiar to Christ, although He admitted
pastors, private men and kings to these actions each in his own
way. But they acted in these cases as different ministers of Christ
and not as Vicars: for "it is the part of the Vicar to produce
actions of like kind with his actions whose place he holds, though
of lesse perfection", while "to a meer Minister it pertaines not
to produce actions of like kind, but such as are serviceable to the
actions of the principall cause".

As to the actions about the outward man, consisting of protection and government of the church, these belonged to Christ's
providence, which was adequate guidance for the church; yet to
demonstrate His Wisdom, He employed the supreme power as
his deputy to preserve the common society of men. For this
reason, the imperium was entrusted with the regulation and
administration of ecclesiastical society.

Grotius had to adapt one more argument to thwart the
opponents of the imperium. If it could be proved that the determination of all doubtful matters rested with the church or the
pastors, then the labour he had given to enlarge the imperium
would have been sterile. Its great power would have depended
upon an external will, and the indirect sovereignty of the church
would have been well grounded on the work of the lawyers. He
would have built for his antagonists. To prevent such a calamitous
conclusion, he attributed to his supreme power a judgment
independent of the church, and authoritative even when it conflicted with the verdict of the church.

Any act of authority[1] proceeded from some judgment, since
a command was the product of a will informed and guided by the
discretion and decision of the individual. Voluntary action presumed a harmony of will and intellect on the one hand, and of
intellect and fact on the other. Uncertainty of mind rendered the
mind inefficacious, while a divergence of intellectual concepts
and human experience distorted judgment and destroyed the
will. Involuntary judgment implied the acceptance of some outward authority by the individual and the subordination of his own
will to its judgment. In this sense, it "properly denotes the act

---

[1] Transl. Barksdale (1651), 69.

of a superiour defining what is just between two parties", whence
the highest judgment was that of the supreme power. Since the
imperium was exercised over sacred as well as secular, the judgment of the supreme power must extend over both; and since all
human judgment was subject to error, and unless all judgment
was eliminated from human relations, there must exist one
definitive human judgment, whose mistakes must be reserved to
God. This was the imperative judgment which rested ultimately
upon coercion for its power of conviction; but in addition and of
totally different character was the directive judgment which
convinced men by a statement of possible consequences, relying
upon persuasive advocacy.

Grotius passionately denied that the imperative judgment
was allowed no place by the supreme judgment of Christ, and
passionately asserted that the directive judgment of the church
was as valid as that of the state. "The Supreme Judgment of
Christ doth no more deny this Judgement of which we speak,
than his Authority, the Authority of the Highest Powers. Legislation carrying with it, by its own virtue, the reward and punishment eternall and finall judgment, according to the Law, is the
prerogative of Christ alone. In the meane time, Christ speaks by
his spirit, by Divine Judgement; yet doth not Humane action
follow that Judgement, unlesse Humane Judgement be inter-
posed. Which as it belongs to every Christian in respect of his
private actions; so in respect of publike, and of private, that are
governed by publike Authority, it belongs to the Publike powers,
and to the Highest in the Highest degree......."[1] As the Architect of the Commonwealth, the ruler should have the final
decision in all human interests. But though he exercised power
over a doctor as a citizen, he as a man must obey the doctor as
the emissary of nature. It was not absurd to Grotius that there
should be two supreme judgments, though of different kinds, in
sacred matters, the one the directive of the Catholic church, the
other the imperative of the supreme power; "for there is no
Judgement among men higher *in esteeme* than that, none higher
than this *in Power*".[2]

Just as Grotius contrasted authority and power, so he also

---

[1] Transl. Barksdale (1651), 74.   [2] *Ib.* 71.

contrasted the righteousness and the validity of any action of the ruler, in order to prove that his imperative judgment was present in his official capacity, irrespective of personal qualities and the use he made of his power. Righteousness proceeded from a well-informed intellect and honest purpose of mind, but validity depended upon the right and the observance of constitutional practice. "We conclude therefore, that the fault either in the understanding, or the affection, makes not void an act of Authority: but the commands out of the Highest Powers are valid still (being not contrary to God's law) though they have not true opinions of things Divine, or serve not God aright." The distinction Grotius emphasised was between the aptitude and the power of judging. All magistrates possessed the power to judge in sacred and secular matters alike, but not the same aptitude, the reward of true Christianity. The Christian magistrate had no more power than the heathen, both sharing the imperium in sacred matters, but Christianity taught the one how to use it properly. The opportunity of the church lay in the conversion of the magistrate by its directive judgment, and never in withdrawal from his official power. Being in the state, it could not "contract out" whenever its claims were not admitted but must be content with its appeal to the conscience. "Wherefore let us also say, when Christian Kings give Commandements about Sacred matters, they have the Right to doe so as they are Kings; the skill, as Christians as taught of God, having the Divine Law inscribed on their hearts......."[1]

It is impossible to follow the application of these general principles to specific problems: a mere hint only can be given of the attitude Grotius adopted toward synods, presbyteries and jurisdiction. In relation to synods, his qualified absolutism is very evident, particularly in regard to their origin and end. "Wherefore we derive the originall of Synods from the Law of Nature. Man being a sociable creature, his nature permits association specially with them, to whom either contemplation, or action is common. So Merchants for Traffick, Physicians and Lawyers to examine the controversies in their Art, hold their meetings by the Law of Nature. But to avoid mistake, we dis-

---

[1] Transl. Barksdale (1651), 80.

tinguish between that which is naturall absolutely, and cannot be altered, as to worship God, to honour our Parents, not to hurt the innocent; and naturall after a sort, that is, permitted or allowed by nature, untill some Law of man interpose; thus all things are by Nature common, all persons free, the next of kin is heir, untill by humane constitutions propriety, and servitude be introduced, and the Inheritance be given away by Will. In this second acception, it is natural to hold synods.......”[1] Since Grotius had already shown that a synod possessed no share of government, its object was to "give Counsell to the Prince for the advancement of Truth and Piety, that is goe before him by a directive Judgement. Another end is that by the Synod the Consent of the Church may be Setled and made known.......A third end may be added to the former:......so synods, beside their native, have an adventitious right from Human Law: whereby they judge of causes as other Courts ordained by the Highest Power; and so, that upon their sentence co-action followes. But now, of all these ends none is necessary, nor is a synod simply necessary to those ends."[2] The relation of the ruler to the synod rested upon the particular end in view. "For first, many Synods are had only for counsell; but naturally it is lawful for everyone to chose his own counsellours.......Synods are also holden for the exercise of Externall Jurisdiction, committed to them by the Highest Power; but this also is naturall for everyone to choose his delegate. In the Synods, that are gathered for procuring of consent the case is somewhat different, in these it seems very expedient, that the election be either by the Churches or by the Pastors, to the end, the acts of the Synod may be more possible."[3]

In this connection, Grotius emphasised the unique power of sovereignty to determine that religion which was to be publicly exercised. "'Tis the Office of the Highest Power alone publickly to authorise the true Religion, and to remove the false. To remove Idols out of private places belongs to the Lord of the place; and upon his neglect, to the King as the Lord generall; but to remove them out of the publick place is the right of the Highest Power."[4]

[1] Transl. Barksdale (1651), III.   [2] Ib. 117.
[3] Ib. 127.   [4] Ib. 142.

Concerning the establishment of the ministry "whose function is principall and most necessary", it is necessary to differentiate four distinct elements: the "mandate",[1] or faculty of preaching, administering the sacraments, and using the keys; ordination, or application of the faculty to a person; election or location of the person in a particular congregation and place; and finally confirmation "whereby a certain person in a certain place exerciseth his ministery under the publick protection, and with publick authority". Of these the last was the peculiar property of the sovereign; the mandate was of God; ordination was by God through the ministry; while election belonged to the pastors by the law of nature "for naturally every society is permitted to procure those things, which are to their own conservation necessary; in which number is the application of functions".[2] This constituted, however, no immutable right.

Grotius' theory, therefore, rested upon his conception of the imperium. It was, in the first place, a unity correspondent to the unity of the state, which in turn was grounded upon the unity of society and of the individual. It was indivisible, and in consequence of one entity alone. Secondly, it was the organised definitive power of the community, and the entity responsible for its exercise was the supreme power. There was only one imperium in a state; to share it among parts of the state was by definition impossible; therefore there was only one sovereign body in the state. The church, unless it was sovereign, could not claim the imperium. Thirdly, the essence of the imperium was a monopoly of coercion, derived from the community and for that reason the only moral expression of force. The church had no moral right to force and, once again, no claim to the imperium. The supreme power was the lawfully instituted body to compel obedience in the interests of associated life. Even when that force was misused, no subject was entitled to resist although he ought not to fulfil the command which violated the express will of God. Fourthly, the imperium constituted the means of architectonic organisation and supervision of the state, and the activities of its members. Through it, the energies of social organs were co-ordinated in one coherent system. Without it, administrative confusion and inefficiency

---

[1] Transl. Barksdale (1651), 190.   [2] *Ib.* 195.

would be the least of many evils which would invade the state; the worst would be a condition of anarchy in which each association and each individual would act as each thought fit according to standards ranging from a self-interested use of force to an ineffective altruism. Fifthly, the imperium was one essential means to realise the eternal purpose of human existence—the salvation of souls; but this indicated more than a theological orthodoxy, a moral conduct and even a religious experience. It implied a good life in society, interpreted in a way which demanded the development of each member for the service and advantage of the community. The imperium was to facilitate this social contribution of the developed personality. Sixthly, the imperium facilitated and fostered this work not merely in a negative way by punishment, by administrative machinery, or even by material provisions, but in a positive way by ordering human life for the greatest good of the community. It existed to command what God willed and to forbid what God had denounced. Its task was to promote spiritual truths by all the resources at its disposal. Nevertheless, it acted and could only act through matter, external activity and social organisation; the normal and natural sphere of the imperium was the public operation of human society. The sanction of the imperium was necessary for any appearance or action upon the public platform of the state; the supreme power was responsible for all activity using and affecting the organisation of the state. Moreover, the method of the imperium was coercion, command and law. So far as these were necessary to regulate matter and public action, the imperium was the only authorised means; beyond them the imperium was impotent. Seventhly and finally, the imperium extended to sacred as to secular subjects so long as sacred possessed matter, and public and external embodiment. The unitary nature of matter and the unitary purpose of life removed all barriers to an imperium regulating visible and external activity by coercion and command; there could be no division into ecclesiastical and civil in order to limit the imperium in its proper sphere and using its proper methods.

The imperium was not universal nor absolute; it was limited by its subject-matter and its method, but also by other factors of somewhat doubtful value. First, the function was beyond the imperium; its principles were derived from some outside supernatural or natural power which no human power could affect. Navigation, medicine and salvation were sciences existing independently of human government, which could not change their innate characteristics. Secondly, internal acts were by their nature uncontrolled by the imperium. The inward operation of the mind was undiscernible and ungovernable. Faith and conviction not being products of force but of inward experience and transformation were subject to no command save that of God. The imperium could not create faith. The spiritual life and spiritual activities were inaccessible to the imperium. Thirdly, God had defined certain actions; some man ought to perform, others he ought to avoid. The imperium by its nature was operative in this sphere, but by God's prescription was bound to enforce His Will. Most ecclesiastical services and most of the essential offices of the church were thus defined, and thus freed from the antagonism of the imperium. Fourthly, the imperium could not usurp the "directive regiment" which persuaded men or convinced them by its directive judgment. That judgment was in no way competent to the imperium. Fifthly, and of less significance, constitutive government by consent belonged by the law of nature to any society; but it must not be conducted in a way contrary to the rights of the greatest society of all. There was, however, a vague and voluntary system of government which possessed an autonomous character so long as it worked within the confines of and according to the interests of the state. The holding of synods and the election of pastors were examples.

To some extent these limitations were illusory, for the imperium retained its legitimate power over all activities of importance to society. The organisation of associations in virtue of natural law was often subject to the ruler, since members could not empower them to act in a way contrary to the conditions by which they had become members of the state. Further, all external actions, even those defined by God, were proper to the imperium; while internal actions might be indirectly regulated by it. Lastly, the function in its environment was liable to imperative government. In spite of these qualifications, certain implied limits—divine, natural and legal—were imposed upon the imperium. The necessity of sovereignty was not allowed to override all life, though a large part of it.

§ V

The *Disputatio* was the one work of Episcopius which was exclusively concerned with the relation of church and state, but it was so summary in treatment that it is a matter of regret that the progress of the debate was not recorded. It is not possible to do more than present his own summary. His method was the formulation of theses which were left without adequate demonstration, and therefore many of his points were framed in a manner so dogmatic that it is impossible to enlarge upon them. This section does little more than present an outline of a highly suggestive scheme which was unfortunately never developed in a truly philosophical manner.

The *Disputatio*[1] began with two axioms from which Episcopius deduced his theory of the magistrate's power in relation to the public operation of ecclesiastical administration. Firstly, there was in every public society an ideal and a necessity of order which must be preserved inviolate. It was the *raison d'être* of the society and the first charge upon the corporate body. The organ responsible for this task and presumably endowed with proper facilities and powers was that person or body instructed and authorised by the grant of a certain power from God, the source of all order. Secondly, not only was it legitimate for any Christian to accept such office in the interests of public order, but also more fitting that a Christian rather than any other member of society should be empowered for this purpose. Both of these axioms were grounded in Protestant thought, and only the Anabaptists would have denied their validity. Later,[2] indeed, the Remonstrant leaders had to meet the argument put forward from within the party that no Christian ought to accept political office, and the necessity of countering this argument occasioned Episcopius' treatise *An homini Christiano liceat gerere Magistratum*. At the time of the *Disputatio* no Calvinist and no Arminian denied either of these basic assumptions of Episcopius.

[1] *Opera Theologia*, Pars Altera, 409; Disputatio xvii.
[2] Haentjens, 66.

Hence he laid down that the Christian magistrate ought to exercise the imperium as much about sacred as secular matters, since obedience was due to his command until and unless he contravened the precepts of Christ. In order to avoid confusion, he defined his use of the term "magistrate" as that person or body to whom the supreme power, ius and imperium in the community belonged, subordinate only to the divine power of Christ. To the magistrate must be subject all inferior officers of state lest that order which was the essence of society should be destroyed and dissolved.

The rational basis of order demanded that the responsibility for and power over sacred subjects should belong exclusively to the imperium of the magistrate. Only one other alternative was possible; that the magistrate did not possess the supreme power, but only a semblance of it, since the church had a power collateral to that of the state. The ministers must either be subordinate to the magistrate or possess an imperium which was independent; for they could not be above the magistrate without violating the express command of St Paul to be subject to the supreme power. The conception of two collateral imperia was inadmissible to reason since the governing principle of order was undermined. Order implied unity, but unity did not exist where society was subject to two equal and independent powers. The very nature of the imperium was contradicted by collaterality, for the imperium worked by binding and coercing men, involving dependence upon one supreme power: otherwise two divergent or antagonistic authorities would regulate the life of the same man at the same time. In that case unity was destroyed for no man could obey two masters; to regulate his life with any consistency he would have to choose which authority he would accept.

Here Episcopius entered a qualification. The whole range of sacred matters was not subject to the imperium, only a narrowly defined part. The substance of religion and the right and capacity to teach its message and to persuade men to live according to its inspiration was no subject for imperative government. The imperium was incapable of determining the fundamental beliefs of religion, and so that formative power and promise of eternal salvation which was the product of grace alone. The supreme power was limited to certain circumstances of place and time, personnel and mode of administration, which were properly included in the public authorisation and exercise of that religion which it approved, at times and in places and by persons it sanctioned. This alone was the power which Episcopius granted to the magistrate, because it was an essential part of his official capacity as lord of all public places, and therefore of the public offices and functions operating within the public body. On the other hand, religion, faith and the revealed way of Christian life were determined by Christ alone and subject to no mortal man, but left, as the Arminians believed, to the individual conscience of every Christian.

This power imposed upon the ruler not only the duty to provide for the free exercise of the sacred services of the church, to prevent abuse of those matters entrusted to the judgment of the ministry and to remove all hindrances and external impediments to the normal operation of the church; but also the greater power of constituting, commanding and enforcing the forms of public worship, the persons to conduct the public worship, and the way it should be conducted. Nevertheless, although the ruler was responsible to no earthly or human power, he ought to submit his will and commands to God, the absolute legislator, and to regulate his ecclesiastical policy in accordance with Scriptural revelation. When his laws and rites were in agreement with the Word, he ought then to institute such government of the church as was necessary for its orderly and efficient administration.

This principle gave to the ruler the right to take care of all public functions in both church and state. He had to choose and appoint persons he considered suitable, and judge, even by deciding peremptorily, their public actions. If it were advisable, the ruler might ignore the officers he had himself appointed to administer sacred services, needing neither their advice nor their authority, being sufficiently empowered by the Scriptures and the plenary power granted by God. In virtue of his supreme power of approving or disapproving, the ruler possessed the supreme judgment and so the supreme power.

It was an important corollary that no Christian might lawfully, in pursuance of his faith and creed, invade the public churches and places, or exercise the functions of a public office if the supreme power was unwilling. No one could usurp the status and sanction of a public preacher if the supreme power was unwilling. Therefore, any holder of that office ought not to preach publicly what the ruler forbade nor publicly criticise what the ruler determined should be publicly expounded; but if he found the obligations of his public office contrary to his conscience, he should withdraw from that office in order to regain the freedom of his own responsible conscience and so privately correct the errors of the public church without defying the public authority.

Episcopius hastened to add that doctrine was not thereby subordinated to the magistrate, nor were ministers slavishly bound to treat his commands as if they were divine. Doctrine was to be considered with regard to its essence, and its public character. The essence of religion was authorised by God alone, and as it was subject to the will of no man, even its public embodiment must be tested by God's Will. If the public enforcement conflicted with the divine command, such human inventions should not be taught from the public pulpit, but neither should they be publicly denounced, since this was unnecessary. It was one thing not to publish these errors publicly, and another to detract from the supreme power, when private propaganda was as effective as public. Public denunciation was unnecessary to truth and intolerable to the imperium. The fact that Episcopius held that every man was free to express his own opinion upon religious topics and principles, and equally free to communicate those opinions to any who would listen, certainly provided the means and opportunity of correcting errors in public doctrine without challenging the power of the ruler. The acceptance of a creed was no longer a test of loyalty, and dissenters could be tolerated without undermining public order and sovereignty. According to Episcopius, the church did not lose, while the faithful could grow more devoutly in the truth. It did not pertain to the state and the imperium to hinder or prohibit this freedom of religious enquiry and criticism. The errors of dissenters would be answered satisfactorily if the ruler took care that the true religion was preached publicly and taught privately. There was no necessity to punish dissenters in the interests of the one true creed.

Since the power of the ruler ought not to be employed to compel belief in one faith, because force could not produce conviction and because in so far as it tried it ventured into the realm of grace which was reserved to Christ alone, that power was rightfully exercised in working the machinery of ecclesiastical government. The ruler was empowered to summon classes and synods, to choose ministers and places of worship, to legislate in ecclesiastical interests, and to determine the method of worship. In the external apparatus of the church, the ruler could act decisively upon his own responsibility to God, reassured by the conviction that God had never ordained a collateral power of church and state to govern human society.

Finally, Episcopius argued that, if collaterality was divinely sanctioned, then it would apply also in other spheres, causing the power of the magistrate to devolve upon the people as the one remaining base for the unity of power, in defiance of the divine command to obey the king.

This outline of Episcopius' theory, framed so dogmatically in the *Disputatio*, was suggestive and stimulating in its novel restatement of a familiar thesis, but hardly adequate to solve the complicated problems inherent in the relation of church and state. Its significance lay in its new attitude toward the church, religion and the conscience. It was, as his editor Curcellaeus remarked, a lasting pity that Episcopius did not have the opportunity of developing more fully and more publicly the ideas which he formulated so briefly and therefore obscurely in these eighteen theses. It is to be the more regretted since they mark an important development in Arminian theory: an Erastianism qualified by toleration. The *Disputatio* was an attempt to preserve the sovereign authority without subordinating religion to its dictates: it was therefore a conscious modification of Arminian theory to meet Calvinist objections which had been undervalued until Arminianism was itself threatened by a hostile political authority.

The *Disputatio* had been one of the last duties of Episcopius as Professor of Theology at Leiden, and the eventful months which preceded the Synod of Dort probably accounted for its

genesis and its limited development. He was too busy to consider
a fuller exposition of its principles, but the times required some
treatment of the vital issue of the decade 1610–1620. When the
Remonstrant party was condemned by the synod and persecuted
by the Erastian but orthodox States, the leaders, driven into exile,
had to publish an authoritative statement of the party's principles.
That was the Confession of the Remonstrants. The Calvinists
could not ignore such a powerful appeal to the conscience of
Europe, and the "Censure"[1] published by the now-orthodox
Theological Faculty of Leiden was intended to vindicate Contra-
Remonstrant convictions by exposing the fallacies of the Confession. Episcopius' pen, which had probably written the greater
part of the Confession, was now turned to its defence and the
Apologia pro Confessione Remonstrantium was the result. It was
a vast polemical work designed to answer each specific objection
of the "Censure" to the Confession: it covered the content of the
Confession, and the entire range of Arminian belief. Theology
was by far the most important part, but here and there the duty
of the ruler and cognate matters were discussed.

In one of these passages,[2] Episcopius felt duty bound to explain
the Arminian theory of force, where and where not it should be
applied. The Calvinists had criticised the doctrine that all force
should be withdrawn from spiritual discipline, because this force
was internal and not external, and therefore inherent in the
church. It was for them a purely spiritual force. Episcopius
replied that the Remonstrants had never denied to the church a
discipline based upon a spiritual authority but had denied that
the church could use a coercive power independently of the ruler.
A spiritual power which convinced the conscience and thus won
obedience was not force. There was, however, an internal force
analogous to such natural forces as magnetic attraction or re-
pulsion, which ruled the mind by the power of persuasion. It was
not an element of the imperium but the peculiar attribute of
ecclesiastical discipline over erring members of the church. This
disciplinary power could possess no carnal and coercive force

---

[1] Wijngaarden, 71; Eekhof, *De theologische faculteit te Leiden in de 17 de
Eeuw*, 68*, 29.

[2] *Apologia*, Cap. xxiv, "De Disciplina Ecclesiastica", *Opera Theologica*,
Pars Altera, 237–243.

since it acted upon the mind and not the body, and since all coercion and physical compulsion was vested in the magistrate alone for the regulation of public matters. Outside the public places there was no right or coercive power competent to the magistrate and still less to any other person, to regulate the conscience or those private activities which were undertaken in the interests of the conscience and for the sake of religion. On the one hand, such a policy would trespass upon the divine prerogative in determining cases which were judicable only by the heavenly judge; on the other, it would make for an undesirable and pitiable government when the members of the state could not live as they felt they should and could not express their innermost convictions upon man's duty to God. To forbid what a citizen feels is his duty and to deny him the right to present it to his neighbours would violate the free activity of the conscience and withhold the necessary means to its edification. In the same way, those common exercises possible only in a corporate assembly and dictated by religion itself should be immune from political interference. The magistrate should permit these assemblies without which religion was crippled, so long as they preserved the original character of a religious communion, but if they became the means of sedition and undermined the existing order, the ruler was bound to interfere in order to preserve the whole.

Therefore, in the discipline of the church, Episcopius saw no need for an external coercive force to protect the church in its operation: the magistrate would undertake the discipline of public worship in public places, while in religious assemblies in private places there was no scope for this external and compulsory force. It was sufficient to declare that any undesirable person was no longer a member of the church. Excommunication was not an act of force, excluding any person from the building and services by coercion or bodily penalty, and compelling a sinner to mend his ways by physical punishment, for the Christian church was in the spirit, and therefore governed by spiritual methods. Its discipline must be truly and purely spiritual. Therefore, excommunication meant separation from defilement and the source of defilement, the demonstration to the sinner of his sin, and the declaration of eternal punishment as the penalty of sin.

Apparently, a sinner might continue to attend the church if he chose, without hindrance, but the congregation would hold itself aloof: if he disturbed the peace of the assembly presumably the public power might be invoked, but the assembly itself had no right to restrain or eject him by force. It was sufficient that he was not in association with the congregation, and showed by his conduct that he did not share in the invisible communion of the spiritual church. Therefore, it was not lawful to any human person or society to punish dissenters by force, nor to leave them freedom of conscience without the right to conduct those exercises in those assemblies which religion required, for such was a travesty of liberty of conscience. The Calvinist idea of toleration for heretical thought but not for schismatic worship was an academic fiction. Their maxim was that of the papacy: where there was one religion, there was peace. Their method was to deny that coercive power could work in the spiritual realm, and yet to rely upon it for the regulation of the church, so that it was exercised by the ministers as a spiritual power and yet retained all the advantages of the imperium. Calvinist discipline was actually external force mis-named spiritual in the interests of ecclesiastical autonomy.

The nature of the church was wholly spiritual, and therefore incapable of a visible imperium. Spiritual matters as such could not be governed by any worldly principle of action, for no human legislator could determine the warrant of the divine law which governed them. In consequence no coercion should be used in matters of religion and the conscience; indeed, it could not, for where imperative government was impossible, the right to rule by coercion disappeared. Religious acts in themselves could not be commanded. The limitation of ecclesiastical action to per-suasive methods and means was an implicit refutation of clerical claims to the imperium, whether vested in the whole church or in the ministry alone. On the one hand, the divine right of the ministry was derived solely from the function of revelation; on the other, the Christian people as a whole had no share of govern-ment save in a limited part of the external polity and external operation, and then without power or authority. There could be no true rule in the church because any member might secede from the church or reject the minister's creed without any action on the part of the church which would affect his freedom of action. There was, therefore, no other imperative government necessary in the church apart from the magistrate's in the external organisation of the church, for its voluntary nature destroyed all other claims. Coercive government existed properly only in the public church: neither the people nor the ministry could use it but only the magistrate. Dissenters naturally had no coercive power in their assemblies, for the voluntary basis of their society was even more evident than that of the public church; nor could the magistrate use the imperium in these assemblies save to confine them to religious worship, while even in the public church he could only enforce external matters of social organisation. He could not compel ministers or members to do what he wished, but he could compel them not to do what he refused to allow in the public places. Religion, conscience and religious acts were not at the mercy of any human ruler.

Under the section "De officio Christiani Magistratus in regimine ecclesiae",[1] Episcopius was careful to point out that the Confession only attributed the right to act in the church to the Christian magistrate in the external ecclesiastical order. He would not discuss what was proper to the magistrate as such in sacred matters, but only whether the architectonic power of the ruler ought to be guided by the church when exercised in ecclesiastical concerns. The Calvinists acknowledged the duty of the magistrate to regulate the external order of the church and to preserve the public worship, but denied that this arose from an absolute architectonic power: so did the Remonstrants, Episcopius added. This architectonic power was subject to Christ. The rational principle of order and the nature of good government logically demanded that this architectonic power should be granted to the ruler in public or external matters. The church ought so far to recognise that power as to do nothing in the field of the external and public without its sanction. If the ruler was a persecutor or unwilling to exercise this power, that sanction ceased to be necessary, but if he would exercise it in the interests of the church, the church must grant proper obedience: for this power belonged to the ruler not as a Christian or as a member of

[1] Cap. xxv; *Opera Theologica*, Pars Altera, 277 (misprinted 377)–281.

the church but in his official capacity, to which Christianity gave only surer guidance.

The fundamental problem was whether this architectonic power in the state, admittedly under Christ, was to be credited to the magistracy or to the ministry. It was generally conceded that the ruler had certain functions related to the external business of the church. Were these to be exercised upon his initiative, knowledge and responsibility, or by the judgment of the ministers? Episcopius declared that there was no way more calculated to detract from the supreme power than by setting up an ecclesiastical authority exercising immediately under Christ the public control of religion and the external government of the church. This would entail service on the part of the civil power, though repugnant to the essential character of its supremacy.

The question was not whether Christ ruled the public and external as well as the internal nature of the church; but whether Christ immediately and alone ruled the external and public polity of the church. The Calvinist critics of Episcopius had asserted this, and deduced that Christ used the ministry in this government as in the spiritual function, giving it a supreme power from and under Him alone. Therefore, the ruler either shared this power with the ministry, or did not possess it, in which case he was subject to the direction of the ministry. The Calvinists attempted to evade the issue by the plea that the ministry alone acted ministerially and not imperatively. But the ministry possessed the architectonic judgment and supreme direction of the ruler, so that it acted ministerially toward Christ, but magisterially toward man. The magistrate likewise was a minister of Christ and acted ministerially under Him but imperatively over men. In so far as the ministry claimed to possess a supreme power from and under Christ without any human superior, to rule the external church, that power was not ministerial toward men but architectonic; which the Calvinists would deny to exist in the church.

The argument is in itself simple although somewhat obscurely put. If Christ ruled His external church directly, and delegated to the ministry immediately that government subject to Him alone, then the ministry exercised a power which was not ministerial in relation to men but only to Christ. If Christ really delegated this power of external government subject to Him alone, then it could not be acted upon ministerially; if the ministry could only act ministerially, they could not receive this power from Christ. The architectonic judgment and power were characterised by the imperium and coercion which the Calvinists themselves denied to the church. Therefore, the power of the ministry in external church government was not architectonic, but under the architectonic power of the ruler. But the Calvinists expressly declared that if the architectonic power of the ruler under Christ was valid, the church and the holy ministry which were properly subject to Christ alone were subjected to the magistracy.

Episcopius was thus able to interpret the controversy between the Remonstrants and Contra-Remonstrants as an antithesis of theories. The Remonstrant thesis was formulated thus: "the architectonic power so far as it affects the public government of the church is immediately competent to the Christian magistrate under Christ, and not to the ministers". The Contra-Remonstrant thesis, on the contrary, asserted that "the architectonic power so far as the public and external government of the church was concerned, was competent immediately under Christ to the ministers of the church, but not to the Christian magistrate". But Episcopius deduced that this implied a supreme architectonic judgment to the ministers, for without that there was no supreme power: whence he further concluded that the universal authority, inspection, care and direction of the magistrates depended upon the judgment of the ministry as a supreme tribunal from which there was no appeal.

Three corollaries followed. First, the Christian magistrate was not only indirectly but even directly bound to follow the decision of the ministry in his relations with the ministers and church assemblies. Secondly, it was the duty of the magistrate to sanction by his public authority all the decrees of the ministers against dissenters. Finally, the subjects of the magistrate need not obey if his decrees were opposed to the judgment of the church. As the Calvinists boldly stated the power of the magistrate was to sanction by law the piety and order of the church to ensure their public observance. It meant no less than Becanus' naïve principle, that "the office of the magistrate in the church is to defend and protect, not as lords but as ministers, not as judges but as executors".

Two principles of Protestant thought vouched for the validity of the Arminian theory. First, it was opposed to the nature of law to have two architectonic powers or legislators: even if one was of a lower status but still independent there would exist two heads to one body. Secondly, the office of the magistrate was intimately linked with the state of religion and with the measures to preserve or reform it, having a responsibility which it would be impossible to meet unless he had the supreme supervisory power. On the other hand, although the ministry depended upon the magistrate, it only did so in so far as he was the minister of God; if he was not, the minister must forsake the public places and teach in private places where the ius of the ruler did not prevail. It was one thing simply to teach, and another to teach in public places subject to that ius. Thus the essential services of the church might be exercised according to the conscience of the ministers, and not sacrificed to the power of the ruler.

Episcopius continued the discussion on the familiar lines of the distinction between public and private places, and the civil authority over each, but forged another link by stating that the architectonic power ought to enforce its decisions by a coercive power in order to avoid becoming a mere shadow. It suffered, therefore, all the disabilities and limitations of coercive authority, which, as he had noted previously, was confined to public places and in no way valid in matters related to a peaceful conscience.

As the epilogue, he defended toleration except for blasphemy. No one should arrogate to himself the right of determining what were heresies, and his Calvinist critics with their views need not worry unduly: were not the reprobate damned in any case, whereas nothing could seduce the Elect? While Truth would not suffer from toleration, there were serious moral disadvantages in any intolerant policy. Liberty of conscience was stifled, reform was prevented and hypocrisy stimulated. There was little danger to the church, as Truth was its strongest support, and it need fear no error; there was less danger to the state since this free enquiry was a common privilege and the solvent of sedition.

In one last work, more rhetorical than the others, Episcopius discussed the duty of the magistrate to preserve religion. "Be unwilling, O Princes, that yours should be the right from God to bespatter your crowns with the blood of the erring. Let it suffice that they approve your sceptre by faith, service and other fitting duties. Religion must be defended not by slaying but by admonishing, not by ferocity but by patience, not by crime but by faith. We hold your power to be great without equal; but the orthodox cherish it as the fulcrum of theirs." The Remonstrants erred, according to their critics, in recognising the right of the ministers to refuse obedience if the magistrate was wrong, whereas the norm should be the Word of God and not the individual conscience. But Episcopius pertinently asked: "If they stood before a king who believed differently, although upon Scriptural grounds, would not their individual conscience prove their ultimate defence?"[1]

The Remonstrants agreed that all public conspiracies should be suppressed, never having asserted in such cases the right of free assemblage. They accepted, too, the obligation to foster religion, but only by spiritual means. It would be illogical to allow private opinions and yet to forbid their dissemination by speech or writing, at home among friends or in society. To compel all to hear the public religion would be tyranny and not religion, to withhold their livelihood to coerce by starvation, while to proscribe would make hermits out of citizens. In their assemblies, the Arminians only met to conduct themselves worthily under the supreme power.

Episcopius[2] valued the liberty of sects as a moral pearl of great price. He ridiculed the Calvinist argument that not to grant liberty to the orthodox was tyranny, while to withhold it from heretics was justice and concern for true religion. Quite consistently he admitted that the sword of the magistrate was invaluable against hate, drunkenness and other works of the flesh, but not against heresy which should be attacked by spiritual means only.

---

[1] *Vedelius Rhapsodus*, ch. IX; *Opera Theologica*, Pars Altera, 367.
[2] In the *Vrye Godes-dienst*, he denied that his position before 1618 was inconsistent with his theory of toleration. See Haentjens, 84, 140; who points out, 126–127, that this theory was not the result of persecution.

Finally,[1] he declared that Christ, desiring His religion to be free, established no corporal punishment; whence nothing was so voluntary as religion. Since it was not religious to coerce men to the true religion, and since the magistrate could not do his duty without force, he could not promote the true religion. Force and religion were opposed, for the latter was love which could not be imprinted on human nature by force. There was no right then to compel those who lived soberly, respectful of authority, tolerant of dissenters and suspected of no evil.

The theory that Episcopius outlined was in its main tenets peculiarly ingenious and appropriate. It was, without abandoning the Calvinist base, an effective criticism and refutation of certain clerical pretensions. Calvin could not have agreed with the principles by which Episcopius allotted the shares of Caesar and God, for he always tended to synchronise the infinite God with the finite church, and conceived the rights of the one as synonymous with those of the other. But while he might have sympathised with the theory of the later Dutch Calvinists, he would have noted that it was a development, and would have criticised it from the logic of his own theory. Just as he was always opposed to active resistance in the political sphere, so he could not have admitted the safeguarding of the Christian church by the exclusion of the Christian state. Indeed, his doctrine of passive resistance was akin to the ideas of Episcopius, and under that pressure to which a permanent and persecuted minority was subjected, might well have developed into a similar theory.

It is well to note that Episcopius was novel only in certain aspects, much of his thought being borrowed from his predecessors. From Vossius he learnt the emphasis upon the divine responsibility of the ruler but he did not accept it fully; from Grotius, he obtained the emphasis upon the public places, as the sphere of the ruler's duty. He probably used their ideas to vindicate his particular and positive teaching. His own emphasis was upon liberty of conscience and toleration of heresies: the distinctions between public and private places; and between force and religion. He did not deny the Calvinist maxims for the Godly Magistrate, but he did qualify their bearing by his interpretations

[1] *Vedelius Rhapsodus*, 373.

of their application and method. His difference from the more
philosophic Arminian theorists was only one of degree, since these
had regarded the relation of church and state from the magistrates'
position, whereas Episcopius, under the goad of experience,
studied it from the view point of a minority expelled from the
church by a tyrannical coalition of ecclesiastical discipline and
state force. It was an important distinction. The Arminians
constructed in persecution and segregation a theory which antici-
pated that of the English Independents, against the same dictator,
Presbytery. Such men as Nye and Goodwin and the others of
the Holland ministers who resisted the Presbyterianism of the
Westminster Assembly had been tolerated in the Netherlands,
had seen the rigidity of the provincial presbyterian machine, had
watched the doubtful struggle of the Remonstrants to gain con-
nivance and had come to understand the practical and theoretical
ideas of toleration which distinguished the Remonstrants.
Episcopius, too, was read in England throughout the century. It is
a natural conjecture that the Independents were directly inspired
by Remonstrant principles, particularly as Nye developed theories
closely related to the argument of Episcopius.

It is remarkable that Episcopius had safeguarded most dex-
terously the rights of both church and state. The ministry was
master of its craft—but so was the magistracy. The character of
each was so portrayed that his division of power was acceptable
to reason. The state was not an absorptive power nor a tyrant over
the church—but its rights as the supreme power and the lord of
public society were asserted. The church was not to claim a
divinity which clutched in its tentacles the whole of life, and
squeezed everything into its own body. It was not an imperium
in imperio but was recognised as Christ's society, when it was
stripped of earthly claims. It had the ultimate responsibility of
salvation and the supreme mode of communion with Christ. It
was holy: and as long as it pursued its holy office in spirit and in
truth, it expressed the Will of God and must bow to no man.
Within that unnatural body, born of Reformation and Renaissance, the church-state or state-church, Episcopius had justly
apportioned their burdens and responsibilities, based upon a
genuine analysis of their respective characters. His scheme

preserved the balance of church and state in that common body
with more skill and success than that of men like Selden or Knox.
Episcopius still accepted in ideal the complementary character
of church and state, each expressing God's purpose and necessarily yoked together. But with him the duel was not of church-
state with state-church but of exclusive establishment with the
liberty of private sects which had been ejected from the established church in response to their conscience.

Episcopius had indeed cut the Gordian knot, which hampered
politicians and churchmen, and falsified the nature and purpose
of church and state. He did not do it, of course, without the
introduction of new principles, because the old dilemma was
insoluble upon the old lines. Episcopius[1] taught the doctrines
of the liberty of conscience and of the voluntary nature of the
church. He distinguished the true function and matter of the
ministry from its encroachments upon state authority. But he
did more than release the church and state from mutual tyranny.
By releasing the individual conscience from the tyranny of both,
he enabled religion to escape the trammels of the church, and
private unblamable actions from the control of the state. He had
placed the individual beside the church and state, and on the
principles of the volition of the one, the voluntary nature of the
second, and the public character of the third, he based his solution.
The full recognition of the individual, on the one side, by involving adequate limitation of the other two, on the other side,
made way for a genuinely successful scheme. It was the influence
of the Arminian belief in Man as being individually ethically
valuable reacting upon political thought, and producing a theory
truer to the basic principles of Arminius than that of his more
politically minded friend Grotius, or philosophically minded
colleague Vossius. Although he never arrived at the conception
of free churches in a free state, his discovery and employment of
toleration and real liberty of conscience enabled him to avoid
the logical difficulties in the theory of the state-church or of
the church-state. Sovereignty and revelation were reconciled
and limited by the independence of the conscience. This was no
mythical nor hypothetical reconciliation which rested upon the

---

[1] Cf. Haentjens, 47; Sepp, II, 190.

valueless concession, that a man might believe what he wished, provided that it was kept within his own mind, but a solid guarantee both of sovereignty and of revelation, founded on a liberty of thought, of expression, and of meeting for the free dissemination of religious convictions and for the free conduct of worship. This was the greatest contribution to the controversy, but it was really wrung from a staunch Erastianism by an indomitable Calvinism.

CHAPTER III

THE CHRISTIAN MAGISTRACY

IN 1642, there appeared a small work by Vedelius which was to provoke a renewal of the controversy upon the relations of church and state, no longer between Calvinist and Arminian, but within the orthodox circle itself. Vedelius[1] was a foreigner, born in the Palatinate, and trained at Geneva, and it has been pointed out that his theory was more Lutheran than Calvinist. But he prefixed to his book two commendatory letters, one from Maccovius, the founder of Protestant Scholasticism in the Netherlands, and the other from Rivetus, the last representative of Scriptural Protestantism. Vedelius seemed to have gained the approval of the old and the new ways of thought, and for that reason his theory was denounced by the staunch defenders of ecclesiastical independence as particularly subversive. Neither of his two supporters, however, had made any notable contribution to the controversy and, save for the vague terms of their letters, had not committed themselves to accept his argument.

It is difficult to find any independent study of the problem of church and state by Maccovius. His attitude was widely known among Dutch theologians as one which favoured the ecclesiastical function of the ruler at the expense of the theory which separated church and state. But among his published works there is only a brief passage in the *Loci Communes* which indicates the line of his own thought.[2] The magistrate was not in such relation to the church that his will was subject to it. His office was supreme in the state, so that his ecclesiastical activities must not be limited by the commands of the church. On the other hand, although this supremacy must be recognised and no policy adopted which would deny his supremacy, no ruler ought to act without consulting the officers of the church. His office is bounded by his

---

[1] See Paquot, *Mémoires, etc.*; Glasius, *Godgeleerd Nederland*. Cf. Sepp, *Het Godgeleerd Onderwijs*, 60, 117–121.
[2] 659; see Kuyper, *J. Maccovius*, 194.

human limitations: nor should his supremacy become an arbitrary and capricious use of coercion. If his task was to enforce justice—the right conduct of his subjects—in those matters in which he was no expert, he could not know what it was right to enforce, and he had necessarily to consider the opinions of those who were competent to give an authoritative opinion. In all problems of a medical character, for instance, the doctor only could advise. In the same way, the officers of the church were the only proper counsellors in their own sphere. But neither commanded the ruler—that was the important point. The ruler followed their advice not as one obedient to their commands, but because he was convinced by their reasons. To the ruler, therefore, was left the ultimate judgment.

The attitude adopted by Rivetus[1] is to be found in his commentary upon the fifth commandment, where he followed a line of argument very similar to the *De Munere* of Walaeus. To him as to the Contra-Remonstrants a separation of church and state was contrary to the Will of God. The rights and duties of the orthodox ruler in the service of religion had to be recognised and respected, though this did not mean that the church was dependent wholly upon his favour. The church, too, had its rights and duties, and the Christian religion was to be forwarded and not thwarted by the civil authority. Rivetus criticised both the papal and the Grotian theory, since the one subjected the ruler to the church and the other the church to the ruler. Both theories were false. He inclined, therefore, to a theory of collateral authority, in which the two powers co-operated, and found in this the ideal of God.

His argument was built upon his faith in Scriptural theology. It was the inspiration behind the principles fundamental to the logical formulation of a theory in which mutual discussion and not command distinguished the relationship of church and state. Rivetus assumed that the revelation of the Bible was a unity because the Will of God was revealed more perfectly throughout; so that he could conclude that the position of the ruler in the Old Testament remained an example of God's Will even after

---

[1] Operum, tom. primus (–tertius), Roterod. 1651–60, p. 1363. Cf. Honders, 134–137.

the coming of Christ. Moreover, the purpose of grace was not to reject but to perfect nature, and thus Rivetus could argue that the New Testament did not imply the destruction of the law of nature. The Christian revelation was partial and did not necessitate a revolutionary conception of society and its problems of organisation. In opposition to the Anabaptists and Socinians, he denied that the death penalty and war were incompatible with a Christian order, because he distinguished the official and personal actions of the ruler. His official duties were not ordered by Christ, and those duties were to protect his subjects in their rights.

The ruler was the foster-father of the church and the guardian of the two Tables of the Law, not as a private person, but as a public officer, who was appointed by God for the protection of the church, to encourage God's worship and the true religion. But neither was this duty part of the ruler's office as such, for Rivetus, though he would not limit the power given by God to pious kings, was well aware of the danger of a new pope in the person of a ruler who was not a faithful member of the church. He might indeed be called the head of the church because he was the head of the people, provided always that he was a member of the church and acted within the framework of ecclesiastical organisation. The faithless ruler who failed in this duty suffered not from a want of power but from a want of will. But the ruler's task was understood in the limited sense of his headship of the church from which the potestas ordinis was excluded, and therefore only within the potestas jurisdictionis. The church was in part an external organisation and only as such was it intimately related to the ruler. The pious king must not interfere with the innermost activities of the church but neither must he withhold himself from that external sphere, since the church would otherwise be powerless within a hostile world.

Thus, Rivetus continued the teaching of the Reformation that both church and state were powers ordained by God with different methods and different functions, the co-operation of which was necessary to the fulfilment of His Will. In that co-operation, there was no room for the imperium: it could only rest upon mutual deliberation and management, since the authority of each was defined by its own capacities.

The *De Episcopatu Constantini*[1] published in 1642 and written by Vedelius is a difficult book to examine. Its general character is a slight summary, dogmatically stated and with little attempt to enter very deeply into fundamental problems, and consequently by no means easy to study impartially and critically. No doubt this obscure brevity and shallow dogmatism is to be explained by the historical origins of the book and by its humble purpose. Vedelius discussed in his class at Deventer the problem of church and state in twelve propositions. When he was not only attacked by his colleagues but silenced by the magistrates, he realised that a private discussion had become a public issue of far greater importance. When his call to Franeker restored his liberty of thought and expression, he did not dare to publish anything in his defence save his original propositions, lest he should be charged with inconsistency. Moreover, Vedelius had never planned an exhaustive examination of the whole problem: he had framed his propositions as part of the students' training in polemics against the Roman church. He intended to provide an adequate answer to Bellarmine's *De Laicis*, and believed that there was no originality in his statement of the Calvinist position. It was not his purpose to do more than state briefly and intelligibly, under certain leading headings, the teaching of the Reformation against the papal theory of indirect temporal power. The gulf between the Roman and Calvinist theories seemed more fundamental to him than a difference of despotic and aristocratic-democratic church government. He assumed the validity of Calvin's premises, the more so since he had come to the Netherlands from Geneva and had practical experience of the arrangement there. In stating what was to him the obvious difference between Roman and Calvinist theories, there was no need for elaborate demonstrations. His purpose, necessary in an age of controversy, was to supply ready-made answers for his students to use, and since a clear understanding of the vital issues was fundamental for that purpose, he grouped the issues under an articulated series of propositions, each of which provided a clear-cut issue for acceptance or rejection.

[1] See Meyjes, *J. Revius*, 77–82; 151–172; and Kuyper, *J. Maccovius* 59–60.

In the edition of 1661, the objections raised by Triglandius were stated and answered briefly, after the proposition to which they were related; but Vedelius' early death prevented him from defending himself more fully against his many critics. It was left to an anonymous writer to justify his argument; but on wholly new grounds.

The premises upon which his thought was constructed were clearly stated in the preface to the 1661 edition and in the opening pages of the book. The ruler, i.e. he to whom was entrusted the supreme and ultimate power in the state, was the head of the political society into which men were organised, and in virtue of his office was responsible for the political interests which underlay the state. Like all Calvinists Vedelius was a constitutionalist and held that coercion, a necessary political fact, could only be lawful if it was the prerogative of the ruler. In this, Vedelius was in agreement with the other Calvinist thinkers. All states were characterised by a supreme power, vested in some constitutional organ, which was subject to no other authority in civil and political matters.

The ruler's office was defined by the nature of the state, and the state existed for the material needs of an organised group. None of these theorists was interested in the state itself or concerned with the problems of its organisation, and Vedelius was no exception. Within the state there was assumed to be a supreme authority, supreme in civil life.

To Vedelius, as to his critics, this civil supremacy was inferior to the supremacy of Christ, and to the work of salvation. In words reminiscent of medieval thought, he compared the object of the state with the object of life, temporal prosperity with eternal salvation and everlasting happiness, and stamped the state as a mere political organisation with a purely human and temporary character, designed to satisfy the needs of the body. It was from this point that he diverged from the Roman theory and from his critics. They drew the conclusion that the interests which the state could not by its nature satisfy could only be met by the church in which Christ was present. Vedelius was not in opposition to this principle as it stood. He fully agreed that salvation was possible only through the grace of God to believe in Christ, and that mysticism and tradition were inadequate in themselves. The Scriptures indicated the means by which Christ's spirit continued to work on earth, and the greatest of those means was the church in which the preaching of the Word, the exercise of discipline and the administration of the sacraments fulfilled the work of God's mercy. He was not, however, prepared to accept the final deduction that this church, this community of believers, was self-sufficient and autonomous in its earthly organisation at all times, in all actions and under all circumstances. It is true that he was prepared to accept this conclusion in certain necessary though unhappy conditions, when the state and its rulers were pagan or hostile to the true religion. In that case, the true church must rely upon its own resources, must entrench itself behind its own spiritual bulwarks, and must wage a ceaseless struggle to preserve its own pure character and to pursue its divine mission. Such was the history of the early church and of its struggle under the Roman empire: and such must be the fate of the Huguenot church. This was a necessary consequence when the state was indifferent or hostile, but it was not the ideal of God in the Old Testament nor of Calvin in Geneva, while the unavailing struggle of the Huguenots revealed only too clearly the sad and inevitable results of the true church separated from the state, in the comparative failure of the true church to order society upon the basis of true Christian principles. The burden upon the church was too heavy when it had to concentrate upon preserving its own existence. So that the difference between his critics and himself turned upon the ideal of the church. He argued that the real ideal was not one of separation of church and state, but of mutual co-operation in which their peculiar services were co-ordinated for a common end. The essential difference was his acceptance of the revelation of the Bible as the Will of God, however difficult it might prove in practice. It was part of the cross that the church must bear that it must strive to work in harmony with the state, and not independently. In so far as it abandoned the attempt, it had failed in its mission.

Vedelius, therefore, refused to accept the separation of church and state without important qualifications, which relegated that conception to a secondary place. But before he stated what those qualifications were and in what way they affected the relations of church and state, he laid down four considerations preliminary to the true understanding of the ideal revealed by God. First,[1] there were two dangers which the church ought to avoid. On the one hand, there was the evil of a hierarchic papacy when the officers of the church drew to themselves an authority in church matters which was not truly theirs and which by violating the law of God offended the consciences of all Christians. On the other hand, a political papacy, no less an evil, was established whenever the ruler possessed authority over the substance of the Christian religion or acted upon his own initiative when he ought to act in collaboration with the ministers. In either case, the danger arose from an excessive demand for liberty and power, so that the right solution was one in which there was due regard for the liberty essential to the proper authority of each.

Secondly, ecclesiastical government was in part determined by the law of God, and therefore immutable, not even the church being empowered to modify these laws in any detail. There remained certain matters left undetermined by the Bible, and necessarily regulated by positive human laws framed by the church and the orthodox magistrate in conjunction. Such laws could be reviewed and modified at any time to meet new conditions. Thirdly, when the state was in a dangerous or misgoverned condition the church had an extraordinary power to intervene: in the same way whenever the church had fallen into corruption or had patently failed in its mission, the state had an extraordinary power to reform and reconstitute it. Fourthly, the possibility that power might be abused was not sufficient to deny the existence and valid exercise of that power. That the ruler might abuse his ecclesiastical authority was no reason to deny that he possessed it. The church admitted its fallibility and yet did not admit that the possibility of the misuse of its authority sanctioned the denial of it. There was an objective test of the legitimate use and of the abuse of the power of either. Whenever the Biblical commands were violated, that power ceased to be valid; but it was necessary that such misuse should be unequivocally contrary to the Bible.

Unless these four considerations were carefully studied, no

[1] *De Episcopatu*, Preface (unnumbered).

stable theory of church and state could be successfully formulated, since it would err either to the Anabaptist or to the Arminian, either to the Lutheran or Roman side. The true Calvinist theory ought not to incline to any one of these extremes, lest it denied that the saints could participate in the concerns of this world; or held that the church *per se* under the orthodox ruler had no spiritual power, the ministers enjoying their office through the magistrate, to whom God had given absolute power in spiritual matters under Himself; or argued that the church alone possessed authority to determine its own affairs where the Scriptures were without definitive instructions. Vedelius attempted in the *De Episcopatu Constantini* to expound the true theory of Scriptural revelation which was truly balanced between these four corners of ecclesiastico-political speculation.

As opposed to his critics, Vedelius assumed two things. First, that Arminianism erred not in giving to the orthodox ruler a voice in religious matters, but in giving an exclusive voice to him. The ministers were excluded from the government of the church, save as deputies of the ruler, to whom was given supreme judgment under Christ in all controversies concerning the Christian faith. This was the architectonic power of the orthodox magistrate, under Christ, in matters ecclesiastical as civil. The error of the Arminians was to give to the ruler the same supremacy in the church as he had by general agreement in the state, save for the qualification that this ecclesiastical supremacy was under Christ. This was to give too much. But the Remonstrants emphasised the second error of giving too little, when they excluded the ruler from all private religious worship. Vedelius' critics were content to pillory Arminianism as sanctioning the authority of the ruler in the church. It was Arminianism not to exclude the ruler from all church government. Both attitudes were unfair to Arminian thought, although there was this to be said for Vedelius that Arminian practice was intended to obtain a lay sanction for doctrines both alien and unpalatable to the church. Secondly, he assumed that the Roman error was to subject the state to the church in all matters of faith and church government. In this his critics agreed with him, but he saw deeper than they, how difficult it was to avoid a virtual supremacy unless the ruler's

judgment preceded any ecclesiastical actions. His critics accused
the Roman church of supremacy, when it ought not to claim more
than equality and independence. They did not see as he did that
an independent church determining the actions of the ruler who
was a member was in fact exercising a supreme authority. To
Vedelius, this supremacy rested upon the claim that the church
alone not only should decide what was the divine law in the
Scriptures but also determine its activity in those matters which
the Bible left to human discretion. The church in the one case
meant the pope, and in the other the church officers: that was the
only difference. Thus, tradition and not revelation governed the
church, and it usurped a power which was without Scriptural
sanction, because it claimed an exclusive right to judge what was
the true religion. The Reformation after all denied that the church
could always and invariably judge rightly what was the true
religion and how the church was to be organised.

The importance of these distinctions was manifested in the
development of the argument. Vedelius[1] explicitly denied what
Bellarmine stated: that the magistrate was merely the executive
agent of the church, accepting in any matters touching church
interests its decision. He denied that the ruler was concerned
only with the civil interests of his subjects, and could not affect
their salvation by one jot or tittle. In consequence he denied that
the ruler's authority was morally unjustified in religious matters,
asserting that the ruler shared by right in the calling of ministers,[1]
in judging of ecclesiastical controversies[2] and in the enactment of
ecclesiastical laws.[2] He denied the church any power to legislate, and recognised only a power of making canons. Moreover,
the ruler had the duty of checking the abuses of ecclesiastical
discipline, and, therefore, his power in relation to the church
officers must be coercive. The ministers derived their authority
from the ruler, not in the substance of ministry, but in the direction of its use, in its external order and incidental circumstances,
and therefore were not independent of the ruler in those matters.[3]
The ruler in his turn was not independent of the ministers
although he was not subject to them in the Roman sense, but
only as the heralds of God.[4] He followed them only in so far as

[1] *De Episcopatu*, Tit. 1.　[2] *Ib*. Tit. 4, 5, 6.　[3] *Ib*. Tit. 12.　[4] *Ib*. Tit. 11.

he obeyed God. No man on earth had an unlimited and absolute authority in ecclesiastical matters—pope, minister and rulers were all incapable of such authority. That absolute power was Christ's alone, and His Human Instruments had no other claim to the allegiance of Christians than that they expressed His Will. Finally, Vedelius held that the magistrate, supreme and orthodox, was not inferior but indeed superior in honour and dignity to the ministers.

This[1] he claimed to represent the theory of the orthodox party before and after the Synod of Dort, and to indicate those respective spheres which if truly observed established full concord between church and state. It met the objections of the Roman church that the way of the Reformation led to the confusion of the essential offices of ruler and pastors, thereby creating discord and reducing the clergy to mere instruments of the state. Finally, there was no basis for criticism when it was remembered that his theory enunciated only what God's Word had determined to be the duty of a ruler, what was the nature of his office and the limits of his power. The church was not subjected to the ruler, since its obedience depended upon the authority of the Word and the extent to which the ruler recognised and endorsed that authority. The rights belonging to the church according to the Bible were fully safeguarded in this theory.

The advantages of the theory were also its valuable recommendations. It guaranteed the preservation of the true religion and minimised the possibility of corruption. There was a greater danger from an independent church than from an independent ruler—the papacy was a greater evil than the Erastian error, and this theory prevented the restoration of papal tyranny. The peace of the state and of the church was more secure when the ministers were unable to appeal to the people under the pretext of religion to effect whatever they purposed. The position of the ruler and his subjects was protected, and through his imperium, the mission of the church and the establishment of God's Kingdom guided the development of the whole society toward the ideal of God. The church was the more likely to fulfil its function according to God's Word because of an earthly supervisor, and because it could

[1] See *De Episcopatu*, Conclusion.

not obtain an unbridled power so long as it had to persuade the ruler that its programme and policy were to the advantage of the church and in accord with the Scriptures.

It is characteristic of Vedelius' method that the only proof he offered was the authority of the Word, and so obvious was the agreement between the Scriptural ideal and his systematic formulation of it, that there was little need for anything save dogmatic reference to the Bible. Nevertheless, the rational formulation of the *De Episcopatu Constantini* implied a basis of first principles by which Scriptures were interpreted and co-ordinated. Although these rational and basic principles were enunciated as axioms and not as theorems, and therefore were never logically proved, their validity was implicitly justified by the cohesion of the whole theory and by the coherence of the different sections which harmonised with each other and with the theory itself. It was the logically rounded and balanced character of the theory which was consistent when applied to specific problems that proved the fundamental conceptions underlying it. In particular, Vedelius relied upon three such principles: the orthodox ruler with a mission under the divine law;[1] the distinction between objective and formal power;[2] and finally the differentiation of ecclesiastical government into the internal and the externally internal, which was really the old division between the potestas ordinis and the potestas jurisdictionis.[2] The interlocking of these principles provided a strong foundation for his theory with its propositions and qualifications, and enabled him to construct the *via media* between Roman and Lutheran, the Arminian and Anabaptist theories. The *via media* was true because it avoided the errors of the four extremes, and therefore the principles upon which it was constructed must be true themselves. Vedelius did not attempt to prove their truth independently.

The basic conception was that embodied in the peculiar nature of the Christian ruler, a faithful member of the true church and a loyal observer of the divine law; the two other conceptions being necessary qualifications to limit this office to the divine purpose. Such a ruler possessed a power greater than his civil authority, and his office was not merely of this world but of God Himself.

---

[1] *De Episcopatu*, Tit. 1–3.   [2] *Ib.* Tit. 4–5.

To remove[1] this divine authority was to endanger his purely human function, and to reduce his office to a fraction of what God had ordained. For this reason, Vedelius could not accept the separation of church and state as the true Calvinist ideal.

According[1] to this conception the Christian ruler was apart from the laity although he had no real office in the church. The Scriptures singled him out for a unique position which was neither of the state as such nor of the church but of God's Kingdom. He was the focus of those divine and social forces which through his co-ordination gave rise to the earthly form of God's Kingdom. He was not to be counted among the ministers of the church since he was not ordained to preach the Word nor to offer the sacraments: the spiritual mission of the church was not opened to him. But he was not a mere member of the laity to whom no duties belonged save those of the individual Christian. He filled an office consecrated by God and set apart by Him for the protection of the church, and for the correlation of the church's spiritual function with the varied functions in society at large. He was the nursing father of the church and custos utriusque tabulae: his was the responsibility for establishing the true religion in the state and for transforming the state into a moral agency of the divine law. Only through his office was the state linked to the divine purpose and given its full character as a divine organ. That office was no more lay than ecclesiastical.

The fact that his power was consecrated to the service of God and to the assistance of the church showed that his office transcended a merely lay nature. Its resources existed to further the society of the saints, and his sword was both the scourge of evil-doers and the stimulus to the moral order. The Bible indicated clearly that the orthodox ruler was an integral item in the divine economy since God's purpose could not be realised in its fullness without his active co-operation. The church by itself could not extend the realm of God beyond its own members, and to deny to the ruler these duties really excluded the external forms of corporate life from the Christian order, on the ground that these forms were inherently incapable of furthering the Kingdom of God. But it was presumptuous to assume that God had never

[1] *De Episcopatu*, Preface.

related these social organisations to His ultimate purpose or that they in no way existed to help forward the communion of saints. It was, indeed, far more probable that the ruler's services were an essential element of God's Will on earth, because the ruler, though an agent of God, was endowed with a large discretion in the interests of the church, whereas the ministers obeyed the divine law alone. To doubt the value of this discretionary power in God's order was to doubt the justification of earthly and human life, and to deny that it was or could be a positive and constructive force in the divine purpose.

The magistrate did not possess this power as a private person, for he was not an insignificant atom in the social cosmos but the corner-stone of the whole structure. He was a minister of God and responsible for the use and direction of all the coercive power necessarily underpinning society. In so far as an imperative authority was needed by the church, the ruler's help must be sought and his conscience convinced by the reasons the church adduced. His was, therefore, a divine function governed by the terms of a divine mandate which made him in his official capacity more truly a servant of God and more active to fulfil His End than the ordinary citizen, because his opportunities were greater, his resources more ample and his responsibilities much heavier. While distinguished from the mass of citizens, his office was also distinct from the church, which had a different sphere, different methods and different limitations. He was commissioned by God to fill an office in His Kingdom which could not be undertaken either by individuals or by the church. To deny the authenticity of that commission must confine the church to its own spiritual resources and destroy the corporate unity of the community before God. If the supreme power in the state was to be used for the glory of God and the enrichment of His Church, there could be only one organ—the supreme and orthodox ruler.

In virtue of this divinely ordained function, the ruler was the principal member of the church, a term intended to signify his peculiar responsibility. His position as head of the state and as the organ of its supreme power, combined with his duty to God in matters of religion and in the Christian conduct of the whole community, marked him out above the ordinary members of the church but not above the ministers in their own divine function. His was a complicated relation, conveyed by the title of principal member. Like the rest of the laity he was a member of the church and obedient to it in all matters of faith. Like them he heard the Word of God and received the sacraments from the ministers. Unlike the laity, who could only act individually according to their own enlightened consciences, the ruler had a grave responsibility for the true religion which set him above errant ministers and required the use of his imperative powers in the interests of the church. His office in its ecclesiastical orientation was that of God's Ephor, a constitutional organ in but not of the church, to preserve the divine law. But also as the source of coercion and, consequently, as the architect of the external forms of society, it was part of his office to facilitate the operation and realisation of divine law throughout his realm. He brought to the church that power in external matters and that control over environment which were beyond the scope of the church, and alien to ministry and laity alike. In each case, he was evidently the principal member of the church, although the authority which he wielded was vastly different in the first from that which he used in the second.

In consequence, the ruler was not inferior in honour and dignity to the ecclesiastics, but in a Christian state enjoyed a position of pre-eminence. Such orthodox writers as Paraeus, Rivetus and Walaeus held this so far as the subordinate magistrates were concerned in their civil capacities. Still more was it true of the supreme and orthodox ruler. His pre-eminence was seen in the universal Kingdom of God, because it was his duty to direct his subjects to the observance of the divine law, if need be by compelling the outward man to obey a uniform order, and in the special Kingdom of Christ because he ought as a member of the church to use that power which he possessed in regno universali, to protect and to help the Holy Spirit present in the true church. Not only should he assist the church with that power which he shared with all rulers as the guardian of public welfare and public order, and which therefore could be given by a pagan ruler, but also he ought as a member of the church to devote his external power to the good of the church as all true members offered their own peculiar gifts.

It was,[1] moreover, inconceivable that the people as a collective unit should not be embodied in the church, since it was the people in their ecclesiastical organisation. As the representative of their corporate character, the ruler delivered or formulated their judgment upon religious as well as civil questions. Through him the corporate conscience expressed its criticisms of social conduct; while in him the knowledge of practical experience, of human limitations and public opinion were confronted by an inspired ideal. By his co-operation society was placed at the service of that ideal, and the church was related to its social context, by which it was furnished with the means for an effective, constructive, and public application of Christianity. Not only was the individual life dedicated to God, but also the public and corporate life of a whole people, the direction of which was in the hands not of the church nor of the private conscience, but of the magistrate, in virtue of his discretionary authority. The state, as the external church, claimed a share in the determination of its own conduct and organisation, and the people as a Christian community had a divinely appointed representative of its ecclesiastical consciousness.

Behind the many strands of thought which Vedelius wove into one pattern of the orthodox and supreme ruler there was the conviction of a covenant between God and the ruler, who thereby received a special mission and became God's agent. The prototype of that covenant existed in the Old Testament and had not been superseded by the New Testament. Thus, he was a chosen vessel of the Lord, the guardian of the divine law and the nursing father of the church, with a function which set him apart from the pagan or heretical ruler. The dominant inspiration of his government ceased to be the temporal interests of his subjects and became their salvation and eternal blessedness. The law of nature taught the same principle, but the Christian ruler had not the same absolute authority in the church, since he was governed by his knowledge of the terms of his covenant with God. The nature of his office was predetermined in the Bible.

This was Vedelius' main thesis and by its application to specific problems it was not difficult to credit the ruler with sufficient

---

[1] *De Episcopatu*, Tit. 4.

authority to prevent serious discord between church and state. But the theory was not so absolutist as it would appear without its two essential qualifications, determining how and where this power was to be exercised. The question "How?" necessitated a distinction between objective and formal ecclesiastical power. There was nothing ecclesiastical which was not in some way subject to the jurisdiction of the ruler, though not in the same way. Political authority could not, indeed, secure penitence and conversion, but it could command that the legitimate methods for that purpose should be faithfully used. In the way of political sanction, the ruler either commanded that some ecclesiastical action should be done, but did not do it himself, or supplemented the action of the church with some ancillary political action. In either case, the ruler did not use an ecclesiastical power: he was only using his political power to secure the proper working of the true church according to divine law, or to facilitate its own action undertaken by its own proper authority. It was not a spiritual power but his political or temporal power exercised for ecclesiastical objects. In that sense it was called an objective ecclesiastical power. It was, to use the distinctions of Vedelius and his critics, political power exercised *around* the church but not *in* it. It was coercive like all true political power and for that reason sharply contrasted to proper ecclesiastical or ministerial power, which was the spiritual authority given by Christ to His Church to work upon souls and save the elect. This was not coercive, since it demanded not external conformity but spiritual regeneration. Such a power could not belong to the ruler and was denied to him by the Scriptures, for he could only obtain outward uniformity. This was the formal ecclesiastical power. The ruler's authority was considerably reduced by this distinction, for he could not use this ministerial power and could only act when his objective ecclesiastical power would be effective. His power was determined by the method of its operation.

In general, his critics agreed with this principle of Vedelius, although it permitted to the ruler a considerable influence over the church. The real difference between them was the answer to the question "Where was the power of the ruler operative?" The answer was implied in the answer to the question "How?" If the

ruler had only an objectively ecclesiastical power he could not
exercise it where the formal ecclesiastical power alone was
operative, and therefore was limited to that region in which his
objective power could work. The method and the sphere defined
each other in the case of both powers. There was even in this
answer a certain amount of agreement, for Vedelius admitted that
the ruler had no power in the substance of the ministry. He
could not preach nor administer the sacraments. The doctrine
and the sacraments of the church were too sacred for his interference. The potestas ordinis was the formal ecclesiastical power:
to the ruler belonged only a directive power to secure the preaching
of the true doctrine and to ensure the proper administration of
the sacraments. Vedelius even admitted that ecclesiastical discipline in so far as it remitted sins or imposed a spiritual penalty
binding also in heaven was a ministerial act. To that extent the
potestas jurisdictionis was also beyond the ruler's interference.
All he might do was to prevent its abuse and to assist its proper
action.

Here agreement ended. The formal ecclesiastical power from
which the ruler was totally excluded was to Vedelius that ministerial function consequent upon the rite of ordination which
imparted to the ministers the spirit of Christ. This spiritual and
divine mission of the church, guided by the Holy Spirit and
revealed in the Bible, was truly internal, being the business of the
church alone. But in the contact of these spiritual forms with
human life and in so far as they were expressed by a human
society there was much belonging both to civil and divine life.
The church in fact used human moulds to substantiate its supernatural inspiration, moulds which were neither wholly external
nor purely internal. They were necessarily related to the spiritual
and internal function of the church since the soul must express
itself in and by means of the body, but they did not lose their
human and civil character entirely. They were the administrative
offices of any corporate body. In the purely internal sphere, the
church employed only spiritual forces and forms; in adopting the
organisation of human corporations, the church passed out of the
purely spiritual realm governed by the inspiration of Christ's
spirit into a region in which human judgment, discretion, needs

and expediency were necessary considerations. Behind this paraphernalia of organisation there was an authority which was not purely spiritual, but that necessarily assumed by any organised community. This was manifest in the Apostolic church in which the character of the Christian fraternity was most developed, and organisation least. It was still more evident in the ecclesiastical organisation of a national church.

The government and administration of the ecclesiastical association was externally internal to the church. It included the calling of ministers, the holding of synods, the making of ecclesiastical canons, the decision in ecclesiastical cases and controversies of faith, and the application of ecclesiastical discipline in matters other than the purely internal. It was the external order and institutional form of the purely internal and spiritual attributes of the church from Christ which were vested in the ministers alone.

Vedelius did not deny that the externally internal matters were ecclesiastical and must be administered by the formally ecclesiastical power. According to his distinction between objectively and formally ecclesiastical power, the ruler had no right to interfere in such matters; and yet he explicitly stated that the ruler had a formally ecclesiastical power by which he could share in their administration, together with the objectively ecclesiastical power by which he preserved the divine order of the church. For example, in the calling of ministers the ruler had both powers. The formal power was acknowledged in the Articles of the Synod of Dort and by the practice of Geneva. The church first sought a faculty to elect a particular candidate, but if the suggested candidate was displeasing to the ruler, the church chose another. This power of approval—for Vedelius admitted that it extended no further into the process of ordination itself— was not of human privilege but of divine law, by reason of his person and his office. In reply to Triglandius' objection Vedelius pointed out that the ruler had as much as the ministers the right to determine the final choice. It was more than public sanction and less than ordination. It was simply the co-operation of ruler and ministers in the nomination of the holder of the divine office of ministry. The objective power should be used to ensure that the presbytery selected suitable men for the pastorate in accordance with the lawful procedure, not only by his consent but also by the consent of the whole church. He was entitled to see that ordination was properly undertaken when a candidate was satisfactory and had been lawfully chosen, but the ruler could not actually ordain.

Again, the ruler had a formal and objective power in religious controversies. To the formal power belonged a threefold judgment: (a) of discretion, which was shared by all men and therefore by the ruler; (b) of definition, which was of the synod, in which the ruler sat as the noblest member and director of the whole synod; (c) of execution, which was subsequent to the decisions of the synod and after its dispersal, and therefore part of the ruler's office to apply those decisions of the synod in making which he himself had participated. The objective power was to be used to direct, so far as the external order was concerned, the public debates of the ministers. When the Biblical doctrine was obscure, the ruler should summon a synod at the request of the ministers to determine the orthodox interpretation. The ruler was to supervise the choice of deputies to the synod and could choose his own counsellors to assist him in the synod. His office constituted him director of the procedure in the synod so that the discussion might be orderly and equitably conducted. The objective power included this external regulation, because the decisions of the synod were without public sanction until the ruler gave his approval.

Vedelius had in fact modified his distinction between the objective and formal ecclesiastical power. It ceased to represent the antithesis of coercive authority around the church and spiritual authority within the church, because the ruler was granted a formal ecclesiastical power in the externally internal matters of the church. Ecclesiastical government was formally ecclesiastical but its authority was not that which Christ gave to His ministers through the sacrament of ordination. For that reason, the ruler could share the formal ecclesiastical power by which the church was governed.

How did Vedelius justify this modification? His answer rested upon two related principles. First, the spiritual power of Christ given to the ministers by their ordination did not extend beyond the essence of the true religion: doctrine and preaching, the sacraments of the Last Supper and of ordination, and the keys. The ministers therefore could not claim an exclusive power to govern the church in virtue of this spiritual authority. Church government was a matter for the whole church in which the ministers played an important part. Secondly, the whole church included the Christian magistrate. As a private person, he had to be granted the power which every other member had. But it was by reason of his office, as the head of the people, and as the principal member of the church, charged with the duty to perfect the external order of the church by means of his official powers, that he had a voice in the government of the church. Thus, he had a formal ecclesiastical power in conjunction with the ministers and members of the church.

The point which was not solved was the nature of his formal ecclesiastical power. Was it the same as his coercive power in the state or was it similar to that of the ministers? It was certainly not merely the power proper to all members of the church, nor was it the spiritual power proper to the ordained minister. If it was the same as the minister's, what was the common characteristic? If, as Vedelius seems to admit, it was the same as his civil authority, was not the whole theory an elaborate artifice, by playing upon words, to introduce his coercive power into the organisation of the church? Vedelius could only protest that the pious ruler would never act in a way that would violate the divine law or the proper liberties of the church. But he could not really give an adequate definition of the pious ruler nor an objective standard by which the church could judge of his piety. In practice, the theory would have opened the way to a secular tyranny.

To summarise his argument: he adopted the differentiation of ecclesiastical authority into potestas ordinis and potestas juris-dictionis, both of which were only indirectly controlled by the political government, save in so far as jurisdictio included the external administration of the corporate interests of the church, when the ruler shared with the ministers the final authority. The ruler ought not to interfere in the proper sphere of the ministers since he possessed in the church only the authority given to him by God. It was, as a positive power co-ordinate with the ministers', restricted to a few specific subjects: as a negative power, it applied to the whole church to correct abuses and to keep it to the strait path meticulously prescribed in the Bible. His responsibility for the public welfare and external order gave him an objectively ecclesiastical power. His position in the church enabled him to share a formally ecclesiastical power in its government.

The significance of the *De Episcopatu Constantini* was its sympathy with the lay character of the Reformation and its pronounced distrust of uncontrolled clericalism. Originally directed against the Roman church, it was equally applicable to the growing clericalism of the Dutch church, which held that to the ministers alone was all authority in the church. The basis of this argument was the spiritual nature of the church, not only in its doctrine and sacraments, but in its government, which required the spiritual power of the ministers for their regulation. Vedelius denied that church government was spiritual in this sense: that was the error of the Roman church. Church government was a matter for the whole church in which the laity as well as the ministers had their part; but how could the laity be adequately represented, unless by the ruler? Moreover, upon the premises of Calvinism, his theory was by no means inconsistent. Assuming an exclusive and established church, a corporate religion, the responsibility of the ruler as God's minister for the true religion, and a divine revelation in the Bible, it was by no means fanciful to link the ruler with the ministers in the ordering of such ecclesiastical matters as God had left to human discretion and local conditions. Where there was only one true church to be maintained by the ruler, where there was no authority which the ruler must obey save Christ, and where certain matters required human interpretation and adaptation, and where neither ministers nor ruler was allowed a final authority, the co-operation of ruler and ministers, such as Vedelius envisaged, was reasonable and even logical. What was fanciful was the belief in an objective divine law which bound both ruler and ministers.

The ideal behind this theory, linking Vedelius and Rivetus and Maccovius with the Reformation and early Calvinism, was indeed noble and inspiring. Life was a crusade of the whole of Christendom to realise God's Kingdom on earth. In its attack on evil and in its construction of the citadel of Christianity, the church used its light spiritual forces in a guerilla warfare against the individual soul, while the state launched its heavy corporal forces against the massed power of organised sin. Each worked in conjunction with the other but by different methods. The assault upon the strongholds of Satan demanded a combined effort, uniting the spiritual vision of the church and the temporal provision of the state. Thus, the church became an organised and endowed body, adopting social forms in order to attain its purpose more effectively, but at the same time giving moral justification to human power. The social system subserved the Christian ideal. In this national order, organised on its religious side as a church, the ruler enjoyed a peculiar function corresponding to his public office.

Such an ideal, however great its appeal, was wholly Utopian, and it was the merit of the critics of Vedelius to have seen its visionary character. The ideal was only conceivable so long as the individual and corporate conscience were sacrificed to divine revelation. The absolute character of such revelation was contrary to human progress and had to be abandoned. With it disappeared the two-kingdom theory as expounded by the Contra-Remonstrants and Vedelius, whose ultimate importance was no more than that the controversy over the *De Episcopatu Constantini* led to the formal acceptance of the principle of the separation of church and state by Calvinist thinkers.

CHAPTER IV

THE VOLUNTARY CHURCH AND THE SECULAR STATE

§ I

VEDELIUS was rapidly answered. Revius, a minister of great literary and scholastic ability, published in 1642 the *Examen Dissertationis D. Nicolai Vedelii*, which refuted Vedelius upon wholly Scriptural grounds. He[1] had criticised an earlier publication of the same year, the *Dissertatio Theologica de civili et ecclesiastica potestate*, by Triglandius, but he welcomed this challenge to Vedelius. Revius was congratulated by Voetius,[2] who referred to the approaching publication of the *Jus Majestatis circa sacra* of Apollonius which appeared in two parts in 1642 and 1643. This book gave rise to a furious controversy of little value. Voetius had not publicly refuted Vedelius: his great work, the *Politica Ecclesiastica*, was completed much later, but the disputations held at Utrecht were used by the critics of Vedelius, and incorporated into the *Politica Ecclesiastica*.

These four writers were active leaders of the church, entrusted with responsible offices and experienced in the actual conflicts of the church and the government. But Voetius was by far the greatest authority in the church, and had a profound effect upon the development of Dutch Calvinism. The University at Utrecht became an international centre for Calvinists under his long academic guidance, and he was throughout his life a strong champion of evangelical truth against Rome. He was at heart "a scholastic sage" who was the greatest controversialist of the century and yet who valued a truly spiritual life through mystic piety more than a pedantic orthodoxy.

The moderation and sanity of his thought upon the relations of church and state were well illustrated by the reports[3] of the

---

[1] Meyjes, *J. Revius*, 152.   [2] *Ib.* 165.
[2] Cramer, *De theol. faculteit te Utrecht*, ch. III.

Theological Faculty which were his work. He was always eager in defence of church rights, as for instance when local magistrates attempted to force their own candidates upon the church, and allowed appeals from ecclesiastical discipline; or when they interfered in the internal government of the church by insisting that organs were to be used in church-services and by introducing into the consistory a greater number of civil deputies to outvote the ecclesiastical representatives. He was equally zealous for the rights of the state and defended them against ecclesiastical encroachment. In the case of an elder suspended by the church for alleged misappropriation, the faculty reported that the elder ought not to have been suspended until he had been convicted by the civil court, since his was a civil offence. It was this keen respect for the rights of both parties which gave interest to the formal scholastic argument of the *Politica Ecclesiastica*.

The subsequent sections of this chapter are based upon the three chief books in which Contra-Remonstrant theory was developed more logically against the idea of a Christian government. In that connection, the *Examen* of Revius and the secondary books of Triglandius and Apollonius are neglected as adding little to the basic theories.

§ II[1]

The ideal of these three theorists was an independent and autonomous church which was free to determine the Will of God, to direct its own function and to decide what organisation was necessary for that purpose, without any responsibility to or connection with the state. Not only was the church to be free from any restriction which might deny its right to govern itself, but it was also to possess the power and means necessary for its independent existence and corporate life. It was not enough to recognise the freedom of the church to control its own forms and institutions, nor to acknowledge that the church was free to use the ordinary means of social life; it was necessary to accept the

---

[1] This section is based primarily upon Apollonius' *Jus Majestatis*, I, Bk 2 and II, Bks 1 and 2. Triglandius (*Dissertatio*, 349–455) was in full agreement, but his treatment was more of a refutation of Vedelius. Voetius started from a contractual basis, but the implications of his argument were also in harmony (*infra*, § III).

innate power of the church as a community in but not of the state,
a community with the power of self-determination, and of binding
its members by its communal sanctions. This implied more than
the obligation of the state to grant to the church the power to
control its own destiny and to use the common benefits of political
organisation; it meant that the state must admit that the church
governed every phase of the ecclesiastical society and every atom
of ecclesiastical matter by a power in no way granted by the state,
but, like that of the state, from God Himself.[1] In so far as the state
assumed its proper duty,[2] it had to accept and provide for the
spontaneous operation of this power inherent in the church.
Therefore,[3] the ecclesiastical like the civil organisation of men
bound its individual members into an entity which was a unity
wholly distinct from any other human association; it absorbed
all human actions which were ecclesiastical in virtue of their
religious purpose and spiritual significance. Outside the church
and beyond its power, there was no organised religion, no corporate worship, and no organ of Christ's Spirit. There was only
one institution which answered the religious needs of men and
the revealed will of God, and that institution existed out of God's
Grace, in consequence of which it possessed the true and legitimate means of salvation. As that institution, the church was
empowered and authorised to preserve the integrity of its social
existence by regulating with its own authority all the detailed
administration and constitution of a vast human society. It alone
could choose its officers, discipline its members, prescribe the
rules of their conduct and association, set in motion the democratic and constitutional organs of the federal society, manage its
endowments, regulate the forms of worship, and, in short, act as
a body as self-sufficient, self-contained and self-complete as the
state itself. It not only had absolute authority of its functional
but also of its institutional character;[4] the two parts were indivisible and integral elements of the one society. The important
point was not that the church was allowed by the state to exercise
this absolute social authority, but that the church alone could

[1] *Jus Maj.* I, 21, 87, 94–95, 327–341; II, 330, 339.
[2] *Ib.* I, 207, 216, 219–221, 279–280, 366–367.
[3] Cf. *ib.* I, 369–373.
[4] *Ib.* II, 129 *seq.*

exercise it.[1] If the state usurped this power, it might indeed control the church; but those acts thus undertaken were not the outcome of ecclesiastical but of civil power.[2] As far as this world was concerned, such usurped power might have the same effect; but in terms of spiritual life and the salvation to come those acts were sterile and impotent. They did not and could not issue in religious life. Therefore, the church, whenever subjected to the tyrannous interference of the state, was not only thwarted in its spiritual service to humanity in general and to the Elect in particular, but also stunted and mutilated in itself, its nature deformed, and its divine spirit desecrated, because its power was violated and its self-development denied. It existed in its perfect form only when its sole responsibility to God for the religious fulfilment of the Elect was acknowledged by the state, and only when it was free to use its absolute power for the satisfaction of the spiritual consciousness of its members. The realisation of its purpose was possible only when the spontaneous and absolute exercise of its power was an actuality, and when this was not possible the church was corrupted and its power vitiated. The vitality, validity and existence of the church depended upon the purity of its power, a purity denied by political intervention.[3] To limit that power was to prevent the self-development of the church and to render abortive the spiritual service which constituted its fundamentally moral purpose: it denied that single responsibility to God which was the essence of its moral character.

Animated by this ideal, these theorists were careful to defend the right and capacity of the church to constitute its own ministers according to the Will of God. Triglandius[4] held firmly that the model provided in the Word and by the practice of the church *sub cruce* was an absolute which must not be altered by human discretion. It was not sufficient to plead that the conversion of the magistrate gave him any share in the true ecclesiastical power through which Christ instructed His Church to appoint His ministers, but necessary to prove that this power of the church *sub cruce* was extraordinary without prejudice to the power given

[1] *Jus Maj.* I, 24–25.
[2] *Ib.* I, 50, 119, 279–80, 298–299, 316, 319; *De Civili*, 361.
[3] Cf. *Jus Maj.* 1–7, 19–21, 32, 36, 98, 113, 116, 119–120, 245; II, 343.
[4] *De Civili*, ch. 18.

by God to the ruler, to show that ecclesiastical functions were civil, and to explain why Christ never stated that the magistrates were His servants in the administration of His Church. But it could never be demonstrated from divine law that the ruler had any share in the election of ministers, or that Christ had counted the ruler as His servant in His spiritual kingdom. It was essential to distinguish the election and calling from the confirmation and approbation. The one was granted by Christ through the gifts which constituted the spiritual integrity of the ministry, the product of His Grace; the other was a matter of worldly status and social concession, which supplemented the inherent spiritual power with human facilities but did not in any way contribute to the divine gifts of the ministry itself. The fact that Christ alone could endow His ministers with grace and that He used the church as the organ by which men spiritually endowed were appointed to the ministry in itself created a ministry which existed without political confirmation or approbation. Since Christ worked through His Church, the election of the ministry operated among men in virtue of its own obedience to His Will; it was an act of divine impulsion and not of human permission.[1]

In the same way, Apollonius[2] defined the call of the ministers as an act of the church by which the office of ministry was entrusted to some particular and suitable person. It was, therefore, an act of ecclesiastical government, prescribed in its constitution, through which the regulation and administration of the church was possible, and illustrated the democratic-aristocratic character of the church's constitution. The presbytery, representing the church, chose the minister, but the whole church endorsed the election. The ministers examined the candidate and, after popular approval, ordained him to the ministry. Thus, the voluntary relation between minister and church was well grounded on voluntary election, and the right of vocatio was recognised to the whole church, so that it might never lack the care of souls nor receive ministers other than from Christ directly. As the Archbishop of Spalatro said, the special act of a democracy was the

[1] *De Civili*, 290. Cf. 269, for the Christian duty to take such steps as were consonant with Christ's Kingdom to obtain the right to worship publicly, even if the ruler was hostile.
[2] *Jus Maj.* I, 2 and Bk II, chs. I, 2.

election of its governors by all the people, and, as Apollonius realised, from this free election there sprang that free will of the church which was the essence of obedience to the ministers. The election of ministers[1] by the church alone was an essential element of ecclesiastical government, which was not civil but ecclesiastical, since it was a power delegated by Christ Himself to the church, for the express purpose of spiritual jurisdiction. To call a minister was to confer that power; that was from Christ alone but through the church as a necessary instrument. Therefore,[2] the church as a society of men organised by the spirit of Christ and endowed with spiritual jurisdiction was the only organ by which that spiritual jurisdiction could be conferred upon the ministry by election. Since the essence of that jurisdiction was voluntary obedience, it must be an act of the whole church, preceded by ministerial investigation, and followed by ministerial ordination. The call belonged to Christ as Head of the church; thence to the church; and so to all the members of the church in their different capacities.

If the church was endangered by a serious shortage of ministers, and if the strictly constitutional method of election was impossible, the pious members of the church might appoint to the ministry, and communicate from Christ the ministerial power in doctrine and discipline. Voetius admitted this same emergency method, even allowing women to act as pseudo-ministers to the unconstitutional congregation; but insisted that once normal conditions were restored these methods lost their validity. It is significant that the congregation was thus conceived as the ultimate authority in abnormal circumstances; the right of election, as part of ecclesiastical power, could not exist outside the ecclesiastical society. Voetius[3] was in full accord with Triglandius and Apollonius—the examination, election, ordination and confirmation were by the presbytery or the church.

To both Apollonius and Voetius,[4] the individual churches were

---

[1] *Jus Maj.* I, 145, 160. [2] *Ib.* I, 169.
[3] *Polit. Eccl.* I, 196.
[4] *Jus Maj.* I, Bk II, chs. 3, 4; *Polit. Eccl.* Part III, Bk I, Tr. 2, ch. 2. Triglandius was merely content to protect the judgment of synods from political interference. He did not discuss the internal constitution of the churches.

equal in ecclesiastical power, one not above another, but meeting in synods and classes as colleagues and members according to a constituted order through which their individual powers were combined into a social and common quasi-power. This collective power was not extrinsic to these individual churches but the product of common deliberation; it was not essentially different from the total powers of individual churches. So that this collective power was not a new power of a new nature but merely a collection of co-ordinated powers of individual churches, as colleges formed a union or the integral parts of the body formed the body. It was a co-ordination of existing powers and not a creation of a new power, though each was to be determined by its place in the collection, and by the good of all. The origin of synodal authority and power was within each individual church, but their exercise and execution were vested in the synod.

Therefore, the synod[1] was a public meeting held by common agreement, constituted by the proper delegation of representatives of the constituent churches, and deliberating in the interests of all. Each church[2] was duty bound to accept its decisions since the synod issued from the divine providence which instituted mutual society for common benefits. The classis afforded mutual association for common counsel.

The right[3] of summoning and holding a synod was with the church and its members alone, for from Christ there came the commission of power, from the magistrate merely civil permission. It was an ecclesiastical institution and had to be conducted in an ecclesiastical way. The members of a synod were primarily those persons specifically ordained to ecclesiastical office, but might include any distinguished by their gifts or vocation. Their selection rested with the church as an ecclesiastical matter, and they were the delegates of the church alone. By this delegation of authority, the intrinsic spiritual power of particular churches was united into a social and common quasi-power through which the collective and combined body of the synod exercised a definitive judgment for the universal good of the church. That judgment[4] sprang from the gift of prophecy, but the public authority of that

---

[1] *Jus Maj.* I, 242.
[2] *Ib.* I, 215.
[3] *Ib.* I, 219; *Polit. Eccl.* I, 187–195.
[4] *Jus Maj.* I, 233.

judgment was from the public delegation of its members by the constituent churches. None[1] but the churches themselves could confer spiritual power upon that union in a synod, and if the members were delegated by some other authority than the churches, the union of the members was no synod but some other body animated by a power not spiritual but derived from the delegating authority. In that case an alien authority determined the needs of the particular churches, subjecting them to a power different and diverse from their own body, contrary to the command of Christ. In the true synod, such alien power did not exist, for the synod did not possess an alien and superior power distinct from the individual churches and operating independently of their power, but was the special organisation of particular churches to combine their powers.

The synod[2] was properly concerned only with spiritual things, directed to the glory of God and the preservation of His Church: either the common needs of the whole church, or the particular needs of each church where it lacked power to settle its own problem, or abused its power, or was suspected of abusing its power. So that this union of the churches was intended to promote the ecclesiastical liberty and power of each church, in consequence of which end the power of the synod could only increase and not diminish the power of each church.

The synod[3] was instituted to treat these spiritual and ecclesiastical matters in a spiritual way by that ministerial authority which could only act in accordance with the divine law. It had no authority if and when it commanded anything contrary to that law: it could not compel individual churches to obey it, for the synod was to excite not only external obedience but also the inward obedience of faith. Even when misused ecclesiastical authority ought always to be reverenced and outwardly obeyed. Though by no means infallible,[4] a synod had the supreme ecclesiastical power of defining and deciding controversies of faith, a power divinely given to avoid confusion, because it was inspired by the Holy Spirit. When the synod[5] decreed a just judgment for the common good of the church and in the interests

---

[1] *Jus Maj.* i, 233–234; *Polit. Eccl.* i, 187.   [2] *Jus Maj.* i, 239, 242–243.
[3] *Ib.* i, 245.   [4] *Ib.* i, 248.   [5] *Ib.* i, 251.

of ecclesiastical administration, the synod had a definitive ecclesiastical power which permitted it to force its decrees upon each church by its censures.

Therefore, the public judgment of all spiritual things was proper to the pastoral office only, and so to those chosen with the public vocatio of the church. Whatever[1] was decided by a council of prophets had the force of canons, and in matters of faith[2] it had supreme, ecclesiastical, ministerial and definitive power, enforceable upon individual churches by ecclesiastical censure. The synod alone could abrogate its canons. Often it punished sins which the state could not. Therefore, the decree and execution were often spiritual actions proper to the church alone. On the other hand,[3] these spiritual actions of the synod were simply "suasoria" which depended upon acceptance by the conscience enlightened by spiritual discipline or spiritual faith.

Ecclesiastical discipline[4] was the application of God's Will to any person who acted contrary to that will and offended the church, in order to remedy spiritual defects by the spiritual means granted by Christ. It was intended to excite repentance and gain salvation, by fraternal correction rather than by anathema. This spiritual discipline was an essential part of the Gospel since it preserved the rule of Christ in the church; but[5] it operated only upon the inward man through spiritual penalties, such as exclusion from the comfort of the church, and only within the ecclesiastical communion. It had no place in civil society, since its object was the correction of those abuses which corrupted or imperilled the spiritual state of the church. In virtue of its divine institution, it was expressly delegated to the church; the gospel message, its own spiritual nature and the common interest of the church demanded that ecclesiastical discipline should be vested in the church alone. Excommunication was proper to the whole church, since it alone could eject whom it had accepted and since excommunication was otherwise vain; but the presbytery as the representative church possessed the executive authority, which was rightly used only when approved by the whole church. This

---

[1] *Jus Maj.* I, 316.   [2] *Ib.* I, 275.   [3] *Ib.* I, 260, 325.
[4] *Ib.* II, Bk I, ch. I; *De Civili*, ch. 20.
[5] *Jus Maj.* I, 325; II, 25, 37, 73; *Polit. Eccl.* I, 31.

executive authority was no more than the declaration of the Will
of God to some particular person; it was therefore ministerial and
not imperative, spiritual and not corporal, from Christ and not
from the ruler, of internal and not external man. Divine and
natural law ordained some means of appeal from any judgment,
but appeals in ecclesiastical cases must be to some higher
ecclesiastical authority—the classis and synod—and not to any
civil court, since excommunication—exclusion from the sacraments—was derived on the one hand from the vocation and
function of the ministry, and on the other from "the instrumental
derivation"[1] of the whole church considered collectively. The
nature of ecclesiastical discipline and natural right must confirm
this teaching of the Reformers; for what concerns all must be
determined by all.

Properly speaking there was no legislative power[2] in the church,
only the power of warning and guiding men. The canons of the
church governed the willing and not the unwilling, and for that
very reason were no true laws. Law implied coercion, and in the
church God alone had the power of compulsion, the pastors only
signifying the commands of God. Their canons[3] were enforced
by spiritual means only, and no human power could make them
binding upon the conscience, apart from their own "ratio"—
manifest utility or charity. Therefore, canons regulating matters
expedient to the church but not divinely prescribed did not bind
save in the case of scandal or contempt, while in matters[4] of divine
worship prescribed by God the obligation was of God, not of the
pastor, who could only publish the divine prescription. There
were, however, certain things instrumental to that worship, some
necessary and instituted of God, others a matter of ecclesiastical
expediency: the former[5] were external acts of ritual which were
not in themselves good except in the worship of God, whence they
were immutable; the latter were those human acts neither commanded nor forbidden by natural or divine law, and consequently
neither good nor evil, but useful and necessary in the public order
of the church. In these matters requiring regulation in the

[1] *Jus Maj.* II, 61, 62.
[2] *Ib.* II, Bk I, ch. 3, 4; *Polit. Eccl.* I, 196, III, 796; *De Civili*, ch. 21.
[3] *Jus Maj.* II, 112, 113, 115.   [4] *Ib.* II, 119, 129.   [5] *Ib.* II, 121–122.

interests of decency and order, the church enjoyed the discretion
but not the power of true legislation.

These regulations in the interests of order must not be confused with those acts of reverence which nature imparted to man.
Natural rites, such as the raising of the hands and eyes, needed
only a rightly ordered adjustment by the human authority, for
any individual could discern them from those acts which were
not in themselves of the moral law. The primary authority of such
acts was from divine and natural law, which established the proper
conduct of human associations, the secondary authority from the
wisdom of each church.

This power[1] of ecclesiastical legislation, confined to matters of
expediency, was competent to the church alone in virtue of its
spiritual discipline, which could only be used to enforce what God
had committed to the care of the church or had left to its discretion. Jurisdiction[2] was the product of legislation, and as God had
given to the church spiritual jurisdiction He must have granted
also the power of deciding those rules which the discipline was to
enforce. The ministry[3] had been divinely instituted not only for
the ministerial function but also for the private and spiritual good
of the faithful and the church; but as these ecclesiastical laws were
necessary for that spiritual good, the power of legislation was
proper to the ministry. Its office was instituted for the government of the ecclesiastical polity through which the spiritual good
of the church could be realised. Natural reason also taught that
the expert alone could formulate the rules of his craft. For these
reasons, none but the church and in it the ministry possessed the
power of ecclesiastical legislation.

Although[4] the legitimate constitution of the church required
rules of orderly conduct in order that the society of the church
might be preserved and its purpose accomplished, these rules
were matters of order and efficiency common to civil and ecclesiastical societies, and not of ritual. The church could not institute
by its own moral power any external rites sanctified to the spiritual
good of souls. That was with God alone, and He had indicated in
the Bible all rites in themselves necessary to worship and spiritual

[1] *Jus Maj.* II, 182.   [2] *Ib.* II, 141.
[3] *Ib.* II, 132.   [4] *Ib.* II, 163–165.

good. What was left to the church was the duty of adapting these rites to the edification of the church, so that its laws in matters of ritual were no more than regulations necessary to establish that order without which the proper end of ritual, the edification of the faithful, was impeded. The church had, in short, no power to sanction the elaborate and vain ritual of Catholicism or to impose rites upon men beyond the general necessity of avoiding anarchy in the church.

The power[1] of legislation proper to the human church regulated particular circumstances which God had not determined, and its laws were binding only in virtue of their reason and end. Whatever[2] in these laws was of certain immediate needs ceased to be binding when those needs disappeared; whatever was of universal reason from nature or the Scriptures continued to bind. Now, the law of charity and the command to avoid offence to the church were of this universal reason, and therefore bound the members of the church to obey particular laws. But these conditions nullified any legislation in the church which bound by pure authority and not by utility or equity, or by agreement with the Word of God. It must never legislate by absolute command, not even in the smallest accessories of religion; for those accessories[3] in so far as they promoted the spiritual good of the church partook of the character of spiritual good, which was entrusted to the church. Thus ecclesiastical law[4] compassed all ecclesiastical action not defined by God, and that law, from the least important accessory to the most important, was formulated by the church.

In all regulations left to the liberty of the church, ecclesiastical laws in themselves could not bind the conscience. God alone possessed that supreme authority. All ecclesiastical laws[5] must be subject to the private judgment of the faithful, who ought to obey such laws only when consonant with the Word and useful or edifying. The norm must be the spirit and not the letter of the law, so that it was not wrong but right to ignore a law when its enforcement would contradict its end and purpose. Only when the law sought justice and the common good was the church justified in vindicating it by spiritual jurisdiction. This was true

---

[1] *Jus Maj.* II, 223.   [2] *Ib.* II, 174.   [3] *Ib.* II, 142, 185.
[4] *Ib.* II, 241.   [5] *Ib.* II, 204 *seq.*

even of civil laws, for the civil legislator did not bind the conscience itself in civil conduct but only the external actions of the body which housed the conscience. This was only an accidental obligation upon the conscience. But the inner man[1] and the church, which was concerned only with the inner man, could not be governed by any but supernatural laws. The conscience was governed by God alone, not by church or state, for it could not be bound by fear of punishment but by true faith. The ministry could only witness to these supernatural laws. In matters of ecclesiastical organisation not imposed on the conscience by God, the church was free to use them in the way best fitted to excite the faithful to ecclesiastical communion.

Voetius went further. He denied[2] that the church as a property-owning corporation was in any way more dependent on the state than any other property owner. Its buildings and endowments were its own property and not the grant of the state. The financial basis of the church was its own matter to be administered according to the wisdom and needs of the church by the officers of the church. But in certain circumstances of national peril the church ought to contribute its all to the preservation of the state;[3] for unless the state safeguarded the community the church itself would be overthrown. There was, however, no right by which ecclesiastical property could be sequestrated without the consent of the church.

The fundamental problem of the early Contra-Remonstrants had been the necessity of preserving the ministerial function without transforming the church into a society which by its self-sufficiency encroached upon the sphere of the state as the imperative authority in the region of matter. They had tried primarily to protect the ministry from secular interference. The function was universally admitted to belong to the ministry alone, but if the ruler appointed the ministers, promulgated ecclesiastical laws, admitted appeals from spiritual jurisdiction, treated ecclesiastical property as in fact civil, and reserved to its own control the financial support of the church, the independent exercise of the function was easily nullified. The revealed religion and the

---

[1] *Jus Maj.* III, 212.   [2] *Polit. Eccl.* Part I, Bk IV, Tr. 2, ch. 1.
[3] Cf. *De Civili*, 442.

miraculous operation of grace through the sacraments and preaching were dependent upon human favour and civil concessions. The early Contra-Remonstrants advanced along the avenue of autonomy, but hesitated to take the broad road of a self-sufficiency parallel to the state. Their respect for sovereignty, divine right and the corpus christianum held them back. Hence arose their inconsistency. The later Contra-Remonstrants were more logical. Their object was autonomy; to them that involved independence and the absolute inclusive nature of the church, since the function of salvation, admittedly entrusted to the church alone through the action of the ministry, could only be freed from human control by the exclusive authority of the church in every part of its institutional activity. The government of the church must be with the church; the state must have no share in the election of officers and similar acts of the ecclesiastical society.

The result of this theory was the absolute independence of the church and a peculiar power for its own government. The miraculous function of the church was the product of grace and only possessed its virtue so long as its human operation was by men designated by Christ and endowed by Him with the peculiar and requisite gifts. No human power could assume this authority of selecting the ministers: God spoke through the church alone. Ecclesiastical jurisdiction was part of the function because it was the spiritual power of producing repentance or spiritual punishment. Such spiritual reaction upon the conscience was not possible save by the power of God through the church. God alone legislated with sovereignty and compulsion in the church, but left to the church the power of deciding circumstances of administration which He had not prescribed. All these activities were the outcome of the inherent spiritual power of the church, acting in a spiritual way impossible to the state.

§ III

An analysis of the meaning to be attributed to the word "church" and still more of its nature and characteristics was the special labour of Voetius, and the foundation upon which he constructed his own theory of the relations of church and state. The ambiguity and vagueness of previous definition had been the cause of much of that confusion which underlay contemporary controversy. It was by no means adequate to rely upon Scriptural terms or upon a straightforward assertion of divinity; for the problem was much more complicated than the Reformers had realised. Until the church was accurately defined, not only as a divine institution but also as a human society, it was not easy to formulate a consistent argument to meet the case put forward on behalf of the godly prince by many Protestants, or on the basis of sovereignty by the Erastians. The principles determining the government of the church were to be found in its essential character, and Voetius was among the first Calvinists to attempt this task of definition by which the divine right of the ruler was to be limited and the social character of the church liberated from external limitations.

The *Politica Ecclesiastica* was a treatise upon the visible church in its many relations and organisation, and this fact was itself significant of Voetius' scrupulous thought. Too often the invisible and visible churches were not properly distinguished and therefore an obstacle to clear thought. From the beginning he defined[1] *Politica Ecclesiastica* as the holy science of ruling the visible church, a study distinct from secular or theological, and from which all consideration of the invisible church was to be excluded. It is true that he did not regard the visible church[2] as differing in essence from the invisible, or the divine decrees in the invisible church as inapplicable to the visible. There was a necessary connection between the two, springing from the divine will and grace to draw certain elect to salvation, but in spite of this common character there was a different place allotted to each in the divine scheme. The visible church was an organisation of men professing Christianity designed to realise in some measure the communion of saints. The invisible church was that communion of saints, independent of time and place and human limitations. The visible church was never more than an approximation to the true communion of saints, and never more than a means to further it among men. Its organisation and government were part of those means

---

[1] I, I (the references in this section are to the *Polit. Eccl.* Part I (Vol. I) and Part III).
[2] I, 61.

and peculiar to the visible church arising out of human needs. The simple worship of God in spirit and in truth was not adequate to satisfy the religious needs of ordinary men nor to fulfil the work of election. While, therefore, the visible church was in virtue of its purpose an integral part of the invisible church and the two identical in essence, both were distinguished[1] by the human circumstances and needs of the visible church organised for the government of men in their spiritual life. The belief that the Catholic church was not wholly invisible, and that its mystical and human aspects were not essentially different, provided the means by which Voetius argued for the spiritual nature and government of the visible church as part of the church ruled by God. Although he wrote only of the visible church, he never neglected the consequences of its connection with the invisible church, by which the church on earth became a supernatural state governed independently of the civil state by its own authority and officers. The church as a society of men professing the true faith was essentially distinct from any other society of men, including the state, since the spirit of God was ever working in it. The core of his doctrine was this expression of faith.

In what way was the visible church to be treated?[2] In one sense it could be considered as an abstraction, or concept, epitomising the essential characteristics of the many visible churches which actually existed, or as the logical formulation of principles partially revealed in the historical churches. In another and concrete sense, the term "visible church" signified a whole made up of similar constituent parts and therefore a whole of the same character as the parts. Thus, the sea was a whole because an assemblage of waters, all of the same character, which was also the character of the whole. The Catholic church could be interpreted in two ways: first, as a "totum universale" by which was indicated the forms of classification; secondly, as a "totum integrale", an individual or singular instance because its parts gave to it its own completeness. In the first case, the Catholic church was considered abstractly or in idea apart from its own

[1] Cf. I, 63, 65.
[2] I, 11 and 218–219. Cf. Ames' *Marrow of Sacred Divinity*, Bk I, chs. 31, 32: also Parker, *R. De Politeia Eccl.* Bk III, ch. 18.

subdivisions, but in the second case, as a definite form of this time or that in virtue of its constituent parts without which it could never be considered.

The point which Voetius was making is best illustrated by enlarging upon his own example. Sea is a totum universale since it is a generic term comprehending all species and divisions and therefore meant of sea in idea. *The* sea postulates a particular and individual sea which is formed by the amalgamation of similar constituents: as such it is a totum integrale. To discuss sea is fundamentally different from discussing this sea or that. Sea is the standard for ordering its own particular divisions; this or that sea is determined by the integral parts from which it is constituted. In the one case, the characteristics are attributes of sea in idea and thence belong to its species; in the other case, the attributes are of this or that sea because primarily of its constituents.

The importance of this distinction was due to Voetius' clear understanding that the totum universale was the product of the human mind and of an intellectual operation. Its conception was a mental process. The unity it established existed only in and through the mind of those conceiving it in idea. It was complete and comprehensive because it was an abstraction existing and valid only in the realm of thought. Its reality was of human understanding. Only in so far as it was idea could it be said to be prior to its parts, being the whole to which the parts were related. The totum integrale was the product of the world of action created by the combination of parts in themselves imperfect, and forming a distinct group of a collective character only because each separate part coalesced with other similar parts. The Catholic church as a totum integrale was constituted by the action of actual and particular churches in combining in ever-expanding groups until the Catholic church existing in the world at a particular time was completed. To argue from the totum universale to the totum integrale was a logical fallacy. The distinction between the two had to be observed lest the qualities proper to the one were confused with the other, and especially lest the completeness and unity of the Catholic church in abstract was identified with the different completeness of the actual Catholic church at any particular time. To apply the principles underlying the idea to the real was to confuse the intellectual synthesis with the living and social synthesis. The fatal objection, to Voetius, was the deduction that the power and nature of the actual Catholic church was derived from the mental concept of a universal Catholic church instead of from the particular churches which created it. In other words, the whole did not exist independently of the parts nor was the individuality of the parts destroyed by the inherent absoluteness of the whole, but in fact the whole was nothing more than the parts themselves, the needs of which it served rather than providing the medium in which the parts found their own true nature. The real and individual entity was the particular church; all combinations of such-like entities were improperly called the church.

The church which was the subject of Voetius' analysis was neither the mystical nor the abstract but the visible church considered concretely, whether the totality made up of many component churches, or the components, each of which was a whole in itself, not only in relation to others, but also in relation to its own members. In either of these ways, the church was distinguished from the mere number of churches or church members: the particular church as a whole was contrasted to the members numerically considered, and the combination of particular churches was contrasted to the number of particular churches. In either instance, Voetius was concerned with the study of the church as a visible combination and with the real individual possession, exercise, and communication of individual power belonging to such particular churches and visible combinations.

A passage of a somewhat similar character in Chamierus' great polemic[1] against the Roman Catholic church and its leading apologists showed the real reason for the Calvinists' insistence upon the distinction between the church in fact and in idea, and upon the fallacy of confusing the universal and the particular. For Harding had asserted in defence of the Roman church that the whole militant church, as the mother of all other churches, gathered all particular churches into one mystical body and united them in itself more than they had been united in them-

---

[1] *Chamierus Contractus...Opera Fr. Spanhemii*, Geneva, 1643, 451 (b).

selves. Chamierus denied that there could be a unity which did
not arise from the combination of particular churches, and that
the whole militant church was something more than the united
churches. How could the whole church, which was not one except
in virtue of the mutual bond between churches, be more one than
the mutually connected churches? Were the sheep gathered
together by the flock, or was not the flock rather the assembled
sheep? The society, whether church or other, was nothing sub-
sisting by itself, but only existed by thought. Only by a figure of
speech was the whole militant church other than the component
churches.

The church in Voetius' theory was primarily the particular
church—the body of faithful men, the constitution of which
formed the visible and instituted church. The church in the
beginning was the parish church; but in its evolution it became
part of a greater combination intended to realise more adequately
the inherent powers of the local churches. Those churches were
the true church, and their classical and synodal groupings were
only described as churches accidentally and improperly. The
visible church[1] was in essence the particular church; in development, the associations of churches for their own greater good and
benefit. His theory of the visible church was built upon the
recognition of the particular churches as the true churches and
of their further associations as defined by their original character.
So that Voetius' arguments returned again and again to the
particular churches as the essential constituents of the visible
church, which was the aggregate of many particular churches.
His analysis of the visible church was mainly an analysis of the
particular church, the indissoluble unit which was in itself a true
visible church, and then of the combinations of such churches for
common interests.

The definition of the particular church proceeded partly by
positive and partly by negative methods. To define the visible
church as primarily the particular church involved the denial of
a representative church[2] by which the person of the particular
church was borne by an organ superior to the local churches.
The pope could not be virtually the oecumenical church nor the

---

[1] *Polit. Eccl.* III, 117 *seq.*   [2] I, 22; III, 120.

bishop the diocesan church. There could be a representative church only when particular churches were actively represented and themselves chose and authorised their representatives. For that reason, the classical and synodal meetings did not form a virtual nor ideal nor representative church which could claim to be called the church in its own right. To argue that the bishop bore the person of the diocesan church was once more a confusion of actual and ideal: for the diocesan church[1] only possessed unity as an idea, and the bishop was not the embodiment of a mental unity but an officer of the combination of churches which was the actual church he administered. Representation meant participation, and was illegitimately used when it was intended to commit the determination of the affairs of many churches to an official who summed up in his official character all those churches because he represented a church, the unity of which was an abstract conception. The whole in which these other churches existed and which contained their being, in virtue of which all were said to be represented in the activity of the whole without their own participation and therefore bound to implement the unity including them, was an idea not corresponding to the facts. Church-officers represented actual churches and not the idea of the church. In so far as they claimed authority in a church which was not visible, they were not truly representatives of visible churches, and could not justify authority in such churches. Thus, Voetius attacked the hierarchic principle of virtual representation by which authority descended from the whole to the particular, instead of being inherent in particular churches by which it might be delegated to elected representatives.

The particular church was not a territorial association, for it did not exist through any territorial bond. Its nature[2] was not a local union due to cohabitation nor was membership the birthright[3] or civil right of any born in the territorial district, although birth, life and upbringing within that area were conditions necessary for the constitution of that church. Mere residence did not suffice, so that the particular church was not a parish church[4] of the English type. Vicinity[5] was a matter of convenience, desirable

---

[1] Cf. Parker, *op. cit.* Bk III, ch. 18.   [2] I, 15.   [3] I, 64.
[4] I, 24.   [5] I, 59–60.

for the enjoyment of mutual benefits, but never the primary condition. Territorial situation and civil ties were no essential characteristics of the church but merely accidental. The church could exist without either and was independent of temporal circumstances.

Since the church was no territorial society, it was not the consequence of political organisation nor dependent upon political principles of association. It was not a political union governed in the same way as the state.[1] Although the church was always in a state, yet the state as such did not always include the church. The two were not to be confounded lest the church was secularised and the world clothed with an ecclesiastical character. Neither ought to be transformed into the other. Consequently, the church-state and state-church violated the principles according to which the church was ordered; neither was a branch of the other, nor were both different organs of the same community. The churches[2] of the Old Testament and of the New were established upon different principles, not only in polity, but also in relation to the state. The church of the Old Testament was a national church complementary to the state, the subjects of the church being the subjects of the state, and the same body[3] constituting church and state. So in recent times had been the churches of Geneva, Switzerland and Elizabethan England. Under the New Testament, there were no national churches save as the collection of particular churches, and no states,[4] the constitution, laws and offices of which were ordained by God and therefore immediately divine. Any connection between church and state was not due to territorial nor national origins, nor even to common membership; for the people[5] did not constitute the church as people nor as members of the state, but as Christians and members of Christ, for which reason the government of the church was not the government[6] of men as men, as dwellers on earth and as associated and united in political society. The church was not the product of the factors which formed political and territorial unions, and was not to be identified with nor included in such unions.

[1] I, 15, 37.   [2] I, 244.   [3] I, 25.
[4] I, 147.   [5] I, 152.   [6] III, 784.

Partly because he denied the territorial character of the church, Voetius was compelled to deny that the particular church was one congregation.[1] If circumstances of place were temporal considerations by which the church was not to be limited, it was not to be confined by the limits of a congregation, nor by the size of a particular building, nor by the strength or weakness of the minister's voice. The essence of the church could not be defined by such accidental features, for the church[2] was not a union in one assembly or body in one place in order to worship God at one and the same time. The particular church might be divided into many congregations when its membership was large enough to warrant it, but none of those congregations contained the essence of the church. The church was not the congregation as the Independents and some of the English Presbyterians had argued.

The church, again, was not the consistory,[3] even though it acted on behalf of the church. To Voetius this distinction was necessary to avoid oligarchic interpretations, and he always pointed to the danger of the consistory acting as the church and not in the church as its agent and open to its criticism. However important the executive was, it was the organ and never the whole, and could not be separated from and opposed to it, as if itself the whole. The whole body containing the consistory was alone entitled to be called the church.

The particular church was a societas[4] established by the agreement of free and equal members for the exercise of the communion of saints or for the mutual communication of everything conducive to salvation. It was, therefore, a multitude, a collection, an aggregate of members, joined together by certain ties. It was a fraternity[5] pledged to brotherhood. It arose out of mutual consent and was only an association of individuals, the mere sum of its members. The origin of the particular church was in accord with contemporary individualistic theory: it was created by the deliberate act by which each and every member bound himself to the others. In the same way as the particular church was a union of individuals, the groups of churches were

[1] I, 27. [2] I, 15. [3] I, 28, 220. [4] I, 12.
[5] I, 58 "Fraternitas seu societas Ecclesiastica"; again I, 70; and III, 133 "fraterna confoederatio".

unions and combinations of equal groups freely agreeing to certain obligations to each other. Nevertheless, the very idea of union implied order and order implied government.[1] The church was not any number of those who came to hear the preaching of the Word.[2] Attendance at the services of the minister was not enough to constitute the church, for a number of hearers was little more than spectators, casually assembled and knit together by no ties. The church was a union of a definite and permanent character which bound the collection together by the terms to which each agreed. The act of union gave to the church-members a character different from a casual and transient assembly, and therefore different from the mere total of its own members considered as individuals without mutual rights and duties. The particular church was a number of individuals collected in a certain order, and the provincial or national church was a number of churches linked in an analogous order.

The church was a visible collection in the sense that it was a number of individuals united by a system of orderly relations among themselves, and not between the whole and the members separately. The church in its origin and creation was a societas, or an aggregate, because the members pledged themselves to each other, and the union resulting was the product of relations undertaken between individuals alone. Collective action arose from the pledge made by each to his fellows to act together in certain matters, and was no more than the action of individual members admitting obligations to each other, and each fulfilling those obligations.

This societas was not the societas as understood by Hooker. Voetius himself did not refer to Hooker by name, but he accepted so much of the argument of a strong English critic of Hooker's position that it is permissible to assume that he also endorsed this particular conception of the ecclesiastical societas.[3] Indeed, Voetius stood upon the same essential grounds whereby the case of Hooker for the hierarchy was implicitly refuted. Hooker[4] had insisted that the church was a societas, and distinguished between a societas and assemblies, which "properly are rather things

---

[1] I, 48, 70, 241–249; III, 153, 179, 804.   [2] I, 31.
[3] Parker, op. cit. Bk III, ch. 17, pp. 189, 202.
[4] Of the Laws of Ecclesiasticall Politie (London, 1604), 124–130.

belonging to a church. Men are assembled for performance of publike actions; which actions being ended, the assembly dissolveth itselfe and is no longer in being, whereas the church which was assembled, doth no less continue afterwards than before." It was a visible society "incorporated into one company", constituting "a sensibly known company" because it was a "number of men belonging unto some Christian fellowship, the place and limites whereof are certain". To Hooker, this society was national; but to Voetius it was a body of Christians held together by a contract and so organised that its members formed a complete religious communion. No such communion was possible in a national church, where the members could not even know each other.

While Voetius regarded the church as a society from the standpoint of its composition and formation, and as unions of such societies, he also regarded it as a corpus in respect of organisation and power, in both its aspects of the particular church and the wider unions of churches. He denied[1] that there were two kinds of government in the church—that of the particular church and that of groups of churches. There was a common principle of government though exercised in different ways.[2] He exposed as a fallacy the contention of the Independents that the power of synods and classes was external[3] to the particular churches and imposed upon them from above; for it was a power belonging to the particular churches which bound them[4] just as much as any exercise of that power in domestic matters which were not common to other churches. The corpus ecclesiasticum, whether of singular or combined churches, incorporated in consequence of the members' consent, was a whole, the organs and the members of which were distinguishable but could not be divided. The consistory or synod or minister or people was only a part of the church, and the power which each part exercised was peculiar and proper to the truly constituted church,[5] i.e. to the corpus ecclesiasticum. Ecclesiastical power was in the whole church, where every part was knit together to form an indissoluble unit or a complete unity. The "subject"[6] of ecclesiastical power was

[1] III, 153.　[2] III, 128.　[3] III, 141, 143, 150.
[4] III, 133, 168.　[5] I, 220.　[6] I, 117, 217–218.

the external, visible and instituted church as such, regarded as a collection, and therefore as a totum corpus including organs and people. It was a unique power because of the ecclesiasticum corpus and of those appointed for that purpose in and by that corpus. That power[1] which was exercised by each and every member was inherent in members as members and in the corpus as corpus. The individual member[2] was bound to submit to the judgment and power of that corpus to which he belonged. But, in fact, Voetius made such confused use[3] of societas and corpus that it may well be doubted whether he understood the corpus to be anything more than the complex of individual obligations, out of which the church was created, although he was fully aware that his theory of ecclesiastical self-determination depended upon that inherent power essential for corporate autonomy.

The essence of the church was, therefore, the bond by which the societas of the faithful was formed, and neither political, civil and territorial connections nor the casual assembly of hearers in one congregation, united by faith and by the profession of faith. The visible church did not arise from transient or temporal or mystical causes, but from the promises made by each member. The theory of Voetius was the covenant theory of the church, uniting into one communion all who accepted the covenant. It was an association established by a contract between individuals for a particular purpose, and it was by this contract that the church was separated from all other societies of men. Any permanent union,[4] as distinct from a mere assembly, was created by a pact and its terms, in consequence of which the societas and its government existed. Without the pact and the union, the visible church did not exist, although there was the communion of the invisible church in the common faith and the profession of faith. Nevertheless, there[5] was no visible church, and no visible communion, without a covenant, just as spectators of different nations meeting in a certain state were not citizens of that state nor constituted an independent polity. The business associates of a merchant did not constitute his family, although they attended his house; nor was there friendship between men of similar habits

---

[1] I, 141, 222.   [2] III, 168.   [3] Cf. I, 206, 214, 222.
[4] I, 242.   [5] I, 14.

and dispositions without a covenant between them; nor did states of the same nation and almost of the same form of government unite in confederation or polity without a union and the methods of union. The visible church[1] was without existence where men were connected only by vicinity or belief; for there was neither union nor government. Membership was not automatic nor in virtue of other qualifications, but was granted only upon an explicit promise.

The visible church was a "coalitio et confoederatio in unum corpus Ecclesiasticum"[2] through free and mutual consent. The "form" of the church was such consent, i.e. the covenant, and Voetius had to explain how such a confoederatio was begun and preserved, and in what manner the consent of each member was to be given. It is obvious that he did not assume that each church would normally be created by the formal consent of members without any aid from other churches or without the presence and guidance of some ministers.[3] Some churches would only be separations from an existing church—as colonies—and others would be chiefly constituted by the classis and officially; but he realised that there were some emergencies when a church would be instituted by unofficial action and by a covenant taken by individual Christians, and that in essence every church was to be treated as the product of such a covenant, since only then would its true nature be understood. The ministers or presbytery or delegates specially sent by a synod, or even the synod itself, might direct the nascent church, partly by working privately upon individuals, partly by initiating a coetus at which business suggested by them might be conducted under their direction, votes taken, and the necessary promises made. Once the church was constituted, those co-opted into the communion of the church had to make a public profession of their faith, before the church or consistory, save when they had been members of another church, whence the minister, or some responsible church member chosen by the consistory when there was no minister available, should examine all intending members in their knowledge of the catechism. In addition, they had to make the confoederatio or stipulatio by which they became members of the church.

[1] I, 63.   [2] I, 16.   I, 17–19.

Voetius rejected the view that some external ecclesiastical body ought invariably to direct the constitution of a church, and that, created without such direction, it was not properly a church and had no power to choose its own minister. There was no evasion of the issue: either the church was the covenant and the body of church-members, or it was tied to the theological conception of pastoral succession by which the church was not the act of church-members; either the church was ultimately the fully empowered because self-empowered unit, or its power was not the result of a covenant but of the hierarchical relation of churches.

His adherence to the contract forced Voetius to modify the rigid clericalism of some Calvinist thought. The ministry and church organs[1] were invaluable for the propagation of the faith, but they were not absolutely necessary for the existence of the church. In the *Politica Ecclesiastica* Voetius included a report bearing upon this problem which he had written in reference to an incident twenty-two years before, when a number of Englishmen living in a Dutch town had formed a new church upon the basis of a new covenant, in virtue of which the minister was selected by the covenanters. The Dutch ministers refused to recognise the combination of Englishmen as a church and urged that the church should be reconstituted in such a way that the whole formation of the church should be either in the call of the minister or in the erection of a consistory, without any recognition of the members who had first been gathered into the holy community. The minister was to be called and then the consistory instituted; or the consistory instituted which was then to call the minister. Thence was raised the question by what authority the church was formed. The English minister denied that the right to elect him should be withdrawn from those who had become a corpus through a contractual union. In this case, an issue fundamental to Voetius' theory had been propounded and controverted: whether a combination of the faithful bound together in a corpus was in essence the church of Christ, with the power to elect their minister. Voetius concluded that both the teaching and practice of the Reformation justified such a creation of a particular church.

[1] I, 42–46; cf. Cramer, *op. cit.* 51, 229–236.

So that under pressure of some necessity, a true visible church could be begun and continued without the offices of a minister or other church organs, and through the efforts of some faithful person, who after the constitution of the church by a formal covenant might act as a leader and even be confirmed as a minister. A church without a ministry was not dissolved; nor could it be prevented from coming into existence for a like cause. This was the essence of the church. Therefore, Voetius denied that a church thus begun without prior co-operation of the classis or synod or neighbouring churches was no true church and devoid of the power to call its minister, and would have to be reconstituted by the classis and synod, since the institutio Ecclesiae and confoederatio Ecclesiastica were null. In essence the church was a corpus formed by the covenant made between the members, and was not dependent upon any other factors or conditions.

The procedure[1] by which the church was established was indicated by Voetius. Normally the ground was prepared by the ministry, for at first there would be only hearers of the Word, but in due course these were assembled in a coetus where the solemn confederation and communion were begun and established by common decisions. The corpus ecclesiasticum thus instituted, the consistory was next erected and finally the minister was called. The fundamental act, whether supervised by ministers or not, was the meeting of all the faithful in one coetus and the formal declaration of their solemn purpose and their own agreement with that. Thence followed the subscription of the covenant. This was the method by which a new church would begin when an existing church was so corrupt that the faithful had to separate from it. The character and origin of the particular church were in essence the covenant between members without any other qualification, territorial, mystical or clerical.

The preservation of the union and the successful functioning of the corpus was not a matter of the covenant but of the organs and the power derived in part but not wholly from it.

The manner in which the consent of each member was given occupied much of Voetius' analysis of the visible church, for, if the contract was indeed the origin of the church, it was of the

[1] I, ch. I.

greatest importance to decide whether that consent was implicit or explicit, whether binding or whether dissoluble, and whether the consent of the father was sufficient to bind the son. Again, Voetius had to discuss whether all kinds and classes of men and women could give their consent, and particularly the terms to which church members did, in fact, agree.

Every member of the church had to make an explicit[1] and actual promise and covenant through which each was incorporated in the people of God and in the visible church; for an implicit and virtual consent did not suffice. Whether a church was newly made or new members admitted into the communion of an established church, the same free and express consent was necessary because[2] none could begin, enter or remain in the "confoederatio et unio Ecclesiastica" save those judged to be holy, which none knew unless each showed it by word and deed. Voetius expressly rejected[3] that tacit contract and implied consent by which political societies existed, although in one passage[4] he seemed to admit it in some degree. He certainly denied that anyone could be committed by a covenant of his predecessors and insisted[5] that all should be free to make their consent for themselves alone. The church was a voluntary society[6] in the sense that no one should be forced to become a member, but[7] it was not voluntary in the sense that any one could leave the church except by transference to another. None could revoke the contract since it had been made freely and expressly by each, and one of the terms was that each member should continue and progress in that communion of saints. By the stipulatio and confoederatio,[8] a member agreed to four things: that the doctrine of the church was the orthodox faith and way of salvation, that he would persevere in it until death, that he would live holy and worthily by that doctrine, and finally that he would submit to ecclesiastical discipline. This promise was made by each to God and the church. A wilful and contumacious breaker of this contract was to be excommunicated and thereby ceased to be a member of the church.[9]

The classical and synodal churches were formed according to the same principles, "ex vi voluntariae conventionis",[10] under a

---

[1] I, 29–30.   [2] I, 47.   [3] I, 48.   [4] III, 169.   [5] I, 64; III, 169.
[6] I, 31.   [7] I, 19.   [8] Ib.   [9] I, 32.   [10] I, 43.

certain system of government and correspondence for mutual edification and preservation, by free and equal particular churches,[1] just as all "socii, confoederati, collegae et membra quaecumque collegiorum" united.

Mutual consent was necessary for mutual union and communion. Such unions were only aggregates[2] of particular churches or of their representatives, and therefore Voetius did not understand how any church considered by itself differed essentially and intrinsically from itself in the collection of other churches exercising the same power as it did in its own body. The essence[3] of these combinations was not ecclesiastical right or statute, not political power, not neighbouring churches nor the impotence and bad administration of particular churches, not territorial connection, but the voluntary consent or pact of single churches which were incorporated, even as individuals formed particular churches, into one corpus. From that union no church was free to depart except in cases of necessity.

Voetius[4] denied the contention of the Independents that the particular church abandoned its own right and voluntarily accepted a subject status when it entered a confederation of churches. He argued, on the one hand, that the English parliament[5] did not exist by the sacrifice of the right of each constituent body, and, on the other hand, that as an individual[6] free from all made himself the servant of all in order to gain many advantages, so the churches strove for some mutual connection in order to free themselves from a human yoke.

The form of the visible church by which the societas of the faithful was organised and distinguished from other societies was determined by its purpose, its foundation, and its government. Its purpose[7] was the exercise of the communion of saints, and mutual excitation for continuance and growth in the Grace of God. Its foundation was the mutual consent of all entering the church without which the divine power could not be given to the church more than to any other body of men. In essence, therefore, the form of the church was a sacred union in the practice of the communion of saints through certain external acts instituted by

---

[1] III, 117–119.   [2] III, 144.   [3] III, 167.   [4] III, 153.
[5] III, 157.   [6] III, 168.   [7] I, 17.

God, a union formed by a covenant, but only completed by the institution of the organs by which the union was regulated in the external acts of divine worship. Voetius[1] emphasised this distinction between the church in essence and the church complete with organs to direct its union. Without ministry or presbytery, the church existed but without the organisation necessary for many acts of worship. The church was only a complete unity or an organised whole when the union was more than the covenanted members because the members had a system of government. The church in essence was the union by contract; the church as a corpus was not only the union or the relations between individual members, but also the relations by which the union and its organs were knit into a unity. In this latter sense, the church was the union in and with one minister or presbytery by which it was governed. If the ministry or both ministry and presbytery were lacking, the church was deprived of the means of Christian communion, but it was not without the essential power of constituting those organs. The covenant by which the societas fidelium was formed was not adequate in itself to create the whole church nor to form that unity arising out of the conjunction of directing organs and directed members; for the covenant was the product of individual acts binding individuals alone and incapable of producing or of exercising spiritual authority.

The visible church enjoyed the attributes of liberty, equality and necessity.[2] The church was not only freely entered without compulsion but also free to reject any who were judged to be unfit. The church as an ecclesiastical communitas had a liberty apart from that of its several members to conduct its own business, choose its own ministers and exercise its own discipline. There was equality not only of ministers, not only of the members of one church, but also between different churches, so that no person or body ruled others without their own previous consent and even then it was desirable to limit and define the exercise of such authority. The necessity of the church was a more delicate problem for Voetius to decide, since he wanted to avoid the Roman extreme as much as the Enthusiasts' distrust of the visible church. Membership[3] was not an absolute necessity for salvation,

[1] I, 14.   [2] I, ch. I.   [3] I, 64.

and therefore the ecclesiastical confoederatio was not absolutely necessary. But in so far as the visible church was a direct means of stimulating Christian life, it was to be deemed a necessary institution—so far as it was in accord with the Word and added to the spiritual life of its members. In the same way the unions of churches[1] were necessary by necessity of precept for the well-being or progress of the churches. Voetius appealed for confirmation of these unions to natural right[2] which taught men that the means necessary to fulfil a divine positive command were to be used by men. So that jus naturale indicated that business common to many churches was to be settled by all those churches, and that any defects or corruptions in one were to be remedied by the collateral churches as members of the same body. Hence, the unions of churches were sanctioned by natural right because only by that means was the divine purpose implemented.

The church thus established had its own peculiar polity or government,[3] accepted and observed by its members and declared in ecclesiastical constitutions, the norms and instruments by which that government was preserved and practised. Voetius defined Politia Ecclesiastica as the definite order according to which the external means of salvation in the ecclesiastical communion were directed. It was the government of the church and not of any other society, and it was proper to the church and not to any other society. It was concerned with res sacrae externae, as such, in order to perfect the communion of the faithful among themselves and with Christ, and to secure peace and security to the church by removing all causes of confusion. It was prescribed by Christ partly in the Word and partly in that discretion of divine permissive law which sanctioned all things prudently and conscientiously undertaken for the benefit of the church; but the means by which a particular constitution was formulated and enforced was the ministers and the church.

The polity and government were intrinsic and proper to the church alone, since both were ordained not for human and worldly but for divine purposes. The Scriptures were confirmed by natural right and necessity; for where there was a multitude there was order, which alone prevented confusion, the source of

[1] III, 153, 171.   [2] III, 130.   [3] I, 241–246.

division and destruction. A multitude was ordered and united only by a system of government. Consequently, church government as such ought in no way to be subordinated to the government of any human and worldly society. The necessity of a peculiar polity was such that it was always the condition of a well-ordered church, for where there was defective government there was no ordered multitude but a promiscuous meeting of men to hear the Word of God, indeed the matter but not the form of a corpus. Great confusion[1] would result if any could enter the church without a solemn promise to conform to its discipline and government, and if a member could leave the church at will. There could be no societas[2] without government, and since the societas fidelium[3] was governed spiritually and not according to the ways of men, that government could not be attempted by the state or any civil society.

The government of the church was partly democratic and partly aristocratic,[4] partly by the people and partly by the officers of the church; Voetius rejected equally oligarchy and popularity. He had no respect for the promiscuous multitude and denied that the people could govern directively or executively; but he was hostile to clerical hierarchies which refused to recognise the share of the people in the government of the church, and for that reason was critical[5] of Gillespie's *CXI Propositions*.

Finally, Voetius attributed to the visible and particular church a peculiar and intrinsic power, distinct from political and civil power, and inherent in it as a complete whole in which members and church organs constituted a system of relations distinct from the relations of each part in itself. The independent origin and the independent nature of ecclesiastical power enabled the visible church to be autonomous, with its own system of government, with the power to determine all activities necessary for the spiritual life in its external communion, and existing solely in virtue of a covenant between its members. The most important part of Voetius' theory was the careful explanation of how all the power needed by the visible church in its government and in its origin was either in or through the church, and was not derived from any external human source.

[1] I, 48.   [2] III, 804.   [3] III, 784.   [4] I, 244.   [5] I, 246.

Ecclesiastical power[1] was the holy ministerial right, granted by Christ as Head of the church and attributed to certain persons or bodies of persons in a prescribed way, to govern externally the church itself and its activities for mutual edification and salvation. But such a definition was too formal and scholastic to explain the complex conception of different powers and different sources of those powers which Voetius' subtle mind so carefully distinguished. In part this was due to the fact that he had defined that power as totum et aggregatum, and in a general sense, although it served to emphasise that the ecclesiastical power with which he was concerned was that of the instituted church as such. It belonged to the external, visible and instituted church in its own collective being, in order to govern its own members and its own activities. It was derived from Christ, the spiritual king of the church, but was only in this or that collection of the faithful and in each single ecclesiastical corpus in consequence of the particular consent and covenant of those faithful. That consent and covenant were the foundation of each visible church and created its form, and therefore the corollary of its form—power to determine its own destiny.

The different powers in the church he defined either according to the subject-matter or according to the body entitled to use them. By the first distinction, he recognised only two powers— that dealing with discipline and that dealing with "dogma", in which last were included preaching, the celebration of the sacraments and other ecclesiastical acts, together with everything necessary for their operation, i.e. the establishment of churches, the determination of times and places of meetings and worship, and the election of officers. He also gave a more detailed method of classification: (1) He separated potestas dogmatica into (a) the power of preaching doctrine out of the Scriptures and of directing the consciences of all and singular, with the power of distributing the sacraments, and (b) the power of deciding doctrinal doubts and controversies. (2) He distinguished a potestas gubernans, the power to make ecclesiastical laws and constitutions, and to govern the church according to them. (3) He defined potestas judicans seu disciplinaris as the power of censuring or excommunicating.

[1] I, 117–122.

The kinds of ecclesiastical power which Voetius classified according to their "subject" or owner were defined with a similar regard for detail. First, there was a power common to all the members derived from a study of the Scriptures by which all were authorised to admonish and reprove each other. Secondly, there was a power peculiar to the different parts of the church.

Some thinkers, Voetius added, held that the power of authoritative direction belonged to the whole body composed of rulers and members quod ad inexistentiam seu inhaesionem but only to the rulers of the church in respect of its execution. This, again, was stated in two other ways: that this power was virtually in the church as such but formally in its rulers, and that it was in the corpus of the church as *principio quod* but in the rulers as *principio quo*.

The power common to the populus ecclesiasticus and apart from the ministry and presbytery was of a negative character. In doctrine, all were to teach according to the measure of the spirit, and to determine controversies by their judgment of discretion and liberty, and by their consent and approval after hearing the decisions of their ministers and elders. In government, they shared in the election of church-officers, voting by voice or ballot or by silence; in the admission of members; in the election of particular delegates, and in common problems of the church, because these were communicated to the people, their doubts referred to synods, and their consent, explicit or tacit, obtained. In discipline the people might act collectively in a matter of public scandal, and had the power to withdraw from any corruption in the church, even from a corrupt synod. Voetius recognised cases in which the people might withdraw their support from a minister.

The power of the ministers and presbytery was the active executive power of government. In doctrine, the ministers had a special authority as ministers of Christ, as alone able to celebrate the sacraments, and as the judges of controversies "judicio antecedente, directivo et praescribente". In government, it was for them to initiate, direct and act authoritatively in their own churches and in synods. In jurisdiction, theirs was the duty to prevent scandal and offence, and in the event of persistent corruption in the church to lead their followers out of it and to form a new church.

So that Voetius[1] denied that all ecclesiastical power was in the ministry or consistory; but he equally denied that it was in the people distinct from, and by them delegated to, church organs. Election of officers did not mean a transfer of power, as if these organs did not have their own proper power, *in se* and *per se*, ex vi ministerii, according to divine law. Nor was all power equally competent to the consistory and the people singly or collectively. But ecclesiastical power, generally and collectively, was in the whole corpus of the church composed by consistory and people, as the proper owner, although not in either of those parts in the same way or degree. It was in both equally as "in subjecto inhaerentiae"; in the consistory or ministry in certain matters, and in its executive operation as "in subjecto et principio quo"; and in some things held differently by the people and by the organs, the former having a power of following and approving and the latter a power of guiding and directing.

The peculiar power of the ministry and presbytery was not in the people primo et immediate, nor was the people the intrinsic means by which it was communicated; for election was no more than the attachment of an office to some particular person and did not create the power, which was competent to the minister as minister ex vi muneris. In like manner, the common power of liberty was proper to the members as such and to the body of the people as such on account of the very nature of membership and holy society, and not from the ministry.

Therefore, ecclesiastical power was neither to be abandoned nor usurped, and the organic and directive power of the ministry was not to be divided but was as such proper to all ministers. The preaching power was not to be separated from the governing powers;[2] for both flowed from Christ, who gave the office of the ministry to His Church. Therefore, he who had the power of preaching was alone entitled to the power of government and discipline. Nevertheless, that executive and directive power was not of an indelible character in the sense that its "subject" surrendered it only at death, for the minister might be suspended

---

[1] I, 220–228. [2] I, 141.

if the people who had attached this power to his person revoked that act. In another reference, Voetius[1] declared that the people who had elected elders and deacons did not commit to them a power which the people could not control; for though he rejected the idea of Suarez and Bellarmine in regard to regal power that it might be resumed and usurped by the people, yet he recognised that the people might determine afresh the application of that power by designating other persons who would use it better.

Ecclesiastical power[2] was primarily and originally in the particular churches, and the combinations of churches arose from the desire of those churches to strengthen their own power in cases where each church had not sufficient power. The power of classes and synods was determined by the needs of their members, and was not wholly distinct from the power of each church nor superseded that power. Moreover, their power existed by the grant and mandate of each church in the union; the mandate being in part general and implicit, in part particular and explicit. So that the power of any classis or synod was the power of delegates, not original but derived from its constituent members, not absolute but limited by its purpose, not inherent but only a peculiar form of exercise of that power, not supreme but inferior to all the churches met together, and not jus rectorium but jus aequatorium for mutual help between equals. In those unions there could be no subjection, obedience or imperium, but only mutual and equal dependence for mutual help. Their power was originally in the churches, but executively in the classes and synods; so that the churches did not owe their power to classes and synods, nor were bound save by social, fraternal, collateral, mutual and spontaneous dependence ex vi spontaneae confoederationis ac combinationis. The different unions and powers did not conflict nor were co-ordinate. While they were not the same, they differed only formaliter and not realiter.

Voetius had denied that classes and synods were external to the churches and that the government of classes and synods was external to the government of the churches; in like manner he denied that the churches were subject to an alien power outside heir own body. Indeed, there was in synods or classes no power

[1] I, 120.   [2] III, 117–231.

separate from the power of churches, which constituted those
organs by their own delegates, and through them collected and
exercised their powers in common. So, that whole power was
and continued to remain in the churches as the source, and was
exercised by them as causa principalis, but was in the classes and
synods by delegation. The directive power was exercised by the
classes or synods, but the churches were justified in giving strict
instructions to their delegates and in expecting reference to
themselves of major grievances for discussion in their own
presbytery. Such mandates were not to be used to prevent a
decision by a majority vote but only to determine how their own
delegates should vote.

Delegates to the classis and synod did not attend in virtue of
their own office nor of an immediate divine law, but by positive
law in virtue of their constitution and delegation by their own
churches. Even pastors had not synodale jus except by delegation; for though the only pastor of a church appeared at the classis
regularly by a virtual or general mandate, according to ecclesiastical constitutions, yet he attended a provincial or national
synod only if given a mandate formally and explicitly by an open
and particular election.

That power of government was a power of commanding
because it was the way by which God commanded men.[1] Voetius
denied that there was no government unless it was supreme and
coercive, for there were many forms of government which
exercised a real and true power, neither imaginary nor a delusion,
although without the sword and the power of life and death.
Again, he denied that all power was a power of legislation, for
pastors published the laws of God, and rulers did not have any
more authority to compel men to obey their laws in matters
indifferent than the pastors themselves: i.e. the divine command
acknowledged by the conscience to obey the authorities instituted
or permitted by God. He denied that any human authority
bound the conscience by its own virtue, but only by the divine
command. Since pastors spoke to men the laws of God and
judged men by divine right, they had a real power of jurisdiction.

Voetius was quite certain that there was a power inherent in

[1] III, 787–799.

the church and in the officers designated by it, proper to it alone and which was not subordinate to any human power. But this power was of three distinct kinds and had three separate sources. First, there was the power of the societas, of the church in essence, to call into being the organs of the church, and to take such measures as were necessary for its existence and continuance. This was the ultimate power in the church but only in the sense that it provided the means by which the church as a whole might be established. The power of the societas arose from the covenant between its members, and therefore extended no further than those actions which a body of individuals bound by mutual rights and duties could determine. For this reason, the second kind of power in the church, the power of the pastorate and presbytery, was not derived from the societas. It was a spiritual power which could not be created by any group of individuals but was a power given by Christ to the body formed by the church and its organs, a power exercised by, though not proper to, the organs of the church alone. The contract did not create this power which was not of the individual contractors; nor did it belong to any part of the church as inherent in it. The power by which the church was governed was not the same as the power by which the church was begun. The third kind of power was that by which unions of churches were governed and was derived from the churches by the delegation of their power to their representatives.

The societas provided the basis for but did not produce the power in the church as a corpus. This distinction was one of the most important points in Voetius' whole theory and explains both the emphasis on the covenant and on the power inherent in the church. Voetius[1] distinguished on the one hand the union and the power of the united corpus in kind, and, on the other hand, the particular application to this and that and some other church. In the first sense, both were of positive divine law; in the second sense both were of divine permissive law, for a human act intervened by which the union was established in a definite and particular case. Marriage, he instanced, was *in genere* directly of positive divine law, but the specific *applicatio* to that man and that woman, not to some other man and some other woman, was

[1] III, 225.

of divine permissive law because the particular consent and contract of those two people alone made that particular marriage.

In the same way, political unions, and the magistrates' office
and power, were instituted by God, but any particular union or
office was the result of consent and contract, in virtue of which
either was of these and not of those men. Without the consent and
contract of the faithful at Utrecht, no visible church of Utrecht
existed; without the designation of certain men to be ministers or
elders by the election of the church, no organs and no power
existed.

The original foundation[1] of classical and synodal unions was
a divine right and mandate, if those unions were considered
abstractly *in genere* and *in se*; but the voluntary consent or covenant
of the churches which were incorporated, if considered concretely
in the individual case and as applied to such and such churches.
The same distinction was true in the case of every contract, pact
and covenant: such as marriage, ministry, church, consistory and
even political power. The ministry was of divine right but that
man was not a minister, nor had that church a minister, without
voluntary election and ecclesiastical organisation. The observa-
tion of fasts was of divine law, but the day to be observed by a
certain church was of human determination. The last example
was, again, the marriage of two actual persons which was not
immediately, but mediately, of divine law, since the application
of the conjugal order and status to two particular persons was
through human consent.

The divine will or reason was only to be realised by human
intervention, which meant to Voetius voluntary consent. The
obligations of the parts and members, in virtue of which the
totum corpus existed and in consequence of which the power of
the corpus determined the relations of its constituents, were
divine. But those obligations were not effective in human relations
and associations until publicly acknowledged to each other by
those concerned as the dictates of their consciences. Men obeyed
the common power because they definitely admitted that in doing
this they participated in the divine purpose revealed to each of
them, and had accepted obligations not of their own making.

[1] III, 167.

It has been pointed out that the contractarian theory in general found it difficult to explain why persons born into society were bound to act as if they had, in fact, consented, and why the minority was held to act according to the decisions of the majority, when all acted only because they had consented. In Voetius' theory, the first difficulty was avoided by his denial that men were, in fact, born into the society of the church, since each had to give a solemn promise to abide by the terms of the covenant. Only in the unions of churches[1] was a tacit consent to the union held to be sufficient to bind the member churches to a government and system of laws, to which the changing personnel of the member churches had not explicitly consented. Indeed, in dealing with these unions, Voetius had passed from the small local society, in which individual consent was practicable, to associations comparable to the state itself, in which explicit consent was not a practical matter. He agreed that a particular consistory was unable to bind subsequent consistories without their free consent, but he could find no means for renewing the contract between churches analogous to the renewal of the contract in individual churches, where the entry of a new member did not require the renewal of the contract by all existing members together with the new member. The individual consent of the would-be member given before all the other members was held to be sufficient. Voetius fell back upon the idea of an implicit contract and tacit consent by daily act and use in order to explain how unions of churches continued.

The second difficulty was obviously of great importance to Voetius. He admitted[2] that there was no unio or communitas without a common power, for where there was ordo there was potestas—just as he had argued in reference to polity that a potestas necessarily demanded ordo. Again, he admitted that where there was potestas, there was necessarily definitive power; otherwise there could be no power, no order and no union. To the single churches acting separately there belonged a definitive power, and therefore to the same, acting conjointly and at the same time, there remained to each its own power. Since he had argued that the power of church unions only differed from the

[1] III, 169.   [2] III, 179.

power of each church formaliter and not realiter, executively and not originally, this could only mean that the unions of churches themselves had a definitive power. In the churches and in the unions of churches, there was a power to act for the whole despite a dissentient minority and to hold all members to obey decisions taken in the name of the whole. This power[1] was in practice the power of the majority which Voetius obviously assumed was an obligation upon all members.

He reverted to the principle of contract to explain why members of the church were committed to this obligation. First,[2] he stated that no church was free to leave a union of churches any more than a member might leave a church. Since the member had voluntarily joined himself to a particular church, he could not by his own will and judgment break that union, but was held to stand by the judgment and power of that body of which he had desired to be a member. Indeed, he had covenanted to submit to the common direction and discipline. Secondly,[3] in the union arising from the nature of the instituted confoederatio and societas, the acts and powers of single members were not opposed and subordinated, but were united and co-ordinated, although the single parts themselves were subordinated to the totum compositum seu collectivum arising out of the combination of all the parts. The good of the whole was to be set before the good of any particular part. Finally,[4] the use and acts of power in relation to other persons were only of divine right when all those persons had formed the whole, in which that power existed, by a contract. First, they had constituted the medium of that power, and, secondly, bound themselves to accept its exercise through that medium.

That the contract served only as the means by which divine obligations were accepted is confirmed by the limitations which Voetius put upon it. Members of the church were to obey the judgment and power of the church only so long as they were consonant with revelation, i.e. the Scriptures. In consequence, the contract was not merely human, and only in so far as it was approved by divine right were members of the church bound to

---

[1] I, 192; III, 124, 188. [2] III, 168. Cf. 159.
[3] III, 153. [4] III, 131.

the power of the whole. By this qualification to the contract, Voetius[1] was able to deny the legitimacy of papal power and polity, even though based upon the contract of the members of the church. On the other hand, he admitted[2] that the power of the classes in relation to the election of ministers and the excommunication of members of a particular church were part of a covenant which other churches in other countries might relax if they so desired.

The foundation of the church was the work of divine creation and human consent in three distinct stages.[3] First, the fundamentum remotum et commune was institutio divina, which willed such forms of churches to be the normal means of salvation. Secondly, fundamentum propinquum was the applicatio of this institution to a particular community. Finally, fundamentum proprium et proximum was the mutual consent of all who entered the church.

The contract was the means by which the divine order was realised among men, and the divine power was transmitted to the whole body of the church.

It was of the greatest importance that a Calvinist theologian of the reputation of Voetius should have emphasised so strongly the covenant as the essential characteristic of the visible church, and, consequently, the share of the people in its government and the primary and indestructible nature of the particular church. Some of the Scottish theologians regretted what they regarded as these concessions to Independency. Divine right was not to Voetius a sufficient basis for the Presbyterians' claims; he insisted that divine right had to be accepted by voluntary consent before it could be the basis of the visible church. The question arises whether Voetius had been influenced by Independent theories, and whether they had been the major influence in the development of his own theory.

No final answer can be given to the second part of the question because two other schools of thought may have had an even greater influence. First, the Spanish Jesuits had adapted the theory of the contract to political society in a way curiously

[1] I, 232.   [2] III, 149, 165.   [3] I, 15.

paralleled in the *Politica Ecclesiastica*. Secondly, Cartwright's influence on the development of English Puritanism had stressed at first the importance of the particular church and the election of ministers by the congregation.[1] Moreover, subscription[2] by members of the church and even the use of covenants[3] were not unknown among the puritans of the state church. But it is no more than a pleasant speculation to suggest that Voetius' knowledge of scholastic theories was adapted to the specific problem of the church in consequence of his study of the conditions of and controversies in the church of England.

It is true that he was opposed to the independency of churches current among many English extremists and was at pains to refute them in the *Politica Ecclesiastica*, but there is little doubt that he was indirectly influenced by them. Two English exiles in the Netherlands enjoyed a great reputation with certain types of Dutch Calvinists, and their works were not only referred to by Voetius but were also distinguished by principles closely akin to those of the *Politica Ecclesiastica*. Both had written in that period of controversy when Voetius was most impressionable. Both were steeped in that scholastic learning and method which Voetius applied with such success. These two exiles—William Ames and Robert Parker—were tainted, at least according to contemporaries, with leanings toward some of the errors of Independency. Moreover, so strong were these suspicions in the case of Ames that Paget, the minister of the English church at Amsterdam, himself[4] admitted that Ames was not suitable for office in the church because he denied the authority of synods and classes.

In *The Marrow of Sacred Divinity*, Ames defined the church as "a company of men that are called". "It is called a company: because it doth consist properly in a multitude joyned in fellowship together, or a community of many, not in some certain one that is called......It is called a body fitly joyned and compacted together of divers members."[5] The form of the church, he said, was faith—a definition explicitly denied by Voetius. The visible

[1] Scott Pearson, *Thomas Cartwright* (Cambridge, 1925), 96, 270, 362.
[2] *Ib.* 337.
[3] Burrage, *Early English Dissenters* (Cambridge, 1912), I, 138, 289.
[4] Hanbury, *Historical Memorials Relating to the Independents*, I, 533.
[5] Bk I, chs. 31, 32.

church was the congregation—again denied by Voetius—"for those congregations were as it were similary parts of the catholick church, and so doe partake both of the name and nature of it". The particular churches, Voetius agreed, were "similares partes". The particular church "in respect of the catholic Church which hath the respect of an whole, [it] is a member compounded of divers severall members gathered together, and so in respect of those members it is also an whole". Such a particular church is "a society of believers joyned together by a speciall band among themselves, for the constant exercise of the communion of Saints among themselves". Again, "believers doe not make a particular Church, although peradventure many may meete and live together in the same place, unless they be joyned together by a speciall bond among themselves....... This bond is a covenant, either expresse or implicite, whereby believers doe particularly bind themselves, to performe all those duties, both toward God and one toward another, which pertaine to the respect and edification of the Church." This covenant only made a church in respect of the communion of saints and a covenant neglecting that communion was no church. "Neither yet doth some suddaine joyning together, and exercise of holy communion suffice to make a Church: unlesse there be also that constancy, at least in intention, which brings the state of a body, and members in a certaine spirituall politie....... The gathering together into an instituted Church is so performed by God, that his command and mans duty and labour doe come betweene."

The *De Politeia Ecclesiastica* was a remarkable defence of Presbyterian ideals against the great Anglican controversialists. It suffered, indeed, from its detailed treatment and from its excessive learning, but it was remarkable for its systematic discussion of an involved argument. Parker was concerned not with the relation of church and state, but with church government. The principles which he emphasised were in large measure shared by Voetius, but in one point Parker was by no means so emphatic.[1] He rejected Robinson's theory of the covenant as the foundation of the church and denied that the church of England was no church because it was not founded on a contract between its

[1] Parker, *op. cit.* Bk III, ch. 16.

members. Nevertheless, he insisted that the church was a voluntary union arising from the preaching of the Word and not from any territorial connection. Its members were accepted only if they were truly repentant, of good life, and provided that they made a solemn pact with God and with the church, to follow the holy communion of the church, to continue in its faith, and to be subject to its discipline. The individual profession of faith and personal *pactio foederis* were the conditions of entry into the church.[1] The communion of the church was the consequence of union, for it could only be among those who were united as if by some kind of bond. In virtue of that tie there was an associated unity in communion. The church was not the congregation, but a *societas fidelium* based upon participation by all its members in that communion. The diocesan or national church was not a church in this sense, nor were particular churches merely parts of either. The divine parish was one congregation constituting in itself an *integrum corpus* subordinate to no other church. The members of churches organised on a wider basis were not united by that visible communion which was the purpose of union in churches; for the members of a diocesan church could not meet together to enjoy personally the external acts of visible communion common to church members.

The essential characteristic of the church was its nature as an *integrum corpus*, i.e. a union which was itself a whole because its members could participate in all the acts of visible communion. Upon this basis,[2] associations of churches were established, but not in any way apart from or independent of these particular churches, which could only be represented by those whom the church elected.[3]

More important, however, was Parker's treatment of the power of the church,[4] which occupied by far the greater part of the Third Book. Ecclesiastical power belonged to the whole church, not to the ministers, nor to bishops, nor to people alone, but to the faithful in conjunction with the ministers. That power was from Christ to each particular church, and it was for the whole church to determine the "applicatio" of that power to this or

---

[1] Parker, *op. cit.* Bk III, ch. 17.   [2] *Ib.* ch. 22 *seq.*
[3] *Ib.* 314, 367–370.   [4] *Ib.* chs. 1–15.

that specific person. Parker quoted[1] from Gerson a passage which distinguished between the divine source of ecclesiastical power and its "applicatio" by the church. But Parker[2] argued that although power was formally in the whole church, it was executively in the ministry alone, for the ministers alone exercised it. Thus, he insisted that the government of the church was partly aristocratic; and partly democratic.

It is true that Parker may not have done more than to develop current arguments by adapting them to Calvinist ideals against the episcopal, but the form into which he arranged them, and the emphasis which he laid upon certain fundamental principles upon which the particular church was to be established, were almost certainly of great influence upon Voetius' own theory of the church. Voetius, however, stressed much more than Parker the fact that the church was created by a covenant of its members.

The question of Independent influence upon Voetius may be pushed back to Henry Jacob, for Ames, Parker and Jacob were Independent Puritans who "sojourned for a time in Leiden; and all three boarded together...".[3] Moreover,[4] in a contemporary complaint, Jacob and Parker were associated in respect of their Independency. Lastly, Independency in New England was, according to Cotton, inspired by Parker and Ames, the friends of Jacob.[5]

In all of Jacob's writings the emphasis upon the covenant as the form of the visible church whereby the body of covenanters had power to direct its common interests was very evident.[6] But as early as 1605, before he left England, he had formulated that principle in its most significant form. "A true Visible or Ministerial Church of Christ is a particular Congregation being a spirituall perfect Corporation of Believers, & having power in it selfe immediately from Christ to administer all Religious meanes of faith to the members thereof." To the question "How is a Visible Church constituted and gathered?" he answered: "By a

---

[1] Parker, *op. cit.* Bk III, ch. 33.
[2] Cf. *ib.* 29, 31, 42, where he also borrowed from "schola Parisiensis in Politeia sua nuper edita, anno 1611" that analogy of the eye and the body which was used by Grotius; see Gierke, *Natural Law and the Theory of Society* (transl. E. Barker), I, 55.
[3] Burrage, *op. cit.* I, 292.
[4] *Ib.* I, 296.
[5] *Ib.* I, 361.
[6] *Ib.* I, 286; II, 157.

free mutual consent of Believers joyning and covenanting to live as members of a holy Society togeather in all religious and vertuous duties as Christ and his Apostles did institute & practise in the Gospell. By such a free mutuall consent also all Civill perfect Corporations did first beginne."

§ IV

Voetius' theory of the church was the basis of what he conceived to be the true relation of church and state; but although neither Triglandius nor Apollonius (save in a superficial and unoriginal way) attempted to ground his own arguments upon the same logical and consistent basis, yet that argument was essentially the same. The position which Voetius fought to make unassailable was the underlying assumption of the other two controversialists —that the church had a form of government and a power binding its parts to the common good which was derived from Christ and not from any political or civil source. But neither felt the logical necessity to explain how this divinely instituted system was adopted by the individuals who composed the visible church.

It is true that Apollonius seems to have some idea of the importance of a church-covenant. It was one thing,[1] he said, to meet together and join oneself to some constituted political society in which the common civil good was pursued, and quite another thing to meet for the institution by a solemn covenant of those offices which were necessary for the edification of the visible church and the communion of saints. The same faithful men constituted a state or city by a contract for the common civil good, and the church by contract for holy communion with God; the one being a ratio virtutis politico-moralis, the other a ratio virtutis spiritualis. Therefore, the government of the church, though external, was spiritual, for its spiritual polity and its external administration were concerned with the holy and mutual communion of the faithful with God and among themselves. But Apollonius was obviously influenced in this by Ames, from whose *Marrow of Sacred Divinity* he made a full quotation. It is true again that he emphasised the importance of consent in ecclesiastical relations, comparing, for instance, the call to the ministry to the

---

[1] *Jus Maj.* I, 244; II, 358–359, 370, 377.

way in which the socii[1] admit into their collegium those whom the statuta fundatoris designate; or to marriage in which the consent of the parties was necessary. But the first comparison was borrowed, and the second was not original. It is very dubious whether he appreciated the real theory of the contract, and very probable that, like Triglandius, he fell back upon the straightforward doctrine of jus divinum by which the church as a multitudo in unum corpus collecta[2] was endowed with the power of Christ. Unlike Voetius, neither was impelled to distinguish sharply between the invisible and visible church.

Nevertheless, despite this difference in regard to the contractual origin of the church, all three were united in treating the relation of church and state as a civil relation common to all societies, which protected but could not diminish the rights of an autonomous church.

Church and state were distinct and not to be confounded. The two communities existed for different purposes, used different powers and had different agents. The church was the supernatural state governed by spiritual laws and the delegates of Christ. So that the mingling of the two, whereby the church was secularised and the state was given a spiritual character, was unnatural, contrary to the divine dispensation, and destructive of the true nature of both. The state was not to be raised above its own character. The first postulate common to all was that a line of demarcation was both evident and demonstrable.

In this postulate there was admittedly no originality, for almost all Christian churches distinguished between the two kingdoms, and all real Calvinists acknowledged that the visible church was a separate organisation. But these three writers went beyond demarcation to self-sufficiency of both the church and the state. The state, in fact, often did not include the true Christian church nor even any Christian church, and yet it was not for that reason imperfect in its organisation nor deprived of any legitimate power. The power of the magistrate according to Voetius[3] was derived directly from God and not from the church. Its "applicatio" to a particular person did not depend upon the church, the pastors or ecclesiastical law, but was determined by permissive-divine

[1] *Jus Maj.* I, 340.   [2] *Ib.* I, 204.   [3] *Polit. Eccl.* I, 133.

law and by human positive law, whether by succession, election, contract or jus belli. According to the principles of the New Testament[1] all forms of the state and all political laws were merely human. The state[2] was truly and legitimately such although it contained no church. Likewise, the church did not need the presence of the ruler to be the church, nor any political power. The two powers were separate and neither was to invade the other. The church[3] was in essence apart from any connection with the state.

Apollonius[4] stated that God had instituted each perfect in its own kind, so that the one did not need the other for the fulfilment of its own peculiar purpose. The civil state was perfectly instituted and governed without ecclesiastical co-operation, even as heathen states were equally instituted by God with a sufficiency of power for their perfect civil government. The state was perfect, absolute and complete in its own sphere and was, like the church, the supernatural state, self-sufficient.

Triglandius[5] was equally ready to recognise that each in essence was able to act in its own interest and according to its own needs without being dependent upon the other, although he was much more convinced than either Voetius or Apollonius that there was a moral connection between church and state which true Christians should strive to foster. However, such a connection was not regarded as absolutely necessary for the effective constitution and organisation of either. It was not an integral part of the divine scheme, the absence or corruption of which disrupted the operation of God's Will in either of·His human instruments.

Church and state were each capable of independent life, government and function, in no way necessary to each other, and so far as essential characteristics were considered wholly self-sufficing. Indeed, it was argued more forcibly that neither was intended nor was capable of undertaking what was the proper task of the other. So that to all three there was no indissoluble nor essential bond between church and state, no divine decree by which each was ordered in a Christian commonwealth, and no relation between the people organised as a state and as a church.

[1] *Polit. Eccl.* I, 147. [2] *Ib.* I, 136. [3] *Ib.* I, 245.
[4] *Jus Maj.* I, 51. [5] *De Civili*, ch. 4.

Such a principle of self-sufficiency required a considerable amount of explanation, for the actual relation of church and state was more complicated than was readily admitted. The greater part of Apollonius' and Triglandius' books was directed to the consideration of the different factors which determined what this sufficiency meant, since both[1] rejected and attacked the Roman theory of theocratic absolutism, denying that theirs was a theocratic ideal and only claiming to rectify the extremist doctrines of the Reformation without abandoning the Reformers' insistence upon the sovereignty of the state. Self-sufficiency, therefore, involved very careful and sometimes very fine distinctions.

Separation and self-sufficiency did not mean that there were no relations between political and ecclesiastical organisations, for the church was not a state in itself, nor ought to mingle political duties with the spiritual function. The church was always in the state but the state was never in the church. Accordingly, the church could not escape its political environment nor evade political obligations which its inclusion in the state entailed. The members of the church were also members of the state, and on that account committed to political duties and shared in political rights. The ministers of the church were citizens and subject to political laws. The church and its members were not related to the state as two worldly powers by a concordat or by an alliance, but were subordinate and bound to the state in all worldly and temporal matters. The self-sufficiency of the church did not mean that the church was independent in its political and civil activities, for that would deny the self-sufficiency of the state. This was as true of a heathen as of a Christian government, for the hostility of a ruler to the church as such did not dissolve its political obligations or those of its members.

Thus, the church was related to the state by its place in the political structure and by its civil ties; while its members could never cease to be citizens and could not form a new political society out of the church. In so far as membership of the church was not adequate to meet merely human and social needs, the church was not the rival nor independent of the state.

The church was subject to the state, Voetius held, so far as the

---

[1] *Jus Maj.* 1, 8–10; *De Civili*, ch. 2. Cf. *Polit. Eccl.* 1, 162.

external man was concerned,[1] i.e. bona et corpora, and in all matters relating to the welfare of the political community. Moreover, he included[2] all external actions and matters which were necessary for the achievement of spiritual ends, for the end did not justify the claim to control every temporal and human matter of service to that end. The church employed[3] purely civil and bodily means which were common to all men as such and without spiritual significance in themselves; in these the church was properly subject to political regulation. The church, again,[4] exercised a power which was characteristic of all societies and was secular in nature. This power included ownership of property and the use of its revenues, and various kinds of ecclesiastical liberties and immunities. This power, being secular, was directly derived from the state. The minister and members of a persecuted church[5] still owed allegiance to the state in those matters of civil and animal life without which it was impossible to live or to live in society. In short, the church was subject in so far as it was a civil society and used civil and political means. But it also enjoyed those civil and political rights which all citizens and societies in the state shared, and could, like them, appeal[6] to those rights against some unjust decision or intolerable act of oppression by the ruler.

Apollonius recognised that there was nothing so ecclesiastical that it was not in some way regulated by the secular state, and concurred[7] with Voetius that everything connected with spiritual matters which was of social intercourse and animal existence was exercised according to political regulations and political authority. But he was particularly interested in the problem of the responsibility of the minister to the ruler, and whether ministers were liable to civil punishments. He rejected[8] the Roman view that any class of ecclesiastics was exempt from the civil courts and power but was to be judged only in ecclesiastical courts. All ministers,[9] like all other citizens who violated the law of the land, might be punished, although the exercise of their pastoral office was thereby suspended. In order to prevent any abuse of this

---

[1] *Polit. Eccl.* I, 131. [2] *Ib.* I, 153. [3] *Ib.* I, 40.
[4] *Ib.* I, 115. [5] *Ib.* I, 153. [6] *Ib.* I, 130, 195.
[7] *Jus Maj.* I, 364; II, 355–356. [8] *Ib.* I, 83.
[9] *Ib.* I, 341, 387.

civil punishment for a civil act, Apollonius urged[1] that the ruler should only be allowed to act as against other subjects—by the lawful process of law—and be limited to the punishment of ministers only for such vices as were corrected by human laws and civil penalties.

Triglandius[2] added nothing original to this view but merely argued that ministers were subject to political authority only in their capacities as men and citizens.

The self-sufficiency of the church was related to its unique spiritual sphere in which it was the authoritative organ of God for the building of the Kingdom of Christ on earth. The visible church was autonomous in that sphere, regulated only by the revealed law of Christ and in no way subject to the secular power of the state. Ecclesiastical government and power was communicated by Christ to His Church, and the ruler and the state had no right by divine law to prevent the church from determining its own destiny in accordance with the divine will, by the means He had provided and through that spiritual power which He alone possessed, to incline the hearts of men to His Will. The church had a function which no other body of men could undertake, which was to be realised by no system of human laws, accompanied, though they were, by a battery of corporal penalties, and from which the state was barred. The church, therefore, ruled itself, appointed its own officers, formulated its own canons, summoned and regulated its own councils, and exercised its own discipline over all who belonged to it, without the participation of the state or its representatives. It alone was able to decide doctrinal disputes and to cause its members to subscribe to its decisions, depriving erring ministers of their office and inflicting suspension or excommunication. It possessed in itself power to reform itself and to reconstitute a corrupt member. Consequently, it had power to meet,[3] to determine the order of its services, the conditions under which new members would be admitted, to regulate the lives and conduct of its members, and to choose its own representatives in the higher ranges of church councils, without dependence upon the state. The function of the church went far beyond the pastoral mission to preach, to celebrate

[1] *Jus Maj.* I, 381.   [2] *De Civili*, 281, 387.   [3] *Jus Maj.* I, 216, 221.

the sacraments, and to withhold the sacraments from those of ill-conducted life. In this, the state had no voice and no right to act either by its own authority or contrary to the decisions of the majority in the true and properly constituted church. The ruler had no divinely ordained office in the church and was not the source from which ecclesiastical power was derived.

Fundamentally, the substance of the argument in favour of the autonomous church was the same. The church as such was the Kingdom of the Mediator. The power of the church as such was a spiritual power, derived from Christ and manifested[1] among men in the particular visible church as a whole in which spiritual power was resident and contained, and the exercise of which was by the applicatio or instrumentalis derivatio of the whole church to certain men called by God and elected by the church. The power was of Christ; the designation of its human possessors was of the church. Christ used the church as the normal means by which men were governed in spiritual matters and as the external and visible embodiment of His Power. To the church was committed all authority necessary to its spiritual edification and to choose freely those who were to exercise that authority on behalf of the church, the instrument and medium for the communication of the ministerial office and power to certain chosen men. Such a power[2] did not spring from the institution of the ministers, although conferred by the church, and was subject to the empire of Christ alone. This ecclesiastical power was distinguished by its inward and spiritual effect upon the soul, and was, therefore, the indissoluble power of the ministry, indissoluble because the power of preaching and of celebrating the sacrament was but a specialised part of that one power given by Christ. The opus ministerii and power to govern the church were one, springing from the one source, conferred by the same means, and attributed equally to all ministers. The unique character of ecclesiastical power and its manifestation in and through the church alone was the consequence of its spiritual and divine institution by Christ

---

[1] For Voetius, *supra* § III; *Jus Maj.* I, 93–95; II, 62; I, 2, 19–21, 24–26, 32, 35, 37–38, 87, 113–118, 127–134, 139, *et passim*.

[2] *De Civili*, 62, 66–76, 84, 112, 179, 201, 207, 265, 281–285, 297–298, 324, 350, 353, *et passim*.

himself; for[1] it was accepted that the external government of the visible church pertained to the heavenly and spiritual government of Christ. Therefore, all right of ecclesiastical power was granted and committed by Christ to the church, for that power was the medium and organum[2] to realise the supernatural good. To the church was granted, and in the church was operative, all power[3] necessary for the essence and integrity of spiritual government.

Moreover, this power was in the church as a spiritual[4] and not as a political flock, as the company of believers and as those who accepted the church as part of their faith. It was not the people nor the state nor a community created and ruled by force. It was not circumscribed by territorial boundaries nor by the limits of human jurisdiction. Membership of the church was the outcome of spiritual gifts, not worldly dignities, and required external profession of faith and conformity of conduct. It was held together as a visible communion recognising a common authority by the consciences of all its members. Therefore, the church was a voluntary communion of those willing to accept it and to live by it. The power of the church was[5] only over its members, who were bound to obey because it was the divine means. Majority government presented no difficulty to these theorists, for only thus were the liberty and equality of the faithful compatible with the observance of that order and obedience which the purpose of the church required.

The significance of this voluntary relation was most obvious in the stress laid by all upon the free election[6] of ministers by the church. It was true that the people's share was formal, but the theory established that the election was an act of the whole church, in which members and officers were related in a particular way. The voluntary relation between ministry and church had no other foundation than voluntary election; for the independent church was not subject to any except by free choice. Moreover, the power to elect by the whole church recurred with every change in the ministry, and, in cases of necessity, the faithful could elect to the ministry and transmit the ministerial power in doctrine

---

[1] *Jus Maj.* I, 87.   [2] *Ib.* I, 116.   [3] *Ib.* I, 280.
[4] *De Civili*, 304.   [5] *Jus Maj.* I, 325; II, 37.
[6] Voetius, *supra*, § III; *Jus Maj.* I, 140–162; *De Civili*, ch. 18.

and discipline. Consent, therefore, even if it was usually tacit, was held to be the bond binding the members of the church, and the church and its ministry.

The fixed determination of these theorists to release the church from any political or territorial or other than spiritual ties was revealed particularly in the fact that each of them denied that the Old Testament bond between political and ecclesiastical society existed under the dispensation of the New Testament.[1] The order and church of Christ superseded the former Jewish polity and removed the servile character of the Jewish law by depriving the ruler of his former ecclesiastical office. Christ prescribed nothing to the ruler in the constitution of the church, and therefore the New Testament church was a church of believers, spiritually governed, and bound by faith. So that the church in essence was the church of the Apostles, the church *sub cruce*, self-sufficient, exercising every ecclesiastical function, owing nothing to an external power, and constituted by the adherence of its members to their faith, and therefore to each other and to their pastors. This was the standard of ecclesiastical self-sufficiency, for the Christian ruler had no right, divine or human, to deprive the church of that which it had in its Apostolic and persecuted state, and to which it had rather return than suffer a diminution of its inherent liberty and power. The church was not to yield to the state solely because the days of its persecution were over.

The great difference between Voetius and the other two writers was the use of contractual theories. Apollonius made a somewhat superficial application of contractual arguments borrowed from other sources, but was acutely conscious that the church owed its self-sufficient character to the fact that it rested upon consent. Triglandius had no understanding of the contractual argument, but he insisted even more strongly than the other two that the church was nothing else than the body of believers, and was independent in virtue of the divine law. Nevertheless, in spite of these differing foundations, the completed structure was the same: the church as a voluntary body possessing power to govern

[1] Voetius, *supra*, § III; *Jus Maj.* I, 26, 30, 70, 78, 124, 373–374; II, 44; *De Civili*, ch. 12 and 374.

itself in every ecclesiastical and spiritual matter, and totally distinct from and without connection with the state in so far as it was exercising a peculiar power to advance the spiritual realm of Christ. This common conception of ecclesiastical power is seen more clearly in their treatment of the state.

First, it was admitted that the ruler was supreme in his own sphere, and that his was an architectonic power and definitive judgment in political society. His power was from God but only because He permitted men to order their own political relations to meet their needs. These theologians were not directly concerned with the theory of the state, although it was a pressing problem for them to distinguish the political power by its complete independence from the church. That they accepted some final and definitive power is not to be doubted, but they had little conception of sovereignty itself. The primary characteristic[1] which Voetius emphasised was its unity and uniformity, and therefore its constant identity in relation to all kinds of persons and matters. The imperium was one, uniform and indivisible; nor could it be given multiple forms, for the essence and form of law was its indivisibility.

From this, Voetius drew two important conclusions. First,[2] the civil power could only act in ecclesiastical matters in the same way as it did in civil and political, so that the church was not the peculiar subject of the ruler's office. Secondly, political power was the same whatever the religion of the ruler and the magistrate might be. The power of the ruler was the power of an office, and was unaffected by the personal inclinations of the individual officer. Therefore, the Christian ruler as ruler had no different relation to the church than had a non-Christian ruler, for grace did not change essentially and intrinsically the nature of things or natural rights. The last survivals of the theocratic doctrine of dominion by grace were discarded and refuted by these strong Calvinists. Political power did not depend upon religion and did not exist for the furtherance of Christ's Kingdom. The godly prince ceased to have a political meaning or a divine call, so that

[1] *Polit. Eccl.* 141, 145, 160, 288; *Jus Maj.* I, 15, 38, 72–76; *De Civili*, 173–175, 207, 243, 254.
[2] *Polit. Eccl.* 145; *Jus Maj.* I, 24; *De Civili*, 211.

a tradition of the Reformation of great influence even among
Calvinist thinkers and developed more fully by some reputable
Calvinist theologians was finally discarded because, as Voetius
saw, there was no guarantee that there would be a succession of
godly princes.

Right, he said, was not founded in grace nor derived from
Christ the Mediator as such; for as grace was not of the essence
or formal reason of power, so it could add nothing intrinsically
to it, but only adorn it with a rank as if of eminence or of beauty.
In the spiritual court and according to the spiritual right of the
conscience before God, the unfaithful had power neither in
relation to ecclesiastical nor in regard to human good; but in the
external court according to natural and civil rights, his title was
as just as that of the faithful.

Christianity and political power were two distinct capacities
associated *per accidens* in the same person, the first as a quality
of mind, the second as an external office, and incapable of fusion
in a Christian magistracy, distinguished from magistracy on the
one hand and Christianity on the other. If such a fiction was
admitted, it[1] was not derived from Christianity for then all
Christians would have it, nor from magistracy for the like reason
that all magistrates could claim it. To say that a man was good
and a poet did not mean that he was a good poet.[2] In the same
way, to say that a man was a Christian and a ruler did not mean
that he was a Christian ruler: he was a Christian as a member of
the church and a ruler as an officer of the state. Therefore, the
ruler was not the primary member of the church nor in virtue of
his office even a member. His political and worldly station did
not set him above other members. In short, the ruler as church
member was in the same position as any church member, and as
ruler was as any ruler supreme in the limits of his office.

The peculiar attribute of his office and power was coercion.[3]
The essence of political society was its involuntary nature because
no member was entitled to deny the validity of any political act
or to exercise force in his own interests without the sanction of

[1] *Polit. Eccl.* I, 137.   [2] *Ib.* I, 38.
[3] *Ib.* I, 122, 131, 136; *Jus Maj.* I, 325; II, 37, 310; *De Civili*, ch. 2 and 79, 103, 179.

the government. The state was distinguished from the church by this power over all men within its territory, for the church had power only over those who entered it voluntarily. Membership of the state was tacit, since the mere act of living within its territory involved obligations and gave rights, which in turn justified the right of the state to subject all individuals to its supreme and definitive political power. Voetius[1] had admitted that tacit consent was a legitimate obligation so far as members of the state were concerned, and the implication of another passage seems to justify his belief in a power binding the members but not created by their consent. The power was of God; the applicatio was by consent; and the people could not resume or usurp this power, although able to apply that power, if need be, by naming other persons to exercise it. But this was not stated explicitly by Voetius; the deduction is only justified in so far as he himself had stated it of the church, and that he himself had treated the potestas and applicatio as valid both in church and in state.

The government of the state was the only coercive government in any particular society; however many voluntary bodies there were protected by the state and governing their own members, none possessed the power of life and death or the right to use corporal punishments to correct their own members. The state existed as the source of coercion, and its government was alone entitled to use force. Consequently, law was external, imposed and penal. It was the standard of external conduct, conformity to which was a matter of social necessity and dictated by the threat of punishment by the political government.

It is true that Apollonius[2] gave prominence to the opinions of many of the Jesuit and Protestant casuists that even the law of the land was not law in virtue of its coercive source but only bound the subject's conscience so long as it agreed with the divine will and reason. Where a human law referred to some matter unde-fined by God and was merely for civil convenience, such casuists held that there was no obligation to obey beyond the general one that all cause of scandal or contempt ought to be avoided because such laws did not bind *per se* in that they did not always bind the conscience. The conscience was subject to God alone even in

---

[1] *Polit. Eccl.* 1; cf. 48, 120, 133.   [2] *Jus Maj.* 11, 214 *seq.*

civil matters. Whence it followed that such laws as were promulgated only by human authority were neglected by subjects
without sin provided that there was no possibility of scandal and
that the common good was not thereby injured. Human laws
were not to be snares and traps of the conscience. Always the
distinction was to be observed between those things ratified by
human law but necessary in themselves as commanded by God
Himself, whether through nature or revelation, and so partaking
of the nature and force of divine law as declarations of divine will,
binding the conscience always and everywhere; and those things
left to the liberty of men and regulated by human laws which
lacked the perfection of divine institution and the just require-
ments of law in every aspect, so that the justa obligationis ratio
was not in them. That ratio obligationis was from the Will of
God, the supreme legislator, and consequently the authority and
obligation of human laws were determined by the moral attributes
which God had willed. Apollonius quoted from Ames' *Cases of
Conscience* two passages in explanation and confirmation. In the
first, Ames stated that nothing except the good ought to be
commanded and nothing except the bad to be prohibited, because
a matter indifferent in itself was the subject of a command or
prohibition only in so far as it was related to some ulterior good or
evil. In the second, he argued that the obligation to obey a human
law was from the divine command to obey the powers that be,
and therefore subjects were to avoid any action bringing the
public authority into contempt or giving offence to others, because either was a sin against the law of God. But human laws,
the product of human discretion, were not to be obeyed absolutely
as if their violation involved damnation, since that would entail
many more sins in political than in primitive society where laws
were few. Those human laws were binding only on account of the
just intention of the legislator, since it was to be presumed that
no ruler intended injury to his subjects. The object of any
legitimate law was always justice, equity and the common good,
whatever the intention of the legislator. Therefore, the obligation
of a law depended upon its purpose, and ceased when that purpose
was neglected or distorted.

Nevertheless, true law was from the point of view of subjects coercive; it established an involuntary relation for the sake of the common good and was not able to influence the motives of human action. Indeed, it had no foundation in individual motives. But penal though law was, it was not merely a law for the reprobate and of no value to the saints to whom the law of God was the only law. Nor was the state of no significance to the Christian; even the most religious person was also a member of society with social relationships and responsibilities, for the regulation of which the state and its instruments were necessary. Religion did not supersede nature—the human life still required regulation in the interests of orderly administration and the common welfare. What was denied was that religious life ought to be determined by social obligations or that the state had a right to influence religion in consequence of civil necessities.

The power of the ruler and of the state had not been challenged nor their independence and supremacy qualified by ecclesiastical control. In its own sphere, the state was in no way made to wait upon clerical approval; but the limitation was important, since the definition of the political sphere led to the conception of the secular state. Voetius[1] stated that political power was human *in se* and formally secular. In its actual organisation it was merely human. Its end was the peace and happiness of civil co-operation and the greatest political good. Its subject-matter was all those relations of persons and things which were of the animal and natural life and of the political community.

Apollonius[2] also defined the state in wholly secular terms. The ruler could not use spiritual means but only the secular arm and such means as civil government and natural reason provided, not what by divine institution had been sanctified for spiritual things. The civil power existed for the natural order; its purpose was that natural happiness, peace and tranquillity which human prudence and the forces of nature alone provided. The immediate cause of the state and its peculiar value were temporal order and safety of the people, and not the eternal and heavenly life and felicity. The power of the state acted in a civil way and through political instruments in all matters dealing with the outward man and animal life. Its results were purely political. Therefore, this

---

[1] *Polit. Eccl.* i, 122, 143.   [2] *Jus Maj.* i, 51–52, 58, 91.

government was political and not ecclesiastical; it was the government of a human society for human and natural ends by civil and political methods.

Triglandius[1] was equally certain that the state was of the natural order, and that political power existed only for temporal prosperity, for which political laws and coercive jurisdiction were instituted. To him the state was an evil necessity, sanctioned indeed by God, but unable to do more than impose peace and order upon the lawless, to regulate the conduct of men acting by the light of natural reason alone, and to provide a natural justice. The architectonic power in the state was only able to act in civil things, and, moreover, in those civil things not determined by God's laws. Its end was only the civil good.

The third characteristic of the state was its limited right in relation to the rights of other institutions and individuals. It was not only limited negatively by the limits of coercion and of its own secular nature, but also positively by the existence of independently established and authorised powers and individual relations. Voetius[2] explicitly stated that the ruler did not possess either virtually or formally all the powers which were contained by the state, but was concerned only with their external character. He denied that all government was coercive, that all power was of legislation, and that all jurisdiction was political. Again, the people as citizens transferred all their power to the ruler but, at least in regard to governments limited by contract, other matters not of that civic capacity were not granted. In such matters, the ruler had a directive but not the functional power.

Triglandius[3] was equally emphatic that the state existed for the preservation of the rights of other institutions. Further, the supreme political power was limited by both Tables of the Law, although it was true that no power save the conscientious and passive resistance of his subjects could enforce those limits.

These points were illustrated by an analogy common to all—the institution of marriage.[4] The husband enjoyed his conjugal rights and power partly in consequence of divine ordination and

[1] *De Civili*, 80, 197–199, 211.   [2] *Polit. Eccl.* I, 150–151.
[3] *De Civili*, 128, 184–185.
[4] *Polit. Eccl.* I, 158–159, 191; cf. *Jus Maj.* I, 28; II, 310–312; *De Civili* 53, 262.

partly of the mutual pledges freely consented to and given by the individual man and the individual woman. The ruler as ruler had no conjugal power; only as an individual and a husband. So that he had not the least share in or claim to the marital power exercised by husbands under his rule; nor did the husband exercise this power as the delegate or minister of the ruler, and therefore the marital power was not directly subordinate to the political power. This formal consent was not in any way a political matter but was proper only to the contracting partners, and thereby constituted the right to conjugal cohabitation, although the state might prevent the actual cohabitation from taking place. Apollonius also stressed the indissoluble and indestructible power of the husband. Even if the wife was abducted or forcibly separated from the husband, yet the conjugal power by right and law remained with him, though it could not be exercised. The bond of matrimony was not invalidated by such an injury, but was perpetuum et indissolubile[1] according to divine law and divine institution.

Since marriage was a divine institution entered into by the consent of one man and one woman, the state was face to face with a union, a contract and a power which came into being independently of the state. Nevertheless, marriages were contracted within the state with and under the approbation, direction, judgment, confirmation and protection of the public and architectonic power which was peculiar to the sovereign. What, then, was the power of the state in regard to marriages between its members? First, there was the subsequent consent and approval; that is, the addition of civil ratification to an intrinsic authority. Secondly, an objective or extrinsic and directive power around the marital power, its constitution and its use. In other words, the state had the power to adjust the marital power to civil conditions and political society so that its operation was properly conducted without endangering the state itself.

In the same way, the ecclesiastical power existed independently of the state and yet in it.[2] In consequence, the state had no part in ecclesiastical power itself but only in its social environment in

---

[1] *Jus Maj.* I, 331. Cf. I, 202.
[2] *Polit. Eccl.* III, 794. See also I, 15.

so far as it reacted upon external relations for the regulation of which the state properly existed. To the state belonged the civil control of a power already in existence, so that political authority could only add to that power and not diminish its inherent rights and privileges. The state was thus limited by the existence of powers and rights which it had to accept and which it could only facilitate or not as its rulers decided. Those powers possessed a validity which the state could not override and a sphere of operation which it could not infringe. Sovereignty was proper only in civil life and was limited by the autonomous exercise of powers which were beyond the range of sovereignty itself. It could act around but not in them; it could facilitate or impede but could not interfere.

Church and state differed in respect of power, scope and membership. Ecclesiastical power was holy,[1] not secular, nor supreme, but the power of ministry by which the conscience was challenged and directed. It was not absolute, for it had to give the reasons of its government by Scriptural precept and to observe the form revealed by God; nor was it to be obeyed unless the members of the church were satisfied that it was exercised in accord with Scriptural principles. Ecclesiastical power was in the church alone, political power in the state; the church was the communitas of the faithful, the state the communitas of citizens. Ecclesiastical power existed for the direction of all things making for union with God in order to reach eternal happiness; political power existed to regulate human matters for the sake of temporal welfare. Membership of the church was voluntary but the citizen was born into the state. The power of each in its own sphere for its own purpose was complete, self-sufficient and definitive. Neither was subordinate to the other; neither was able to usurp the office of the other; neither could participate in the other. The church as such and the state as such were exclusive, independent and self-sufficient institutions. So that neither was part of the other nor to be confounded, and neither as such was capable of taking part in the activities of the other.

The connection which these theorists desired was no more than civil protection, and this point was aptly made by Voetius in one

[1] *Polit. Eccl.* I, 122, 136; *Jus Maj.* 24–26; *De Civili,* ch. 4.

of his analogies. The father[1] of a minister had the responsibility and burden of his education and support. The military officers protected his congregation, office and person from enemies. Both the father and the soldiers, therefore, had a necessary office in relation to the ministry and its function, for without their services the ministry would be impossible; but neither possessed on that account the ministry or the ministerial function. In the same way, political power was necessary to the church, but could not use this necessity to usurp ecclesiastical power nor to deprive the church of it.

The relationship between church and state was the external connection between two associations existing in the same social framework. For that reason, that relation was accidental, although in most circumstances inevitable. Temporal and spiritual were in essence wholly distinct and no connection through external factors affected the essence of either. But in spite of this fundamental antithesis and complete differentiation, none of these thinkers believed in isolation. They sought to distinguish but not to separate church and state. Voetius[2] held that both were always distinct, although not always separate, whence one was not of the essence of the other nor could they be blended nor intermingled nor transformed from the one into the other. But this distinction in character did not entail separation. Apollonius also admitted that there was a connection in spite of a formal distinction. Triglandius was even more emphatic that the fundamental difference in character did not mean hostility or indifference in their mutual relations.

It was this additional theory of co-operation which obscured and complicated the original and fundamental conceptions of a voluntary church and a secular state. That relation was understandable and reasonable, and the case for it had been ably presented. It was not so easy to graft on to this stock the theory of co-operation and at the same time to preserve the independence and self-sufficiency of each. It was in virtue of this attempt that the suspicion of an ecclesiastical supremacy innate in the whole theory seemed plausible to contemporaries.

[1] *Polit. Eccl.* I, 140.
[2] *Ib.* I, 147; III, 219; *Jus Maj.* II, 311 *seq.*; *De Civili*, ch. 5.

The ideal relation of church and state was co-ordination and not subordination. While there was no intrinsic subordination of the two institutions, there ought to be a common understanding to co-operate, or, in other words, coercion and religion should be linked for the good of the state and also for the good of the church. The state would gain from the teaching of the church and find that its coercive power was given a moral foundation in the consciences of its members; the church would have at its disposal the resources of the state for the extension and stabilisation of its spiritual mission. Then mind and matter, and the spiritual and temporal forces, were harmonised. But it is in this idea that the transition was made to a new theory with theocratic implications; for, this theory of co-operation and co-ordination did not mean that the church was really to assist the state to realise more adequately its secular character and end, but that the state was to become the instrument of the church in a higher and spiritual endeavour, so that both together should realise the ultimate purpose of God. The state in the service of the church had a purpose which was no longer really secular, although it could only act in a secular and political medium and manner. This transition was revealed in each writer by his treatment of the argument: each discussed not how the church helped the state but how the state helped the church.

Apollonius developed this point in great detail. First,[1] he explained that the duty of the ruler as custos et vindex legis was common to all, even unfaithful, rulers and was instituted by the divine law in order to preserve the rights of others under that law. Therefore, he was not empowered to undertake the ecclesiastical function himself, since it was given to the church by divine law, but only to take such steps as were necessary to ensure that the church faithfully observed its function. His was an external and directive power around the conduct of these functions; he had no power in the function itself.

Secondly, Apollonius defined the duty of the ruler as nutricius et defensor ecclesiae, which title he shared with all Christians in so far as he himself was a faithful and orthodox Christian; for as such he brought all his authority and rank to the service of the

[1] *Jus Maj.* I, 28–33.

church. In this capacity, the ruler's power was to add to, and not to deprive the church of, the liberties which Christ gave to it, since the condition of the church ought not to be worse under a faithful than under an unfaithful ruler. Again, he ought to satisfy all the material needs of the church, but this did not allow him to alter the polity of the Apostolic church. Moreover, he had to protect all the rights and liberties of the church and to obtain civil satisfaction for any injuries to it. Not only did this include the duty to punish any who interfered with the legitimate execution of ecclesiastical power, but also the removal of all impediments to that power, e.g. false religions, persecution and oppression. As nutricius and defensor the ruler ought to cherish and observe the spiritual rights of the church by attending, and fostering attendance at, its services, and submitting himself and his own (*se et sua*) to its spiritual power. He had, therefore, to stimulate among his subjects a proper piety and respect for the church and God's worship; but not to act in the church and its function in virtue of his political office.

Thirdly,[1] the ruler as director ordinis externi ecclesiae had four duties: (*a*) to institute, promote and regulate the external order of the church; (*b*) to ensure by the imperium that the church observed this order; (*c*) so to regulate the church that the order instituted in the assembly of the faithful should be adopted and made effective, and the administration of ecclesiastical affairs entrusted to the church; and (*d*) to punish the disobedient and contumacious.

Lastly, the ruler as such had political power to establish a church as the public church in his territory.

Triglandius[2] was not less anxious to prove that the ruler had a duty to place his power and office at the service of the church. He insisted that the ruler was by his office vindex justitiae and had to guarantee the rights of all. The ruler was not to follow his own will but the norm of justice and equity, and in respect of the church to give political force to the divine laws by which it was ordered. His duty was to use his power to direct his subjects to the worship of God;[3] his was the sword,[4] to be used by divine

---

[1] *Jus Maj.* I, 20.   [2] *De Civili*, 129, 186.
[3] *Ib.* 49.   [4] *Ib.* 54.

command to stabilise and strengthen ecclesiastical government.[1] He was to recognise in his own life the spiritual guidance of the church and to submit to its authority. Therefore, the real relation of the ruler to the church was the establishment of the public church,[2] supported by the political power, provided with material assistance, and freed from all impediments, so that the church was able to perform its own tasks the more easily. The duty of the ruler was to ease the work of the ministers; his power extended no further than to give public recognition and support to what was already of divine right.[3]

Voetius did not differ in any of these points. The power[4] to reform the church was in the body of the church itself, not only in doctrine but also in government. The ruler as ruler had the peculiar power, but no more, to remove all impediments, whether secular or pseudo-ecclesiastical, in order to reform, and to give a public status to, the true and reformed church by ratifying and defending politically what the church had freely determined to be the law of Christ. His power[5] went no further than to enable the church to reform itself. If the ruler desired to have a reformed church where there was "Pseudo-Ecclesia et Pseudo-Potestas ecclesiastica, seu usurpatio (e.g. Papalis)", his power was properly used when he removed that impediment and opened the way to the establishment of the true church by its own action, whereby it could institute its own proper power and government.

The state had become more than the means of social regulation and political association for certain elementary necessities of civilised life; its true function was to prepare the social environment of the church so that its spiritual power was free and effective. In so far as the state was natural and an association of men as men, not as Christians, and in so far as the ruler as such had no place in the church, it would have seemed that political responsibility for the morality of subjects would not have extended to spiritual and religious welfare but have been limited to the preservation of political society and its real object, efficient government. Human prudence and natural reason, but not the revelation of the Gospel, should have dictated the ruler's policy since his

[1] *De Civili*, 80.   [2] *Ib.* 109–110; 379–381.   [3] *Ib.* 129.
[4] *Polit. Eccl.* I, 182, 196.   [5] *Ib.* I, 210, 214.

government had to take account of human nature, and the facts of social life. The natural state, it would have been assumed, was governed by human laws formulated according to worldly wisdom and political necessity. The very emphasis laid upon the degradation of human nature seemed to imply a morality, a law and a policy adapted to it. Then, the state was no more than earthly and transient, although a divine device to meet human needs, and to facilitate a higher life to which political society itself made no direct contribution.

The state ceased to be a religious organ directly concerned with the spiritual life when it was admitted that the ruler only acted by force, and that force did not promote spiritual conversion and willing obedience to God's Law. Eternal life and happiness were beyond the reign of force, and therefore beyond the state. The church alone possessed the supernatural powers to work upon the spirit of man. The state could not use spiritual means in the exercise of its office around spiritual matters, but only the secular arm and those means which civil government and natural reason permitted, not those which the divine institution had sanctioned for the realisation of spiritual life and the administration of spiritual things. But, because the state ought to use its power to create a monopoly for the true church and to foster it by all the means proper to the state, it would seem that its secular self-sufficiency and natural purpose were in fact to be subordinated to theological revelation and ecclesiastical regulation. Indeed, Triglandius and Apollonius did argue that as the supernatural end of the church was nobler than the natural end of the state, the state was subordinate to the church in regard to the Kingdom of Heaven and was to be directed by the church. Yet, in that case, how could both claim that the state was independent and supreme in its own sphere? How was secular independence to be reconciled to the duty to serve the church?

These writers were not unaware of this seeming inconsistency, and sought to meet it by two distinctions to show that this service to the church was merely secular and political. Both distinctions also vindicated the claim of the church to self-government in church matters.

First, it was argued that whatever the state did in the interests of the church was done in a political way by the same power as that by which the state was ruled, and therefore could be done by all rulers of whatever faith. Ecclesiastical power[1] was to be understood either as that which was exercised by ecclesiastical methods or as that which had ecclesiastical persons and matters merely as the "object", though itself not acting in ecclesiastical ways. The first was the formally ecclesiastical power because it was a power given by Christ to determine church subjects according to ecclesiastical forms and was proper to the church alone. The second was the objectively ecclesiastical power which was only a civil power acting upon and not in ecclesiastical matters. This distinction was not valueless, although it meant no more than that the spiritual power in the church itself was to be distinguished from the civil power around the church. It served especially to emphasise that the ruler's power in regard to the church was only the political power of giving the sanction of political law and protection of political coercion to that which had been determined by the church itself; and this power was wholly political and secular because it was exactly the same as that used around "objects" which were not ecclesiastical. It was political because it was action in the state, not in the church, and through the law and force of the state. To favour the true church and to persecute the false church was only a matter of force and law, wholly political and secular, and proper to the state but not to the church.

Secondly,[2] not only did the ruler who observed his duty to the true church act only in a political way, but also he acted only in political matters, for the regulation of which his power and office were instituted. The external order of the church was open to two constructions: the first being the disposition of all visible external matters necessary to the organisation of the visible church and therefore proper to the formally spiritual and ecclesiastical government; and the second denoted the extraneous adjuncts and activities extrinsic to the ecclesiastical polity and common to temporal existence. In this second sense, the external

---

[1] *Jus Maj.* I, 2–4, 7, 28; *Polit. Eccl.* I, 115, 139–142, 148.
[2] *Polit. Eccl.* I, 16, 118, 143, 146; *Jus Maj.* I, 18, 26, 40, 114, 364; II, 142, 355, 369–370; *De Civili,* ch. 8, 270.

order was the sum of the external and political circumstances associated with the spiritual order, by reason of the fact that spiritual society did not exist nor function without such means and instruments as were directly and *per se* subject to the external human order. The ruler had no part in the external ecclesiastical order proper, which was regulated by the church alone. All that the ruler had the power to do was to take care that in the state the true church was able to control its own external actions. This power was purely political, since it was a political action to incorporate the church order into the political order.

The ruler had no more than a political power and only acted in a political way for the civil benefit of the church. In serving the church, he did nothing outside the legitimate limits of the state and nothing which was contrary to its secular origin and character. In making the state the instrument of the true church, the ruler was fulfilling his secular function; in accepting and giving political countenance to that church, he did not exceed the political power of his office.

These two distinctions, taken together, excluded the ruler from any ecclesiastical office or function; for the objectively ecclesiastical power could only confirm the external ecclesiastical order proper, while by his civil power, he determined that external order which was common to the physical needs of men. It was an important point, because the church was left free to use its formally ecclesiastical power to control the external forms of its own organisation; and the church decided what was of the external ecclesiastical order proper by its interpretation of the Scriptures.

All that constituted the integrity of spiritual government through ecclesiastical power was peculiar and proper to the church. That power was spiritual because it was of Christ in the spiritual kingdom, and the autonomous visible church was part of that kingdom; but, although the power was divine, it was granted to the church and exercised through its intermediary action. The supernatural and the human foundations of the church were linked together and made to vindicate ecclesiastical independence and self-government; as a supernatural state governed by supernatural power, and as a voluntary society constituted by consent for the use of visible and social means to manifest on earth the spiritual communion of saints. The two were linked by the miraculous action of God's Grace, which created in the Elect a willing people apt to spiritual government, out of the reprobate people of the world, who had to be coerced by the state.

The transition from the voluntary to the state-established church and from the secular state to the ecclesiastical instrument was the consequence of stressing two different principles. The principle of differentiation was used to contrast the spiritual power of the church over willing members and the coercive power of the state over unwilling members; or, in other words, to contrast the institution of the church as a body of Christians, and the institution of the state as a body of men. The principle of co-operation was used to stress the duty of the ruler as an individual member of the church to submit to the power of the church and of ministers as citizens to submit to the power of the state. The ideal relation of church and state was twofold. First, each as an institution was separate and self-sufficient, and the power of each was not subordinate to the other. Secondly, the governors of each were subordinate to each other in so far as the governors of the one were also members of the other. Emphasis upon the first principle enabled the church to claim the same independence and self-sufficiency under a godly as under an ungodly ruler; the second principle was used to obtain civil privileges in addition to its fundamental rights. The theory was based upon the assumption of an ungodly ruler, but also upon the hope that the ruler who was a true son of the church would reinforce its power.

Differentiation of church and state culminated in the idea that there was no intrinsic subordination of the two institutions or of the two powers. Voetius[1] insisted that the one power did not contain the other nor could produce the other. The church was the church and as such possessed all ecclesiastical power for the building of the Kingdom of Christ. Likewise, the state as such did not need to include the church to be the lawful political society. Each held its power directly from God; not the ruler but the church was the intermediary between Christ and the ministers,[2]

[1] *Polit. Eccl.* I, 136, 238, 242, 245.   [2] *Ib.* I, 146.

and therefore neither was directly, *per se* and intrinsically subordinate to the other.[1] He held[2] that the best way to avoid the confusion of the things of Caesar and the things of God was to state roundly that nothing which was of the church as such was competent to the ruler as such; and nothing which was of the ruler as such was competent to the church as such. Apollonius and Triglandius[3] agreed that the powers were independent and that the ruler as such was not of the essence of, nor in, the church. A sharp distinction was made between the office and the individual; only as an individual was the ruler a member of the church.

The co-ordination of church and state was the consequence of the mutual subordination of those who held the different offices and exercised the different powers. When the ruler as a member of the church submitted to the ministers as the ambassadors of Christ, and when the ministers as citizens submitted to the ruler as ruler, then was there the true co-ordination of the two powers. But the validity of this argument depended upon the consistency with which the relations of the ruler in his two capacities to the church was observed. If the ruler as a Christian and church member was made ecclesiastically responsible for the conduct of his office and the use of his power, and in addition was to govern the political society by the guidance which the church ministers gave to him as a church member, then the argument broke down and with it the independence of the state. Political power was in that case at the disposition of the ministers. It would have been just as logical for the ruler to have transposed that argument to his relation as ruler with the ministers as citizens and expect them to order their religious power and office according to his political guidance of their lives as citizens. But this these writers had expressly rejected. Again, they had claimed that the church ought to be in no worse condition under the faithful than it had been under the unfaithful ruler; and it might be urged with equal logic against them that the Christian ruler ought not to be any less independent in his actions as ruler than when he had not been a member of the church. In short, the accusation that these

---

[1] *Polit. Eccl.* I, 155.   [2] *Ib.* I, 198.
[3] *Jus Maj.* I, 46 *seq.*; II, 283 *seq.*; *De Civili*, ch. 4, 207, 243, 253–258.

thinkers were advocates of a virtual theocracy, although church and state were formally independent, rests upon their answer to the questions whether the official policy of the ruler was to be separated from his personal conduct as a Christian, and whether the ruler was to submit to the guidance of the church only as an individual and only in his personal life.

There is little doubt that Apollonius in spite of all his qualifications and ingenious distinctions did believe that the ruler who was the true son of the church should bow to pastoral guidance, even in his office. First,[1] he declared that his power and its use were not granted but, in fact, necessarily imposed upon the civil magistrate, if he wished to fulfil his function according to divine law. Again,[2] the ruler endowed with spiritual gifts and who used his office as custos, vindex and nutricius rightly and legitimately, was praised and respected as an outstanding member of the church, because he furthered its liberties. Thirdly,[3] the Christian ruler was to prevent any confusion of ecclesiastical and civil offices or functions, to order his government so that it did not conflict with the faith and habits of faithful men or damage the liberties of the church or oppose the Christian religion, and consequently to remove all impediments to the church and all moral sins from the state. He ought to promote the true religion even though it was not for political felicity and even though the false religion was more advantageous to him. Thus, the ruler enlightened by faith sustained the church with his official power. It is true that Apollonius added that in doing this, the ruler acted by an immediately divine and not by an ecclesiastical mandate, and by his own architectonic power, not by a power derived from the church. But this independence was made somewhat formal by another line of argument.

Apollonius[4] rejected the argument of Bellarmine that the art of ruling men ought to be subordinate to the art of ruling souls, not because its power was derived from that, but because its end was inferior to the *ars artium*. This was denounced as the foundation of indirect temporal power, but Apollonius substituted an argument which was even more fictitious. He distinguished

[1] *Jus Maj.* I, 7.   [2] *Ib.* I, 17.
[3] *Ib.* I, 56–58.   [4] *Ib.* I, 48 *seq.*

between the art and the "subject" or him having the art. The purpose of one art was not subordinate to nor determined by the purpose of any other art: the regal art or the end of the art of ruling men was neither subject nor subordinate to the end of ecclesiastical government, just as the end of the sculptor's or navigator's art was not subordinate to eternal life. Nevertheless, he said, the king, the sculptor and the navigator, if faithful, ought to direct their art for the attainment of eternal life; for the ultimate end of the faithful artist or "subject" of the art was eternal life, though it was not the end of the art itself.

Again,[1] Apollonius argued that the office of magistrate had not as its purpose eternal life; but that was the purpose of the holder of the office, i.e. the Christian magistrate. All members of the church were bound to contribute and direct "omnem suam potentiam et dignitatem, et media, et facultates, etiam externas et corporales" for the furtherance of the Kingdom of Christ. The magistrate had to use "omnem suam potestatem" to promote and cherish the piety and eternal life of his subjects. This service[2] was civil and external, i.e. to use coercion, not the spiritual power.

There was an obligation upon the ruler to serve the church; it was an obligation which was real only when the ruler was a member of the church. What was to be the attitude of the church toward the ruler who was a member, if he did not use his office to serve the church? Who was to decide what that service ought to be? Was the ruler to be informed of his duty by preachers from the pulpit? Was his policy to be scrutinised in the presbytery, the classes and the synod? Finally, if the ruler neglected the advice of the church, was the church able to suspend him from the sacraments and eventually to excommunicate him, not for the conduct of his private life, but because he had not put into political operation ecclesiastical advice?

Apollonius had little hesitation in answering that the ministers[3] ought to correct the ruler, as a faithful man, for the abuse of his regal power to the detriment of the spiritual welfare of his subjects. The ruler had a corresponding power to punish the minister as a subject if he abused his ecclesiastical office to stir up civil disorder. The civil power was subject to the church when its

---

[1] *Jus Maj.* I, 62–63.   [2] *Ib.* II, 310.   [3] *Ib.* I, 51.

ministers were the mouthpiece of God, but not when they spoke
only with the authority of men. In those things enjoined directly
by God in the Scriptures the ministers[1] were to admonish and
compel by spiritual discipline; but in matters determined ecclesiastically, they could only admonish and reprove, and in the last
resort leave the ruler to the divine judgment unless he voluntarily
submitted. Therefore, the rulers were to be stimulated and
reproved by pastoral admonitions and censures; "non tantum
ut abstracte considerantur extra considerationem muneris, quo
funguntur, et quasi materialiter quatenus homines christiani,
quomodo reliqui fideles. . . . . . . Sed etiam quatenus considerantur
formaliter, qua tales. . . . . . . docendi, monendi terrendi ex verbo
Dei ipsum etiam Imperatorem habet ecclesia potestatem etiam
in actionibus muneris ejus." He denied[2] that rulers and their
civil government were not subject to the ministerial power, for
it was "pastoris officium monere, adhortari, reprehendere reges
delinquentes in Deum, et ex verbo Dei docere quid fieri debeat;
protervos et pertinaces deserere, ex Christiana communione
excludere, eosque quoad officia fraternae et Christianae familiari-
tatis vitare. . . . . . ". But the church was not to use other than
spiritual discipline; it was not to release subjects from their civil
allegiance, nor to excite them to act against the civil power, nor
to appeal to any other ruler.

Triglandius was hardly so clear in his argument but he seemed
to conclude that the ruler, in his capacity as a Christian man, and
as the ruler, was to submit to the ministers in so far as the ministers
were the ambassadors of Christ. But he made no real attempt to
distinguish between the two capacities. In matters commanded
by God, the ruler was not free to decide according to his own
discretion, but was a minister of God, and therefore to be rebuked
by the church if he exceeded or failed in this duty as minister.
The reason Triglandius[3] gave was that this power as minister
was defined by the Scriptures, but it was for the ecclesiastical
power to administer the Word, and to admonish each in his office.
The ruler[4] was to ensure the civil good of his subjects by the
administration of justice according to the laws, and also the

---

[1] *Jus Maj.* II, 314–316.
[2] *Ib.* II, 321–322.
[3] *De Civili*, 185–187.
[4] *Ib.* 211.

spiritual good so that in the same state the pure religion was publicly preached according to the Word. The civil ruler[1] could not perceive that spiritual good, which was revealed to him through the ministers. There would be no conflict and no injury to the conscience of any subject if each power functioned according to the Word.

The scholastic method of Voetius led him to state certain important objections of his opponents relating to this problem, but in his answers he hardly met the real issue. First,[2] it was objected that any one who had to follow the decisions of others did not rule but was ruled, and was the slave of him who decided: therefore, all the authority attributed to the ruler depended upon the judgment of the church as from a supreme tribunal. Voetius met this argument by an analogy. The ruler was held to follow the opinion of the lawyer or counsellor by whom some fundamental law of the state was interpreted. The faculty of interpretation was with the counsellor; the power of commanding was with the law. Whether the ruler recognised or rejected the empire of law, the counsellor had no judicium dominans aut imperatorium above the regal power, but only ministerial, so that the ruler as such was not the slave of the counsellor. The same was true of ecclesiastical judgment. Again,[3] Voetius insisted that ecclesiastical power was ministerial and not architectonic. Any person supreme or superior in the political sphere could be subordinate to such power "ratione fraternitatis et symbiosios spiritualis in corpore et communione matris suae Ecclesiae", without injury to his political position and power because the two powers differed in kind. Thus, a consul was subject to the patriarchal power of his father, and a ruler to his doctor. Why should he not be subordinate to pastoral care for the safety of his soul?

Was the ruler, then, to sanction all the decrees of the ministers and act simply as an executioner?[4] No: because he was to sanction and execute those decrees only when he was convinced in his conscience that those decrees were consonant with the Scriptures and materialiter the decision of Christ. The ruler was not to obey

---

[1] De Civili, 204.
[2] Polit. Eccl. I, 154.
[3] Ib. I, 152.
[4] Ib. I, 154.

the ecclesiastical judgment directly but Christ, who alone commanded consciences, and to obey the ministers only as ministers
of Christ. When the ruler commanded the execution of ecclesiastical decrees by his political judgment, he did this as a free
and supreme judge and lord, not as a slave or executioner.
Ecclesiastical power over a king was of the same kind as the marital
power of a consort over a reigning queen.

The two powers of ministers and rulers were distinct. The
ministers[1] had by divine institution potestas antecedens which
decided matters in the church for the church; the ruler had no
such power, but in so far as he followed Christ was bound to
observe these decisions of the ministers. He could only act
politically by a potestas consequens which could not precede
ecclesiastical judgment, but only confirm it. But in its own place
(i.e. of political confirmation) his power was "prima et antecedens, immo sola et solitaria". In time but not in kind was it
subsequent to ministerial judgment. So that the ruler was free
to decide independently whether to give political sanction to the
judgment of the church, although he was as a faithful follower
of Christ to follow that judgment. Was he to follow that judgment
himself only, or was he expected also to follow it as a magistrate?
Was he to be visited with ecclesiastical censures if his political
judgment did not conform to the minister's ecclesiastical judgment?

To these questions Voetius gave no unequivocal answer. He
admitted[2] that the ruler had a definitive political judgment as
whether the church was to be simply tolerated, or supported by
his full political power, or otherwise. He admitted[3] that ecclesiastical discipline was not to affect the civil office, civil rights and
civil goods of any man, nor consequently the political power of
the ruler. He declared[4] that Christ was caput regis aut Mariti
fidelis not qua Rex or Maritus, but so far as he was membrum
Christi; and the king or husband was not caput subditorum or
caput uxoris qua faithful or members of Christ, but qua cives or
qua uxor. Again,[5] the ruler as "subditus spiritualis Christi seu
quod ad actus externos Christianismi" was subordinate and

[1] *Polit. Eccl.* I, 158. [2] *Ib.* I, 134, 148, 158. [3] *Ib.* I, 163.
[4] *Ib.* I, 161. [5] *Ib.* I, 161.

subject to Christ as Head of the church, and to the pastor as His minister and legate. But the ruler "qua Magistratus, seu quod ad supremam Potestatem sive circa negotia saecularia, sive circa ecclesiastica", was subject to no power or ministry directing potestative aut peremptorie. Voetius agreed[1] that the ruler was not to sanction publicly any religion, of the truth and goodness of which he was not conscientiously convinced. But he also insisted that the ruler was not to further a false religion; at the most he ought only to approve the toleration of the evil, not to approve the evil which was tolerated. Again,[2] the relation of the ruler as a member of the church to the minister of the church was a voluntary relation in so far as he wished to be the son of the church; but it seems to be implied that the ruler was bound by his assent to the church covenant as much as any other member. Lastly,[3] Voetius answered an objection that if the ruler did not approve of and put into operation the decision of the church by his political authority, but acted in the contrary manner, did not the church judge of his decision and action, thereby subordinating the whole power of the ruler to its own definitive judgment? He replied that the church did not subordinate the power of the ruler; but, after many vain attempts to persuade him to change his policy, would judge that he was no brother but an apostate and enemy of religion, to be treated by the church as a heathen and a publican. It is doubtful whether Voetius did, in fact, admit the distinction between the official and private capacities of the ruler, and therefore that the theory which he was at such pains to construct upon principles emphasising the fundamental difference of church and state had an ultimately theocratic character. The civil favours which the Christian ruler might grant were the religious duties of the church member which he had to provide.

Visser[4] has pointed out that the weakness of Voetius' theory was the power which the ruler exercised over corrupt elements in the church, and that Voetius allowed to the ruler a final political judgment of what was his duty to the church. But Visser has not emphasised sufficiently that this political judgment was either

---

[1] *Polit. Eccl.* I, 134.
[3] *Ib.* I, 163.
[2] *Ib.* I, 153.
[4] *Kerk en Staat*, II, 401.

political confirmation of what had been determined ecclesiastically
or was a refusal to give political support. There was no political
determination of ecclesiastical matters; for even if the ruler was
convinced that the majority in the church was right and gave to
it political support, if that majority was corrupt the minority
ought to secede and govern itself in spite of persecution. Here
was the real weakness—for Voetius assumed that the majority
in the Calvinist church of the Netherlands, if that church was
absolutely free to decide, would always decide in strict agreement
with the Scriptures; therefore the duty of the ruler went no
further than to confirm that decision of the majority. Voetius
made no provision for the possibility that the minority was alone
Scripturally justified and that the ruler was convinced that the
majority was in accord with Christ, except to fall back upon his
original principle[1] that the minority should constitute itself by
a covenant into a new church, and at the very worst to hold secret
meetings.

Now, this hypothetical case illustrates the essential weakness
of his theory, a weakness due to the fact that he based it upon
what were normally consistent but which might be wholly inconsistent principles. The first principle was the self-determination
of the church. The second was the political recognition of the
true church and elimination of false churches. He wanted both
self-determination and the absolutely true church of Christ. For
instance, self-determination in the Roman church was not the
way to the true church, so that Voetius called upon the Christian
ruler (i.e. the Calvinist) to purge the church by force. If the ruler
was a Catholic, the true church was constituted by a covenant in
spite of possible persecution and therefore had self-determination.
Self-determination as such, however, was no guarantee that the
church was the only true Scriptural church. The coercive power
of the state was to be at the service and disposal of the self-
determining church to prevent ecclesiastical self-determination
from forming false churches. But there was no theoretically
complete way of preventing self-determination from leading to
a false church; for the majority might be false Christians. If it
was supported by the ruler, the true church did not exist save in

[1] *Polit. Eccl.* I, 184.

the persecuted minority; if the minority was supported by the ruler, self-determination was not of the whole church but only of the true church.

There were only two ways to break this vicious line of argument. One was to provide an unquestionable and obvious test of the true church which the ruler was to preserve and purge by force so that it might become autonomous. This was what Voetius assumed but did not provide. But it would have subordinated self-determination to the duty of the ruler to ensure that only the true church existed, for only the true church was to be autonomous, and if by that action it degenerated into a false church because of majority rule, self-determination ceased to be valid until the church was purged of the majority. Voetius had assumed that the Calvinist church was the true church and that the majority in that church was always right; therefore, the ruler who fulfilled his divine duty had only to establish the Calvinist church, eliminate all other churches, and sanction the decisions taken by the majority.

The other way of avoiding these pitfalls was to have relied solely upon that line of argument which Voetius developed in the case where the ruler was not a member of the Calvinist church and was indifferent or hostile to it. That argument relied upon self-determination alone when the relation of the true church to the state was the same as that of any other association, with the rights of any association. It would mean not only that the true church was not supported by the state but that false churches would be allowed because the ruler had no means of deciding whether self-determination was of the true church or not. The church or churches would arise by a covenant and be free to govern themselves. If members seceded and formed a new church by covenant, it also had the right to be self-governing. So long as it decided only its own activities and was a law-abiding body, any church was to be treated by the state as a voluntary association in the internal affairs of which it was not concerned. If Voetius had followed his basic and original principles of the covenant, and the consequent right of self-determination, and not sought to obtain ecclesiastical control of the political power of coercion to establish the monopoly of the true church and to preserve the true church, he would not have been forced into an untenable position.

The fundamental defect of the theory of Voetius, and still more of Apollonius and Triglandius, was the substitution of jus divinum for the original ideas of the voluntary church and the secular state. Self-determination and the one true church were incompatible: the dilemma led to a modification of the idea of the voluntary church and equally of the secular state. It led to the attempt to obtain more for the voluntary church from the secular state than the voluntary church as a civil association ought to be granted. If the relation of the voluntary church to the secular state was as these writers contended when the ruler was not a member of the Calvinist church—as any other association—then it was contrary to that principle to claim or to be granted any civil privileges which violated the civil rights to which all other associations voluntarily formed were entitled. In so far as the church in order to assert its own independence and inherent power of government claimed to be in the position of any voluntary association, it set itself in a relation to the state by which it could claim consistently no more from the state than the civil rights which any voluntary society could claim: the protection of law and order.

The relation of church and state envisaged by these theorists was really inconsistent. It rested upon the conception of a secular state, concerned with the external man alone and unable to use its power in the Kingdom of Christ because that Kingdom was ruled by a spiritual, and not a coercive power, which persuaded but did not compel the consciences of those who voluntarily submitted. At the same time, the secular and coercive power was to be used not only to give ordinary civil rights of protection and justice and freedom to act in regard to its own members, but also to deprive citizens other than members of the true church of these same civil rights and consequently of their religious freedom from the state. But if the state could so control the external organisation of such heretical churches, it controlled religion itself, and the only way to deny a like control over the external organisation of the true church was to distinguish the true church with its divine right to survive and false churches with the civil duty to suppress them. Actions which were denounced as encroachments upon the spiritual realm and unlawful for any but a spiritual power were applauded as proper to the ruler when directed against other churches. If the state was concerned only with life in this world, it had no more right to control heretical churches than the true church. Moreover, the voluntary church ceased to be truly voluntary since it claimed and was to be granted an exclusive monopoly backed by political coercion. The truly voluntary church, really ruled by spiritual power alone, needed no more from the powers of this world than strictly civil rights which any citizen claimed. The spiritual power and the covenant itself were binding not really from consent but from the power of the state to enforce the contract. The whole theory suggested that the design was to give to the church the virtual control of force which it dared not claim outright and which was not the spiritual power of Christ. The Kingdom of Christ and the one visible church in the state were not identified, and the attempt to identify them forced these writers to introduce an extraneous principle in the duty of the Christian ruler to support the true church.

It is, therefore, to be doubted whether Voetius[1] was really the first to formulate what later came to be known as collegialism. His contractual theory of the church was ordered by divine right: if the Christian did not contract into the divine institution, the mere act of mutual consent and contract did not establish the true church in which was divine ministerial power and the power of self-government. He never really treated the church as a voluntary association except when the ruler was indifferent. It served as a basic minimum; it was not the ideal for which the church was to strive.

    [1] Gierke, *Natural Law and the Theory of Society* (transl. Ernest Barker), pp. 89, 92. Cf. Nauta, *De Nederlandsche Gereformeerden en Het Independentisme in de Zeventiende Eeuw* (Amsterdam, 1930), 30–32, where the difference between Voetius and Apollonius is treated as a matter of emphasis, and Voetius is held to be in full agreement with the Reformed Church.

CHAPTER V

THE ERASTIAN CRITICISM

§ I

A LOW CHURCH THEORY

THE theory of the two kingdoms formulated by the opponents of Vedelius was in turn subjected to considerable criticism. The controversy was, indeed, carried on with great bitterness and with diminishing attention to the essential principles at issue, but the works of three writers in particular were suggestive of new developments in the Erastian argument, and of the new free-thinking attitude toward religion. In consequence of this tendency, the church was treated as a human association to be regulated by the same principles as were all other human associations. The natural conclusion of this line of argument was reached in the theory of Constans, to whom the church was a mere civil department of a secular state.

The first of these Erastians was an anonymous champion of Vedelius and a savage, even scurrilous, critic of Apollonius. While his first work—the *Grallae*, translated into English as *The Supreame Power of Christian States Vindicated, etc.*[1]—was a rational refutation, in spite of its sarcastic tone, the subsequent pamphlets on both sides became tedious and unprofitable exercises in personal abuse to which no new argument was attached. This anonymous author has been identified with Salmasius,[2] the distinguished classical scholar of the seventeenth century, whose humanistic, Huguenot and royalist sympathies produced a theory much more palatable in an age of absolutism than the collegial theory of the church. The principal feature of this theory was the rationalist interpretation of the church, which was, however, joined to a more commonplace argument of divine right.

---

[1] Brit. Mus. Thomason Tracts.
[2] Visscher and van Langeraad, *Het Protestantsche Vaderland*, I, 199–208. Cf. *Nieuw Nederlandsch Biografisch Woorden-boek*, "Apollonius".

The *Grallae* was primarily a vindication of the lay reaction to the growing clericalism of the Calvinist church. It was a careful examination of the claims of the clerical party to a sufficiency of revelation, of which it itself was the exclusive channel to laymen. The *Grallae* denied any peculiar sanctity in the vocation of pastors and reduced the ministry to a condition of service like that of any worldly trade. It refuted the claim of the ministers to a divine right of church government upon the grounds that the "modern" church was a human society without miraculous powers and organised in the light of worldly prudence.

From the beginning, the *Grallae* identified Calvinist and Roman theories of the church. The "old leven of popery concerning the wonderful sanctity and spirituality of the external ministry of the visible church"[1] was responsible for the belief "that all clergie appointment is sacred and spiritual, and that the clergy themselves are all spiritual and holy". There followed, first, "a superstitious conceit that it was neither lawful nor possible for laymen to intermeddle with ecclesiastical affairs", and secondly, "that this charge belonged by divine end and inviolable right to clergy or spiritual men only, as the fruit of their vocation and confirmation (which imprints a spiritual and indelible character upon the soul and body of clergiemen) by the privilege of which they are preferred in holiness to all other Christians as being but laymen". In the same way, Apollonius[2] "extolls the outward business of ecclesiastical ministry for holy, spiritual and divine among men", because "the external things of the church reach into the soul and are so sublime that they cannot be done by the magistrate". Apollonius was accused of wanting to "obtrude superstition after a popish manner when he searcheth after such abstruce mysteries of spirit in the outward works of ecclesiastical dressing", whereby "what is performed by Ministerial function of the church is of higher nature than man's capacity can reach unto".

The *Grallae* was framed to disprove that there was any peculiar spiritual character in the organisation of the visible church, because Christ did not prescribe one unalterable form but allowed human discretion to adjust the fundamentals to circumstances. Salmasius rejected the principles of high churchmanship. The

---

[1] *The Supreame Power etc.*, Preface.   [2] Preface, 6 (unnumbered).

vocation of the ministry conferred by the imposition of hands was
no basis for "that spiritual right and prerogative to perform the
spiritual offices of the church". He rejected also that peculiar
church government, which though in the world and only too
often exercised by worldly means and by men whose ordination
failed to restrain the "carnality" of their natures, Apollonius
"would have us believe is not earthly but heavenly, absolute, and
of its own power by reason of the inseparable subjection of
churchmen to Christ as his legates". Salmasius stated explicitly
that the imposition of hands altered in no way the character of
a minister.

Salmasius denounced the methods of reasoning adopted by
Apollonius. "In logic he plays but a canvasse merchant",[1] as
was to be seen by the construction of his argument. "The church
of Christ is holy and spiritual: therefore are all her affairs, and
so chiefly her government. *Ergo*, the government and business
of the church which he calls church-dressings belong only to the
Saints or spiritual men, and ministers, that is because they by
special privilege of their vocation are sanctified and consecrated.
Ergo, these affairs belong not to the godly civil magistrate because
they were not sanctified to this work but are altogether unfit as
being but mean members of the church, worldly, whose power is
dispoticall, or Lordly, Architectonicall and corporal, earthly, not
heavenly, which can produce no spiritual effect or touch the
soul."

This summary of Apollonius' thesis was by no means accurate,
for it exaggerated the importance which was attributed in the *Jus
Majestatis* to the ministry and ignored the more significant
distinctions by which the ruler was made a servant of the church.
But Salmasius had seen that the theory of Apollonius was based
upon the right of the church to order its own polity because that
was spiritual. The subsequent argument of the *Grallae* therefore
was not really falsified by the logical form into which Salmasius
had cast the assumptions of his opponent. In attacking that
logical construction, Salmasius developed a thesis which undermined the claim to a divine right made not only by Apollonius but
also by Voetius and Triglandius. In doing so, he abandoned both

[1] *The Supreame Power etc.*, 10.

Scriptural Protestantism and Calvinist Scholasticism in favour of a humanistic rationalism.

The *Grallae* rested upon a preliminary enquiry into the nature of the church, of sanctity, of spirituality, and a comparison between the Apostolic and "modern" church. Its method was to destroy the jus divinum of the church rather than to justify the jus divinum of the ruler although it was asserted that the ruler had a power by divine right to regulate "modern outward affairs of the church".[1] In these early chapters, Salmasius' thought displayed a rational character strangely at variance with his later and traditional treatment of the ruler's claims.

Of the numerous definitions of the church, Salmasius accepted only two, and was careful to distinguish between them. The word "church" was used in the Scriptures to signify any meeting for any purpose and in any form, so that it was not properly defined as a mystical and internal union with Christ. In general, it described "the Assemblies of men gathered together for the publick worship of God, whether this Assembly be great or small......".[2] Accordingly the "form" of the church was "the externall union which these men have among themselves, when they meet to worship Christ, and to make profession of their faith". Salmasius did not explain the nature of this union nor the manner in which it was formed, problems with which he was little concerned so long as the church was regarded as an association. The peculiar acts of the church—"consisting in the preaching, reading, expounding, or any ways meditating in the word of God, in administering the Sacraments upon occasion; lastly in exercising the workes of charity among themselves......"—were the acts of an external union. The visible church was a society of men differing from other societies not in its constitution but in its purpose and practices. Distinct from the visible church, the word "church" signified especially "the congregation of all that have been, or shall be saved from the beginning to the end of the world", the form of which was "a true union with Christ by faith, being spiritual, mysticall and indissoluble". The gulf between these two conceptions of the church was the gulf between natural and supernatural, and between

---

[1] *The Supreame Power etc.*, 16.   [2] *Ib.* ch. II, p. 11.

human and divine. The glorious Scriptural epithets—"One, Catholick, Holy, Spiritual"—were peculiar to the invisible church alone, for the visible church was more commonly corrupted by human errors. The first and fundamental defect of Apollonius' theory was to apply to the visible church principles true only of the invisible church, and thus to fall into the Roman error of acknowledging no other church but the external, and no other "form" but outward profession and government. In particular, Apollonius' attack upon Vedelius broke down because he endowed "the whole furniture of the outward Ministery, which everyone knowes to be the externall and visible businesse of the visible church"[1] with the spiritual power of the mystical church.

It was, therefore, with the visible church that Salmasius was concerned, and with a church which was human and open to corruption. He refused to describe it uncritically as either holy or spiritual, until he had enquired into the meaning of sanctity and spirituality. It was not sufficient to argue that a "modern" church was constituted exactly like the Apostolic or had a direct and unbroken connection with it, to justify its sanctity.

Sanctity was a relative conception used of many different subjects, all varying in degrees of holiness. The standard by which Salmasius determined sanctity was "a perpetual and inherent perfection, and ordination for promoting God's worship and man's salvation".[2] Primarily it pointed to "the inward and perfect integrity of a thing, such as God eminently", and was transferred to the worship of God through the holy virtues, infused into men by the Holy Ghost. In this way men were holy because they were inseparably united to Christ by faith imparted by God Himself.

Next in order of holiness was God's Word, "in itself perfectly holy" since it was "uttered and written by the instinct and motion of the holy Ghost"; but the reception of the Word alone was not enough to make men holy: that was due to its conjunction with justifying faith. The "outward workes and meanes of worship" were only sanctified by the ordination of God for certain times and places, and were not in themselves holy: theirs was a relative

[1] *The Supreame Power etc.*, 13.   [2] *Ib.* 18–20.

sanctity dependent upon the Will of God. No act of, or conducing to, worship was holy unless God had so ordained. Moreover, not all the instruments of God were holy because He had used them for His Purpose. God did not bind Himself to sanctify those agents inwardly whom He called to a holy function, although their acts were possibly efficacious in producing faith despite their corrupt characters.

Holiness was a product of faith and of revelation, whereas Apollonius treated all things in divine worship as possessing a uniform and intrinsic sanctity. He put such a high mystery of dignity and perfection in the external means of worship that church discipline was elevated in sanctity above all worldly business, and the ministers were dignified by a vocation which gave to them alone the right to administer the forms of outward worship. Salmasius insisted that only such things as God had ordained were to be counted holy; "outward church-rites are not therefore to be held sacred, because of their order or reference to Religion and Worship".[1]

Salmasius had worked out a scale of "externall and relative sanctities", but he also distinguished holiness and spirituality.[2] Not everything in church matters was to be accounted spiritual, for in that case another Scotus would be needed to follow the trail of spirituality into all the trifles of its connections. Because, for instance, the communion was a holy begetting of faith and divinely consecrated, was the bread or the baker's boy spiritual? By this reasoning the "cuticula or epidermis of the fingers" was the most spiritual part of man as nearest to the communion substance. Salmasius argued that the instruments of God were not inevitably spiritual, but required three essential conditions: that they were ordained by God, for His worship and human salvation, and "done after a spirituall manner".

It was clear that the whole work of creation was not spiritual; but "Hope, Charity, but chiefly Faith, and its seed, God's word", which were the true means of promoting God's worship and salvation. The work of the Apostles was spiritual because their supernatural gifts were such that God "did speake, write and doe" through them; this spirituality existed only because of the

[1] *The Supreame Power etc.*, 30.　　　　　[2] *Ib.* ch. III.

spiritual gifts they possessed, gifts which had since passed from the earth. While it was true that anything ordained by God for human salvation was spiritual, it was not proper to conclude that everything subserving this "principall end" was itself spiritual. The degree of spirituality was only to be ascertained in the modern church by its operation "whereby we see more or less sparkles of spiritual light", in spiritual things or persons, by comparison with the less spiritual.

Spirituality was to be graded.[1] The Word was the most spiritual in virtue of its source, and since it promoted faith, faith itself was spiritual. Inferior to this was the spirituality of "Hope, Charity, Prayer and Confession", themselves the offshoots of faith. Inferior to all these spiritual powers were the external and visible means of "begetting faith and other vertues in us", such as study and exposition of the Scriptures, and the administration of the sacraments, in themselves serviceable instruments to gain salvation, but not spiritual, except in so far as they were instruments of God's Word and Faith, and ordered and employed in a spiritual way. Finally, and in the least degree of spirituality, were the parts of ecclesiastical government designed for the well-being of the church, or more properly for removing "the evil-being" arising from confusion and scandal. Salmasius here meant "the calling of Ministers, Discipline and appoynting of Lawes", not one of which was "absolutely required to the internal form of the Church". Therefore, these negative and external means of salvation possessed spirituality solely "as they do exactly answer the Rules of holy Scriptures, especially so long as they carry plainly the markes and Badges of the Holy Ghost".

Salmasius was prepared to recognise a certain sanctity and spirituality in the visible church, although strictly conditional upon the prescription of the New Testament and the spiritual method and end through which they were manifested. The presence of certain spiritual gifts, visible in their conduct, was his condition for the recognition of the ministers' and church's spirituality. Even in this limited sense, Salmasius had struck at the very faith of Apollonius and his colleagues, but he went further when he denied that the Apostolic Church could have

---

[1] *The Supreame Power etc.*, 39.

been imitated by later churches unless the Apostolic gifts had
been continued in the ministry. The church was no longer to be
viewed as spiritual and holy in all its forms, and accordingly
differentiated from secular materials or secular agents.

Salmasius[1] used the simplicity of the Apostolic church as a
standard of ecclesiastical purity, and by it the complex organisation of the Calvinist polity revealed a superfluity of human and
clerical contrivances. The modern church had not only permitted
specialisation but had also exalted a selected and consecrated
body of experts as the lawful administrators of the means of
salvation and also of every interest of ecclesiastical society. Thus,
the ministry claimed a mandate from God to rule the church,
a mandate granted because of the vocation of the ministry,
in which neither the body of the church nor the magistracy
shared.

Salmasius concentrated his attack upon two points in this
theory. First, he maintained that the evolution of the modern
church necessarily denied the intrinsic spirituality and sanctity
of its instruments. It had departed from the Apostolic vision of
a church founded upon a common service according to the variety
of individual gifts. God had chosen His own preachers and did
not limit Himself to those selected by the church; all endowed
with suitable gifts were divinely empowered to preach. In the
time of the Apostles the body of Christians was permitted to share
in the external business of the church according to their capacities
and "without the solemnity of outward calling", so that the most
sacred affairs of the church were debated and determined by that
body. "Nor was it held absurd by these great lights of the Church;
for the same to call and be called; to send and be sent; to help and
be helped."[2]

Salmasius denied that the Baptism and the Supper were to be
administered iure divino by those "specially sanctified".[3] Likewise he denounced the modes of discipline invented by the
modern church, transforming a brotherly and charitable duty of
all members of the Christian fraternity into the authoritarian
judicial office of overseers. The early form of discipline was verbal
reprehension and separation from sin, partly to avoid contagion,

---

[1] *The Supreame Power etc.*, ch. v.   [2] *Ib.* 15.   [3] *Ib.* 53.

partly to give the sinner occasion for repentance by the act of public separation. Sin was only to be expiated by prayer and repentance; the censures of the church were unnecessary human inventions for the sake of ministerial power.

The claim to a disciplinary power implied a legislative power. The Calvinist contention that there was no more power in the church than to make rules was set aside: "for because they prescribe to Christians under most grievous punishments, what they must doe or not doe,... who seeth not that these ordinances have the nature of Lawes".[1] There was no justification for any human law-making power in matters of salvation, since God spoke only in the "plaine termes" of the Scriptures. The only law-making power in church matters was in those indifferent matters which were not necessary for salvation, and were only regulated in the interests of order. But in that case, why was the ruler denied any share in this power? Apollonius had resorted to the principle that church laws were to be made by spiritual jurisdiction. "So that", Salmasius said, "necessarily some mystery of spirituality must lye hid in Church men, that the same Lawes of the same things (whether these things bee necessary or indifferent) they become spiritual, if they be given from spiritual; that is, churchmen but profane if given by Godly Magistrates."[2]

In the second place, Salmasius[3] denied that modern preachers were true legates of Christ to be accepted as if He himself was present. The most excellent means of begetting faith was the reading of the Scriptures, the more so since it was not subject to the will or command of any man. Such legates were limited to the Apostles alone, whose miraculous powers testified to the fact that God spoke in them. Their successors, however, were not granted the virtue, even if they received the form, of ordination, unless God had added the necessary gifts. Thus was the assumption of Apollonius destroyed, for as there was no exclusive spirituality in church business, neither was there any in churchmen. The church, indeed, had been trained by the Apostles in human and ordinary methods of government to meet the situation when their own gifts should be withdrawn. In this manner, the normal rules regulating ecclesiastical organisation were invented

---

[1] *The Supreame Power etc.*, 92.   [2] *Ib.* 95.   [3] *Ib.* ch. VI.

to preserve an orderly progress. The claim of Apollonius that vocation and consecration "imprints an indelible character not only on the body but on the soul as well" was the source of an exclusive pastoral right to govern the church and to exclude the laity, especially the ruler.

"Church dressing or furniture"[1] was not of any special sanctity by which it was to be regulated by some and not by all Christians. Its sanctity was that of Biblical study or prayer, either of which might be undertaken by any suitably gifted person. Moreover, all ecclesiastical functions were a matter of training and experience, like any mechanical trade. The modern selection of ministers was wholly human. Thus, Salmasius exposed the mystic circle[2] of ecclesiastical internals and internal externals in which no unconsecrated layman was allowed to tread, and which gave all church-government to the ministers.

In the *Grallae* there was little attempt to defend the right of the ruler to a share in church-government upon independent principles. The ruler was held to be a part of the divine order "for the preservation of natural society among men but chiefly to maintain the church of Christ entire here on earth".[3] He was not to be excluded from spiritual things unless, both as ruler and as secular man, he was in a state of nature "the property of which is to be blind in their minds, perverse in their wills, enemies of God and sons of wrath".[4] Nor was there any fundamental difference between the aims and instruments of the church and the ruler. The ruler's power was not "corporal" and "carnal" merely because it was commonly expressed through "rods, wracks, halters and swords",[5] for "they may have much spirituality joyned with them". Again, the "end and intention of the Agent"[6] were of great effect; the most carnal instruments of power "become spiritual in the Author, subject and end", so that a pious ruler had a claim to share in the government of the church. Finally, Salmasius insisted that the ruler's function was to co-ordinate the different parts of his state. For that purpose he had a "power in his own precincts subject to none",[7] a power of jurisdiction in which was implied a power of examining, judging

---

[1] *The Supreame Power etc.*, 128.   [2] *Ib.* 168.   [3] *Ib.*80.   [4] *Ib.* 170.
[5] *Ib.* 176.   [6] *Ib.* 177.   [7] *Ib.* 194.

and putting into execution. The "secular accident",[1] as Apollonius had called the ruler, in fact "sustains the ecclesiastical substance or else it would fall to the ground".

Salmasius exalted the ruler above the church, and placed a political above an ecclesiastical loyalty. The lay power was of a divine origin and form, however it was obtained;[2] the church was primarily a human institution and often lacked any divinity at all. Obedience to the ruler was absolute but to the ministers conditional. "For God hath appoynted the former to be his Embassadours and Vicars upon earth, and Gods in his name; under which Tittle hee gives them this power, that not onely every soule, but also for conscience, is bound to obey them, that is absolutely, not onely as they command justly, and lawfully, but as they command. Therefore he hath armed them with the sword, that they may force men. For if the civill Magistrate commands things, either just or indifferent, the subject is bound to obey for conscience. If hee commands what is unjust, the subject is not bound to performe but to submit either by suffering the punishment or by flight; but the obedience due to Church-Rulers is farre other; for they are not to bee obeyed absolutely, because they command, but conditionally, if they command lawfully." Therefore, he concluded[3] "that there is now nothing in the whole church-government not lawful to them (i.e. the magistrates) by divine right, both for matter of action, rule and care".

The significance of the *Grallae* was in its secular treatment of the church. Its attack was directed against the most important assumption of his opponent that the external church had a spiritual power to order its own affairs because these were spiritual. But in reducing the church to the condition of a society of men, without any particular divine right, Salmasius had also prepared the way for treating the state itself as a mere society of men equally devoid of divinity. The means he adopted to destroy the claims of the church were to be of equal force against the conception of divine right in any form.

---

[1] *The Supreame Power etc.*, 210.   [2] *Ib.* 104.   [3] *Ib.* 234.

§ II

THE CHURCH AS A HUMAN ASSOCIATION

A second critic of the Calvinist two-kingdom theory, whether in its French or Dutch or Scottish forms, was Louis Du Moulin, who made it his lifework, after his settlement in England, to expose the Calvinist theory of church and state as another variant of the ancient papal claim to dominate the state. Originally, his argument was an almost unqualified Erastianism, but his experience of Independency during the protectorate persuaded him that the congregational ideal of church-government was easily reconciled with the claims of the state. His principal objection to Calvinist theory was the Erastian fear of an independent ecclesiastical discipline exercised by a national church without any political supervision. He identified this discipline with an independent exercise of coercion and argued that in any one state there might be logically no other system of coercion save that of the ruler.

The more elaborate presentations of this thesis were published during his tenure of the Camden professorship of History at Oxford, under the Protectorate. The most learned work was the *Paraenesis ad aedificatores Imperii in Imperio*, which was followed by an English writing *Of the Right of Churches and the Magistrates' Power over them*. The argument was very similar. A third book, *Papa Ultrajectinus*, was published under a pseudonym to refute the *Politica Ecclesiastica* of Voetius. In this refutation, Du Moulin concentrated upon the nature of the ecclesiastical power which Voetius claimed for the church, and denied that it was either ecclesiastical or political power. The pope of Utrecht[1] differed from the pope of Rome first in that the real pope exercised a real power, even over the unwilling, whereas the Voetian pope had a power neither coercive nor truly ecclesiastical; and secondly because Roman theory demanded the subordination of the state to the church, while Voetius created a collateral system, both impracticable and illogical. The argument of the *Papa Ultrajectinus* rested upon principles laid down in the earlier works, and according to which the ecclesiastical jurisdiction outlined by Voetius was not only erroneous but also fictitious.

---

[1] *Papa [Ultrajectinus]*, chs. I, II. Cf. Duker, *Gisbertus Voetius*, III, 74–77.

Du Moulin's purpose was only to reinterpret the two-kingdom theory, recognising, indeed exalting, the divinity of the church, but distinguishing between the divine and the human. The solution of the problem of the relations of church and state was the logical formulation of the antithesis between the supernatural authority of the church and its human organisation. In consequence, he was not treading in the secular path of the *Grallae*, for he did admit the divine mission of the church and did not treat it merely as a human association. He recognised that the Kingdom of Christ was active on earth through a truly divine authority, but denied that the church in the Calvinist theory was to be identified with that Kingdom. The separation of the two kingdoms was not the separation of church and state; it was the separation of the spiritual and supernatural function from the human and natural association, which was properly of the same character as any other association of men. The Christian revelation did not include that which arose from the common rational nature of mankind, although both were rightly joined in the church among men. Therefore, the church as an association was not subordinate solely and directly to Christ, even though its function was never subject to political direction.

By the use of this distinction, Du Moulin[1] hoped "to make the right and power of private churches consistent and sociable with the magistrate's power over them, and so to sever by divine right the sacred function of Ministery from that of Magistracy as to make both their jurisdictions but one, and derive it from the sovereign power of the state, and this from the Lord Jesus Christ who hath given unto the Magistrate the sovereign power and authority for a sovereign end".

He[2] willingly admitted that the Scriptures mentioned two kingdoms but denied that both were visible and that Christ was called Head of the church in reference to the visible congregations of Christians. Christ's Kingdom was not a visible government of men; it was the kingdom of grace entered "by the door of utterance in the ministery", the weapons of which were not "carnal" but the Word of God, and directed "to the pulling

---

[1] R[*ight*] *of* C[*hurches*], Dedication.
[2] *Ib.* 66 *et seq.* Cf. *Papa*, ch. III.

down the strong holds of sin; not by tying a man with church-censures, but bringing into captivity his imagination to the obedience of Christ". The authority manifested in this Kingdom was the spirit of God "working in the heart by the Word preached or read", the "power that translateth from darkness to light". God had many instruments, and no governors, in this Kingdom, and as instruments the known part of their work was the least part of their ministry. The directing power in the church, there-fore, was the spirit of God, which used men often without know-ledge of their part, and which was itself beyond any human control.

In this Kingdom, the jurisdiction of the Word alone had a claim upon the Christian because the conscience was subject to Christ alone and to no man.[1] The ministers had no part in their jurisdiction save as its instruments by which grace in the Word spoke to and worked upon the conscience. The pastor discharged "the part of a messenger, and not the part of a judge in a court ......and such is the nature of the court of conscience, when it justifieth only where it knoweth itself clear and condemneth where it is conscious of its guiltinesse. But no pastour hath a particular knowledge of any persons evidence for heaven, but what he gathereth by outward signs; and so all acts of his, either of absolution or of condemnation, are meerly upon supposition, and no acts of a judge, and therefore no acts of a court." Thus, the tribunal of the conscience, to which the minister was no more than an usher, was the means by which the spirit of God judged men. This was the only jurisdiction sanctioned by Christ in His Kingdom, and therefore there was no system of human discipline imposing penalties upon Christians by an external authority. In so far as there was such a system of discipline, it was an external and human contrivance which was properly of the same nature as all human jurisdiction.

Du Moulin acknowledged the jurisdiction of the Word in the conscience but rejected the jurisdiction of the priest or minister in the church. "I do not quarrell against the spirituall jurisdiction over the inward man in the ministery; when a minister doth command from Christ, and the people yields obedience, being

[1] *R. of C.* 121; Paraen[esis], 108.

at once inlightened and convinced: all is done on both parts willingly and not by constraint: the weapons of that jurisdiction are not carnall, and yet very mighty; not by putting away by excommunication, but by pulling down the strong holds of sin, and bringing into captivity every thought to the obedience of Christ."[1] The essence of this spiritual jurisdiction was the conviction of the individual conscience through the working of the Spirit. It was the product of a voluntary submission and a genuine repentance, in which the ministry played a part only in so far as it was the vehicle of the divine grace.

The jurisdiction of the Word was to be distinguished from the external ecclesiastical jurisdiction of the Roman and Calvinist churches. The true ministerial power "is the noblest power and the greatest power in the universe, next to that of creating and redeeming the world; a power that the Son of God had and managed in this world: none have such warrant of authority as to be Ambassadours from Christ; none have such an errand: there is no type of obedience like to that of their commands. But still this ministeriall power, commands and authority, and the obedience due to them are not of the nature of the power and obedience observed in churches or magistrates judicatories."[2] The reasons which he gave for this distinction illustrate his conception of the church. First, ministers were only to communicate the Will of God whereas "church judicatories" enjoined their own will. Secondly, a church-member obeyed God and not the pastor. When the latter gave his own opinion, it was advice and not command; yet every church had need also of "a power of magistracy" which the church-members had to obey. Thirdly, church judicatories "require obedience and submission, without arguing or disputing the case, or having liberty either to yield to them, or to decline them if they list: But true pastorall power commandeth only understanding, free and wise men, that are able to judge......" Finally he argued that "the ecclesiasticall presbyteriall power, like that of the magistrate, requireth obedience to its lawes, ordinances and decrees, not because they are good, just and equitable, but because it so pleased the law-givers; for a man excommunicated never so unjustly is to submit

[1] R. of C. 54.   [2] R. of C. 148–151; Papa, ch. 1.

to the validity of the sentence, and not to the equity......: But the true ministeriall power requireth no obedience to its commands, but of such as are persuaded or convinced of the goodnesse, truth, and equity of the law and sentence."

In this spirit, Du Moulin interpreted the necessary acts of the church. The call[1] to the ministry was by the direct authority of God, and the church and the ruler had no power other than "publickly to declare their willingnesse and readinesse to accept of his ministery among them". In like manner,[2] the deposition of a minister was no more than a refusal to acknowledge, and a withdrawal from, a ministry unworthily exercised. Lastly,[3] the act of excommunication was an act of the divine spirit and not of the ministry, which was unable to apprehend the work of the Spirit.

Du Moulin had distinguished true ministerial power from the external ecclesiastical power, but he had yet to show that this last, necessary as it was for the welfare of the church, was nevertheless identical in character with the power of the state. Ecclesiastical jurisdiction was in his theory a part of civil jurisdiction, in as much as it issued in an external system of punishment and legislation. The church had properly speaking no power, no laws, and no definitive judgment; at the most it had authority, canons and the capacity to advise its members. The difference was that between the compulsory and a voluntary organisation of men.

According to Du Moulin,[4] power was exercised over men even against their will, and was expressed as a command to be followed by active or passive obedience. Authority claimed the voluntary obedience of minds which were persuaded and convinced, and by its exhortations directed them not by constraint but freely and voluntarily, not because of punishment but by fear of God and by strength of reason. These two methods were the only possible ways to obtain obedience—either by mere force or by a rational appeal, either by command or advice—and law without command was no more than advice influential only on the willing mind. Therefore, ecclesiastical jurisdiction was either command upon the unwilling or a rational appeal to the willing. If it was the

---

[1] R. of C. 134; Paraen. 166.   [2] R. of C. 141; Paraen. 169.
[3] R. of C. 144; Papa, ch. III.   [4] R. of C. 2 et seq.; Paraen. 5 et seq.

latter, it was not properly jurisdiction, if the former it was dependent upon the civil power since its decisions could be violated without any penalty. The only "co-ordinate" powers which Du Moulin recognised were, on the one hand, the internal power of divine origin revealed in nature or the Bible, and working upon the conscience to make the unwilling willing, and, on the other hand, the external power of the state based upon its power to punish the outward man, and alone able to make the unwilling man conform in his outward conduct. Church and state were not co-ordinate powers.

Nor had the church any independent power to legislate, because "the law is a rule of life and of moral actions, made and published by a legislator armed with a judicial power commanding things to be done, and forbidding things not to be done, under recompenses and penalties".[1] Canon law never had the form and sanction of law from ecclesiastical authority, since the church could only issue counsels, lacking any coercive power to translate them into laws. Its decrees were only to be obeyed if just and equitable, and in as much as the ministers were not infallible, the reasons for obeying had to be stated so that each man might judge of their justice and equity. The validity of law did not rest upon its justice, nor was obedience the consequence of approval. The division of law into civil and ecclesiastical was equally vain. There was no distinction in kind. The source of law, moreover, was political; and if law may be called ecclesiastical "because it handleth laws for the government of the church", there would be as many kinds of law as there were societies, whereas it was the nature of law to constitute one system uniting social activities despite distinctions based upon the subject-matter.

Du Moulin accepted the conclusion that the church had no definitive judgment. He distinguished[2] the private judgment of the individual which was the deliberate conviction which governed his actions, from the judgment of the ruler which appeared in the form of a command, and which was to be obeyed actively only when endorsed by private judgment. But the ruler's judgment was the chief means by which the public decision, endorsed by private judgment, was put into execution; for unless the ruler

[1] *R. of C.* 35. Cf. *Paraen.* ch. 3.   [2] *R. of C.* 45; *Paraen.* ch. 8.

was a mere executioner, the so-called definitive judgment of the ministers had no validity until both the ruler and private individuals were convinced of its agreement with the word of God. Pastoral judgment, however, was valuable. "The ministers of the Gospel have by their education, function and ministeriall duty, that publick judgement to declare either in churches or synods, what by the judgement of discretion they conceive to be the mind and ordinance of Christ; but this judgement inforceth and obligeth no man to assent to it except they also by their private judgement of discretion apprehend it to be such. So ought neither magistrates, nor the power of magistracy seated in churches, to command or enjoyn it as a law to be obeyed, or a doctrine to be believed, except apprehended by the judgement of discretion to be the mind or an ordinance of Christ."[1] Their authoritative judgment was that of experts, without powers of compulsion, and valid only for them that were persuaded and convinced.

The peculiar character of the church was determined by its function and not by its organisation in a human association. Christ alone was the Head of the church as the communion of saints and in virtue of His Power the church in that character was alone able to witness to His Teaching.[2] The work of salvation was a peculiar function, serving all men, even the ruler who ought to "stoup his will" to the Word.[3] But this functional authority was not able to institute and preserve the church as an association, which called for powers common to all associations and arising from the law of nature. Every society possessed a unique function and shared in common means of organisation.[4] To each society belonged the unique authority of its function; but that authority could not organise the society. In becoming a society, a power distinct from authority, i.e. a power over the unwilling distinct from the functional authority over the willing, had to be assumed. It was a power shared by all societies; it did not issue from the function and therefore was not unique. The feature of an association was a power of government by which the minority might be

---

[1] R. of C. 52.   [2] Ib. 92, 134.
[3] R. of C. 83, 148; Paraen. 15; Papa, ch. 1.
[4] R. of C. 30, 171, 217, 224; Paraen. 22, 37, 107.

held to the will of the majority. "For if a member of a society be obstinate and refractory, and will not be ruled but by coercion and compulsion and it be more than church-members as such can do, to reduce him by exhortation and good advice; then church-members must act also by a power of magistracy, either assumed or delegated; however it be, that power of magistracy is subordinate to the soveraign magistrate."[1]

Any member of a society was present in a dual capacity—as a member of a craft and as a member of an association—and possessed authority in the one capacity and power in the other, by which he could participate in the functional and in the collective activities of the society. "It is known that men do not sit and vote in Parliament as merchants, phisitians, silkmen or drapers, and that if there be new lawes to make, or old to alter, suppose about some manufacture, as clothworking, a member of Parliament being professour of that craft which is in agitation, is the most able to discourse upon that subject, and to state how the thing may be regulated; and this he doth as a professour of the craft about which the law is to be made: but when the thing to be debated is to be carried by vote, and receive the stamp of law, and of publick authority, then, I say, none of the members give their votes as professours of the art and science which they exercise in the Commonwealth, and which is debated in Parliament, no not if a member were a chief justice of England, but all sit and vote as men invested with a power of legislation, and at that time a physitian voteth not in the quality and capacity of a physitian, no not when lawes are made for physitians and apothecaries although when they are in debate, a physitian may discourse pertinently of physick, as a physitian and skilfull in his art."[2]

In another passage, Du Moulin distinguished the dual nature of the church as a body of church-members and as a society of men, and consequently the functional authority of the pastor as such and the power of the pastor as the chosen officer of a society. "A man being at once a member of a family, hall, city, Parliament, church doth not act alwaies according to the quality of his relation, function and place, publick or private; not acting as a physitian,

[1] *R. of C.* 225.   [2] *Ib.* 171.

father or husband but as a judge: and not as a church member, but as a free member of a society. Thus, a member of a colledge of physitians joyneth with his brethren in case of physick, as a physitian; but in making lawes, regulating the practise of physick, and the apothecaries entrenching upon the physitians, he doth not act as a physitian, but as a judge, and as a person invested with judiciall power from the state." "In short, ministers and people have many actings within the sphere of Christian duties, which are not proper to them as Christians and members of churches."[1]

The power of the church[2] was no different from that of other societies, the orders of which passed for laws to themselves if made by the major part. Even if Christ had prescribed the method and means of church government, they were acts of church-members only if done willingly and in obedience to God and not men, and were acts of members of a society if done by a majority decision requiring external obedience.

Nevertheless,[3] the independent rights of the church as a body of church-members were fictitious; for these rights were hardly to be exercised without a power of magistracy on the part of the church. The very acts of the ecclesiastical function were indirectly subject to the ruler, from whom the power of magistracy came, since the function required that power for its own fulfilment. But Du Moulin meant only that these acts were most efficiently ordered when joined with a power to bind the minority. He did not mean that the secular power might determine the function; "properly the magistrate is not head of the church, more then of other societies; for as the calling of a physitian, merchant, smith, seaman, so of a Christian, as Christian and church member, are not subordinate to the magistracy, but only under the notion of, and as they are members of families, societies, corporations and commonwealths: in all which magistracy is virtually and eminently resident; in regard that no society of men can be imagined to be governed either without a power delegate from the magistrate, or without assuming magistracy within it self".[4] In that sense, the ruler was the head of "a visible nationall church". It was his task to provide the church with the means to

---

[1] R. of C. 29. Cf. Paraen. 453–454.
[3] Ib. 226.
[2] R. of C. 220.
[4] Ib. 70.

realise its high purpose, to remove all hindrances, and to give a positive direction to human efforts to build the Kingdom of Christ. His power and final judgment were in the external organisation of the church. To the ministry alone belonged the sacred function and the spiritual jurisdiction of the word in the conscience.

The conclusion of Du Moulin's argument was the establishment of those rights of the church arising out of the conviction of every individual Christian conscience, and of those rights of government shared by any society within the state by virtue of political recognition. This conclusion[1] rested upon his fundamental distinction between the internal power of God in the conscience, giving rise to the pastoral function without jurisdiction, and the external power of the ruler, exercising jurisdiction but not function; for the relation of church and state was then transformed into simpler relation of the individual enlightened conscience and the imperative power.[2]

Du Moulin's general position is sufficiently clear. His was the argument of Erastus against excommunication save as a civil act derived from the ruler and, in wider points, of Grotius, to whom the function was something wholly apart from the power. Du Moulin favoured the legalistic theory of the state and the pietistic theory of the church. To the state was all coercive power since it was the one and only association endowed with power even over the unwilling. Its laws were commands universally applicable; its judgment definitive since there was no appeal from it save to the conscience governed by God.[3] The church, on the other hand, was a body of willing worshippers, admitting the authority of pastors in so far as the consciences of its members were convinced, and in itself having no power of binding any of its members apart from the power of the Word. The saints had no government but were held together by a common allegiance to Christ, whose spirit working in each conscience was the rule and bond of union. The church in this sense embodied the authority of Christ, and Du Moulin was a champion of its duty to worship and obey the Will of Christ. The function of the

---

[1] *Paraen.* 37.   [2] *Paraen.* 144 (misprinted 134).
[3] Cf. *Paraen.* 130, 135.

pastors was to open to the flocks the way of salvation, to lead the flock along that way, and to cherish the weak and chide the obstinate. In this sense, the ecclesiastical function was unique, and its authority extended to all human acts. But even Du Moulin admitted that the church could not exist without delays and obstructions to its work unless it also possessed a power to determine matters of common policy and to make those decisions binding upon all members, whether convinced or not. This power belonged to the church not as a body of Christians or church-members, among whom authority and obedience existed only in so far as the unwilling were made willing by the appeal to their conscience, but as a society of men, since every society possessed certain natural rights to frame and conduct its common interests. All associations were to be regarded in a twofold aspect; on the one hand as exercising a peculiar function, and, on the other hand, as exercising a common power of legislation and discipline. The peculiar function was not directly controlled by the ruler, but the common power of all associations was regulated by him whose specific function was power. Therefore, Du Moulin's ultimate position was that the power wielded by any association within the state over members of that state was derived from the ruler, who had as such acquired all force which henceforth could only be used with his consent. Power had belonged to man as man, being a unity not to be partitioned according to his various functions, and being the same whether used by the same man as a father, or a member of a college of physicians or as a member of a church. But this power or force belonging to every man as a human being had been invested in the ruler, whose very purpose was to regulate this power by the surrender of which men had become subjects. The state meant to Du Moulin two things. First, it existed by virtue of the surrender of all power, and not merely parts such as civil in contradistinction to ecclesiastical or medical, by all men who became subjects, and not merely by some men. Power, therefore, had one centre, the ruler, and one circumference, the state. Secondly, the state represented the generality of power but not the generality of functions. The multitude of functions in which subjects shared,[1] and in many of

[1] *Paraen.* 60.

which one and the same subject might share, were directed by that functional knowledge and authority which led reason and conscience to recognise it. It was the authority of the expert in relation to those consulting him, or the counsels of a body of experts freely and voluntarily accepting the consequences of principles recognised by all in relation to the diffusion of that knowledge among their own number. Such functions lacked all inherent power of government, although they had an authority over all who were convinced of their value and skill. In their functional capacities, these experts could neither bind themselves nor those whom they served. Such binding decisions could not be made by them as experts but as men, i.e. as members of an association; and this power to bind human wills to submit had been surrendered by all men in constituting the state. The power which alone made such decisions binding had belonged to men as men, and, therefore, was after the establishment of the state in that association which represented all men subject to it as men. Because the state was the supreme association in this sense, all other associations were necessarily subordinate.

Such a position was fortified in Du Moulin's argument by the particular purpose of the power vested in the ruler. If power was retained by different associations of entirely different membership, conflict might follow; much more certain was this danger if membership overlapped. Du Moulin foresaw chaos; for the power to bind members of different associations spelt corporate anarchy unless the use of those powers might be regulated, in which case differences in policy would cease to be a social danger. How could such powers be regulated so that there should be neither continual conflict nor the supremacy of some over others? How could each retain and use its own powers without destroying the loyalty of the same members? In other words, how could these powers be truly co-ordinate, binding the same members but not infringing the independent power of each association? Du Moulin held that such co-ordination was possible only if the co-ordinate powers were subordinate to a common power. The very act of co-ordination implied subordination. What co-ordinating power could there be, unless that supreme power containing all men and all their associations? "Among those that live under one sovraign power, and within the precincts of one jurisdiction",[1] there is so great a confusion of human relations, functions, and jurisdictions, that every action of a subject in some particular capacity involves not only his other capacities but his fellows also. It is impossible for the manifold social reactions of some individual or functional act to be regulated and co-ordinated in order to harmonise with these wider social relations in which all subjects in all their capacities are necessarily involved, "except they all are modified, ruled and directed by one supreme jurisdiction". On these grounds, his Erastian conclusion was inevitable. "Granting that the same persons are members of the Commonwealth, and of the Church, it is not possible to make these two jurisdictions co-ordinate, and yet subsist together in peace, love and amity: and without one disturbs the other, they must joyntly agree to have one power over them; or the law, injunction and commands of one, must be subordinate to the lawes of the other."[2]

The basis of this Erastian doctrine was Du Moulin's repeated denial[3] that there was any "medium" between the external jurisdiction of command and the internal jurisdiction of the Word working on the individual conscience through the admonitions of the pastors. There was no medium between power to compel obedience even of the unwilling and authority to win obedience of the willing. The only way in which a transgressor might "incurre any penalty, and thereby be deprived of life, liberty and goods"[4] was either because he had to bow to a truly coercive power or because he had willingly acquiesced in the verdict of his fellows. The only way in which he might be legally punished was for a breach of the law of the land; and therefore legal penalties could not be imposed for a breach of God's law unless that law had become part of the law of the land. The church, without the ruler's assent, could excommunicate no man without his own consent, which Du Moulin pointed out was not very likely. The church was not governed by church members in that capacity; for as Christians they were bound to act according to their conscience and to direct their conduct according to their

---

[1] R. of C. 22. Cf. *Paraen*, 76; *Papa*, ch. III.　　　[2] R. of C. 21.
[3] *Papa*, ch. I.　　　[4] R. of C. 8.

reason enlightened by divine grace.[1] So that motives were more important than works and therefore church-membership implied a supremely individualistic attitude. It was not obedience which counted but the motive underlying any action, while motives, themselves the fruit of the indwelling grace of God, were known to each church-member alone. Acts of church-membership could not be ordered, much less enforced, without the conscientious agreement of each member. Since human motives could not be affected save by persuasion and by appeal to the court of conscience seated in every man, and since right motives were all important in the Christian life, church members were unable to bind each other to a certain course of action. Du Moulin thought that the Christian obligation was individual examination of any proposal put forward in the church, and of individual judgment. Each church member was to guide his own activity in the church by what "he by his reason inlightened by the word conceiveth to be most good", and not by the number of his fellow-members. For this reason that the acts of church members could not be determined by a mere majority ruling, the church as such had no means of government. In the same way, no function as such constituted any government.

Government was the regulation of external action by the reason common to every man. It sprang from "a liberty and common prudence, that every rationall and free man maketh use of in ordering"[2] the affairs of any society. It employed the same "judgement, prudence and discretion"[3] in all its forms, and those qualities were a uniform standard by which men were governed, uniform because in every man, a standard because all societies of whatever kind necessarily founded government upon them. Government, therefore, was based upon that common reason which taught all men whatever their station or vocation that society depended upon order, and order upon the regulation of external action of all members according to the decision of the majority, whether that decision was right or wrong. The motives underlying the individual judgment were unknowable to fellow-members. Only the outside was seen, and a society of Christians

---

[1] R. of C. 217; Paraen. 145–153.
[2] R. of C. 28.   [3] Ib. 58.

in that respect could not be distinguished from a society of merchants. From the outside both were societies of men and the decisions which each took were decisions of men acting as rational beings. Since the order implicit in every society was framed according to the outward aspect of members as men, and not in accordance with internal and unknown motives, all government was of the same kind—an arbitrary device based upon reason. So that all associations possessed the same character and all were constituted in virtue of that power common to all as bodies of men, the actions of which were determined by a reason common to all men and to all their associations. Once it was realised that motives were beyond the sphere of government and could not be taken into account in the relations of the members of any association, those relations constituting government were based upon that which every member saw—the outward face of members which was only the aspect of men. All the actions of any association were no more than the regulation of the outward man. The essence of association was the binding nature of the decisions adopted which demanded an obedience apart from the rightness of the decision and apart from the convictions of the member. Such decisions and such obedience were possible only upon the minimum assumption that all members were men and as such recognised the need of such external regulations. So that all government was the government of men, and all associations were associations of men, in which motives were excluded and everything was determined in virtue of that reason common to all men, and therefore to the members of the association. The affairs of Christians, merchants, and citizens could only be determined if the reason which members had as men was invoked, and therefore as associations they used common rational principles uncoloured by their peculiar function. Therefore Du Moulin concluded that since all associations were of the same kind, all government of the same piece, all external obligation due to the same cause, that the government which was in the state, the widest association of men as men, must not only include all other government and all other associations, but must also be the one by which all other government and associations were regulated. Government ordered the relations of men as men according to the dictate of reason in men as men, and the greatest expression of that dictate was the state.

Du Moulin himself recognised that this Erastian argument was the primary constituent of his thought, but he also claimed that it was easily reconciled with the right of particular churches. Baxter, while not hostile to the man, was contemptuous of his theories. "The good Man", he declared, "meant rightly in the main but had not a head sufficiently accurate for such a Controversy, & so could not perceive that anything could be called properly Government which was no way coactive by Corporal Penalties."[1] Here was the problem. How could Du Moulin protect the right of churches to determine their own affairs if all government was derived from the ruler? How could those rights exist unless there was a medium between coercion and counsel; jurisdiction and function? Even if the state was alone possessed of force, was there not a capacity among the members of a church to govern themselves by agreement which involved no coercion at all?

It seems clear that Du Moulin's regard for the rights of churches was an afterthought, but his writing was so obscure and piecemeal that it is difficult to find a genuine consistency save on the basis of one interpretation. Congregational churches did not form a rival organisation to the state which could readily permit the small particular churches adequate freedom to govern themselves, even as many other small associations in the state were regulated by the state but only in very general terms. In this case, churches had rights merely because the state was not sufficiently interested to deny them, and because the churches were in fact too small to be dangerous. The very title of his chief English work thus becomes significant. *The Right of Churches* implicitly rejected the rights of one national church. Moreover, congregational churches had no means save the arm of the magistrate to bind a minority, since secession and the constitution of a new church were not easily denied upon their principles. The rule by persuasion was more important in each church and in the relations of churches than any rule by compulsion. Nevertheless, there were excommunications and other acts manifesting a power

---

[1] *Reliquiae Baxterianae*, III, 85.

more than the authority which Du Moulin would grant, and
which according to him could only be exercised by a delegation
of power from the ruler.

The rights of churches were little more than parochial, and
existed either because the ruler lent a positive aid or because he
was content to allow the church freedom to determine its own
domestic matters, though holding his power in reserve. In this
connection, two points in Du Moulin's argument are important.
First, he distinguished public external power, which the ruler
alone possessed, and private external power which was "that
freedome in every private man or society to act things and in
things, wherein the publick is little or nothing concerned, and no
way disturbed".[1] Obviously, this power was intended to be
subordinate to the ruler's. Secondly, Du Moulin recognised that
the churches had the same rights as other associations, rights
which were natural because consonant to reason. Such rights
were to meet in order to conduct business in an orderly way
through chosen officers and by means of majority decisions,
which were to be obeyed under penalties. It is by "the law of
nature and nations, that every assembly and convention of men
should have power to chuse, admit, and exclude members of
their own society, and to perform all acts conducing to their
subsistence".[2] Nor were members of a society to yield these
rights unless commanded otherwise by the positive law of God
or man. From this it is legitimate to conclude that Du Moulin
admitted a right of government so long as the ruler did not deny
it, but there is no explanation of how this natural right was
subordinate to the civil power. It is clear that the natural right
of self-government had no standing against the law of the ruler,
but even when this is accepted it is difficult to reconcile it with
Du Moulin's thesis that the ruler was "the fountain and spring
from whom all human jurisdictions, lawes and constitutions do
flow".[3] At one time, he seems to admit the source to be the
members themselves, and rising from below, at another time to
be the ruler and delegated by him to all societies. It may be that
Du Moulin assumed that the ruler was originally set up by those
same natural rights in order to be "the last to judge and command

---

[1] *R. of C.* 12.   [2] *Ib.* 27.   [3] *Ib.* 65.

anything, propounded and debated in whatever assembly of men ",[1] so that the subsequent exercise of those rights were to be regulated by that purpose. Again, the distinction between right and law may supply the answer: natural right being what is consonant to reason and law being what is enforced, right can only be effective in a framework of law, so that what arises from below becomes effective only by a power from above. However he reached it, his real position was that natural rights could not be the basis of any independent and inherent power of government in the smaller associations comprehended by the state. In so far as these associations were possessed of rights of government, and Du Moulin[2] never denied such rights and their necessity, they were rights arising from and realised within the state. In so far as the church was an association of men, it exercised a power in no way different from that of any other association and therefore was subordinate to the co-ordinating power of the supreme jurisdiction and definitive judgment of the ruler. When the church made laws, it was acting as any other association under the supreme legislator in the state, since its laws, like all laws, were obligatory not because of their justice, equality and honesty but solely because they were enforced, whereas Christians were concerned not with the power to enforce but with that justice, equality and honesty, of which they must be convinced before obeying.

Du Moulin denied that the church had rights of government independent of political supervision, but he did not deny a different class of rights—rights grounded on the law of God, sanctioned by the individual conscience, and in no way derived from the common rational nature of mankind. Christians who willingly obeyed God's law were possessed of certain divine positive rights whatever the attitude of the state, and a congregation of Christians had certain rights only because each member willingly recognised them. The essence of the divine positive rights was the conviction they carried in the conscience of each Christian, and a body of Christians acted together in virtue of these rights because each and every member was bound by his conscience alone. Whatever was done in common because each

[1] *R. of C.* 72.   [2] *Papa*, ch. III.

member was convinced that it was done according to the Word
of God arose from rights of conscience and not from rights of
government. Hence, a pastor had a right to gather a body of
converts, and Christians to choose their pastor, so that in common
they could exercise the rights of a congregation of Christians.
Of such right was the pastoral act to preach, to celebrate the
sacrament, and to comfort or reprehend members of the flock.
Likewise, the people owed due respect to the pastor and to the
convictions of each other. But the exercise of all these common
rights depended upon the actively willing consent of each member
of the congregation, none of whom was to be bound in the exercise
of these rights unless his conscience acknowledged their exercise
to be of God. The relations of Christians which constituted acts
of the congregation were wholly voluntary, and the church
possessed these rights because it was a voluntary communion.
The pastors had a power of ruling and governing only in the same
sense as philosophers had over the minds of their disciples, who
yielded a voluntary submission to the precepts of their teachers.
In this voluntary manner, pastors exercised a spiritual jurisdiction
over the inward man because the conscience of him subjected to
such jurisdiction willed him to submit. Indeed, "to see the mind
of Christ fulfilled"[1] by way of His Grace, and not by way of
natural reason, required always a voluntary action on the part of
each member of the congregation. Not only was such action
actively voluntary, it was also recurrently voluntary; that is to
say, no Christian could alienate his own individual responsibility.
Every act of church membership had to be self-imposed by each
individual member, and he could not evade that duty by delegating his own responsibility and judgment to the whole congregation, represented by the majority. He alone knew the message
of Grace spoken by his conscience and no other person ought to
dictate his conduct as a church member against his own conscience. The contractual idea was ruled out.

The church as a congregation of Christians had no proper
corporate character because it could not formulate decisions to
which members were committed. It was no more than a loosely-
knit group held together simply by the authority of the Word, the

[1] *R. of C.* 220.

interpretation of which was ultimately a matter for the individual
conscience. Its character was continuously and completely
voluntary. It did, however, possess certain negative characteristics as a group—it could refuse to admit the profane and
ignorant to membership; it could withdraw from the services of
an unworthy pastor; and it could separate from members leading
obviously non-Christian lives. But these acts were really acts of
individual members obeying the general Christian obligation
"not to have communion with such unfruitful workers of dark-
nesse".[1] None of these acts were positive in the sense of excluding
members from the sacraments as a discipline, or of expelling
members or of subjecting them to similar penalties. There was
no compulsion, only withdrawal. Positive acts of compulsion
were proper to the church only as an association of men.

The real issue was, as Baxter saw, the right of government by
associations upon the basis of agreement and without coercion.
But Baxter was a great admirer of Grotius, treating the *De Imperio
circa sacra* almost as a gospel, and was not any the less anxious to
assert the rights of the ruler in religious matters than Du Moulin,
although his Presbyterian ideal would not permit him to adopt
the legalistic arguments of the Frenchman. To Du Moulin, the
issue was not the rights and relations of associations and the state,
but the old controversy about the Two Kingdoms, and it was
because he wrote with that alone in mind that his theories seem
so illiberal. His was an attack upon the Dutch and Scottish
Calvinists, and a protest against theories which treated the state
as the instrument to create a monopoly for the church, to give
reality to its definitive judgment, and to prevent secession, without in turn giving to the state any effective supervision over the
use to which its powers of coercion were directed by the church.
If the church desired more from the state than the rights of any
association, if it desired more than civil protection for the exercise
of its own function; and if it would have the state deny similar
protection to other groups which claimed to be churches, Du
Moulin was justified in his protest. If the church demanded not
only freedom for its own members but a political prohibition of
like freedom for non-members and even non-Christians, the

---

[1] *R. of C.* 215.

assertion of the rights of the state by Du Moulin were not without
their value. When secession was to be denied, and with it the
right to exercise powers identical with those exercised by the body
from which a secession was made, the ultimate sanction was
political and the government of that body was also quasi-
compulsory, at least, in virtue of the threat, more or less remote,
of corporal penalties. For in these cases, the power of the association did not, in fact, spring from the active and willing consent
of members and thence upward to the government of the association, but downward from the government sanctioned by the
state. The point really raised by Du Moulin was the rights of
minorities and by what rights majorities could prevent the
minorities from constituting new associations, and his answer
was that such acts being virtually coercive, they must be valid
only by reason of the supreme political power which prevented
minorities from forming new societies. If, indeed, it was desirable
that minorities should be so prevented in order that the authority
of a function should be safeguarded within the organisation of
one association, there was some reason for Du Moulin's argument
that the constitution and conduct of the association should be
ultimately under political supervision, the more so since it was
for the state to co-ordinate the powers of the many associations
within it. Since he accepted with his opponents the necessity that
the true churches only should be admitted by the ruler, he could
no more than they recognise religious toleration, and he could
more consistently than they deny the rights of minorities. His
theory was necessarily no more illiberal than that of the Calvinists,
and can only be understood in opposition to it. This, it is true,
merely means that both theories were partial truths which might
more readily be reconciled in practice with goodwill, than in
theory with a logical insistence upon uncompromising principle.
So long as it was generally held that the state ought to establish
the true church, the Calvinist two-kingdom theory was open to
the attacks of increasingly secular theories, which (despite their
own constructive weakness) served to show how unreal was the
Calvinist solution. No theory of church and state constructed
upon that axiom of Scriptural Protestantism was logically consistent and equitable. The increasingly secular conception of the

state and spiritual conception of the church, notable among later
Calvinist and Erastian theorists, marked the new stage in which
the church was to be treated in theory as a voluntary society. In
this development the contribution of Erastianism was of as much
value as that of Calvinism, and it was only when the two-kingdom
theory was abandoned and Calvinist claims modified that Erastianism lost its inspiration and value. In the seventeenth century,
Erastian speculation was by no means lacking in social significance,
however inequitable and illiberal the practice of statesmen may
have been.

§ III

CONSTANS

These Dutch controversies continued to the end of the century
in an increasingly secular and sceptical atmosphere. The Calvinist church was on the defensive, while its critics were advocates
of absolutism without any pretence of defending the rights of
the godly prince. The age of Spinoza had little respect for
Calvinist theories, and treated the organised church as a part of
the state and its officers as civil servants.

The modest book of Constans[1] was notable only as an example
of these absolutist and secular theories, in which the contract and
natural rights were used to destroy any power other than that of
the ruler. Constans marked the transition from the theological
to the rational controversies, grounded upon principles wholly
antagonistic to Calvinist tradition. He examined the rights of
the church according to principles of an independent study of
politics based wholly upon the rational nature of man, and
regarding religion as little more than theological reasoning.

The pseudonym has been thought to conceal the identity of
four different writers. Spinoza denied that he was the author,
and Thomasius'[2] belief that Louis du Moulin was the real author
seems to be wholly conjectural. A third writer was a free-
thinking doctor of Amsterdam, Louis Meyer,[3] to whom the *De*

---

[1] *De Jure Ecclesiasticorum, Liber Singularis*, Alethopoli, 1665.

[2] *Historia Contentionis inter imperium et sacerdotium*, Halle, 1722, 418.

[3] Cf. A. Wolf, *Correspondence of Spinoza*, 50; and *The Oldest Biography of Spinoza*, 88.

Jure Ecclesiasticorum was attributed by Colerus, the biographer of Spinoza. Finally, van der Hooft was suspected to have written it in order to discredit the Dutch clergy, the strong supporters of the House of Orange against De Witt.

The argument of the *De Jure* was both simple and straightforward. It began by distinguishing between internal and external religion, meaning by the first that inward communion of the soul with God, of which no man had knowledge and which was beyond human regulation; and by the second, the external and social worship in assemblies organised according to certain rules. This external religion depended upon the favour of the ruler, because it was his responsibility to give to it his peculiar sanction, but the normal conduct of the church's organisation was in the hands of trained administrators—the clergy. But no authority was granted to them in the personal and inward religious exercises or beliefs. The ministers of the church had no authority except that of greater knowledge and probity, which was no more than the authority which all experts possessed. Whatever was decided and promulgated by their authority was no more than advice, the truth of which was to be judged by all who listened to their exposition, for the ministers had no power to enforce their decisions. Indeed, the right to teach religious doctrines was a privilege granted to those who held their office in the name of the ruler and by his authority, in the same way as all public offices were held. To teach without this public authorisation was an act of a private and personal authority which had been surrendered by every member of the state.

To Constans, the church existed in virtue of its civil establishment, and no member of the state had any power to act in religious matters contrary to the policy of the ruler. To preach without his consent was to withdraw from him that power which every member of the state had committed to him. The ministers were those individuals to whom the civil power granted the right to preach publicly.

This conception of the church and its ministers was the application of the general proposition laid down by Constans that the ruler was the source of all power in the state, and consequently that the citizens had no power which was not derived from that source. If that proposition was proved, it was only necessary to show that ecclesiastics were in no way exempt from this obligation in order to prove that they, like all citizens, owed their authority to the state.

To prove that general proposition,[1] Constans examined the constitution of the civil state out of the natural state. God created all men so that none was subject to another; all were born equal, not in their powers, but in being possessed of that power necessary for self-protection and of the right to use so much as each thought necessary for that purpose. Freedom was defined as that condition in which each exercised his own power without subjection to another; and equality was the relation between men who were free in that sense. This natural right was abused by the stronger to deprive others of their right and to subject them.

Apart from this unwilling deprivation of natural right by a brute force presumably exceeding that amount which was necessary for self-protection, there was another way by which natural right ceased. By agreement, men surrendered their particular natural rights in order to escape the disadvantages and evils of the natural state, and from the hope of a better state. Natural right was not inalienable nor were men bound to use it. God had given to man not only that right and power to protect himself, but also reason by which he could determine the use of that right. Therefore, men resolved to change their natural state were justified in meeting together in order to agree to transfer their particular rights either to all indivisibly, or to some selected from them or to one. After this agreement, there followed the actual transference of natural right by the promise of each and all not to use that right against the constituted ruler but to commit the use of that right to the ruler alone.

Whenever this right was committed to all indivisibly or to some who were their equals, this double convention was necessary; first, for the two parties to meet and covenant; secondly, for the transference itself. But Constans did not insist upon this order, provided that the procedure was in two separate stages. What was necessary was some convention of society, tacit at least, by which the many might govern the state without those divisions which

---

[1] *De Jure*, Tit. II.

otherwise would constitute separate states to the disruption of the original state.

To all states, however constituted, there was the same right to demand from their members the surrender of so much natural right as was necessary for the protection of the civil corpus, and, indeed, the members of the state formed one corpus for that protection; so that the surrender of their natural right was accepted by each. Moreover, Constans insisted that it was for the ruler to judge of the amount to be surrendered, since the members had agreed not to govern this civil corpus by their own singular wills but that it was to be governed by the will of the ruler. It was contrary to the common will of those constituting the state for it to be governed by the judgment of each, since those contracting did not transfer their natural right to each other separately but to all collectively or to some or to one. The state meant that each member had ceased to desire to exercise his natural right according to his own will and judgment; for he desired to surrender as much as was for the advantage and utility of the common body. Constans identified unwillingness and powerlessness to exercise the natural right. He also argued that although faculties of the mind could not be transferred to another person, yet members of the state had agreed not to be governed by their own judgment or will, but by those of the ruler.

No conditions were lawfully imposed on the transference of natural right to the ruler, since anyone making such conditions violated that equal surrender, agreement upon which principle was itself the basis of that society preceding the actual surrender. Therefore, the fact of such conditions set those making them outside that body of men agreeing to surrender their rights. Moreover, such conditions implied that those making them were acting and would act according to their private utility instead of the common utility. Even if any conditions were made it was for the ruler to interpret them lest they should conflict with the common interest. This was consistent with the principle laid down by Constans that in entering the civil state each member had abandoned the intention and means of acting according to his own judgment and will.

This analysis of the origin of civil society Constans admitted to be a rational construction to justify the right as distinct from the fact of the ruler's power in those states, the historical origins of which were unknown. To him the proof of the transfer of rights to the ruler was the fact that the state was continued by the entry of new members who would not have been allowed to enjoy the advantages of civil society unless they had surrendered their natural right. He met the argument that there was no manifest transference of right by claiming that the state did not cease when its original members and rulers had died, but had been originally constituted because of the multitude of advantages which time would bring and which alone compensated for the original surrender of natural right. The purpose of the original contractors was to be realised only by their descendants, and that implied the continuity of the state upon the original foundation. The actual rather than the formal acceptance of the obligations of citizenship was the more important, and in so far as any one was a citizen he had accepted obligations which involved the surrender of his natural right.

The surrender of natural right to the ruler alone meant that all civil inequality was the result of his institution;[1] for all his subjects were equal in their relation to him as the ruler, and unequal only because he had given to some certain privileges which were not given to others. Subjects were not unequal among themselves nor subordinate to some except by the authority of the ruler. No subject had claim to a position of superiority which was not granted by the ruler; for in the civil state there was no perpetuation of those voluntary agreements by which inequalities were possible in the natural state. After the civil state was constituted, no man was free to agree to any other system of inequality and authority; he had surrendered this freedom by entering the state.

Constans argued that civil inequality was the consequence of power and rested upon the control of the bodies of men by bodily punishment. Those who could coerce—the ruler and his delegates —were the superiors. The superiority of ecclesiastics was just as much a matter of power over the body and was identical with the power of the ruler.[2] External religion was ordered by the deter-

---

[1] *De Jure*, 38. [2] *Ib.* 55.

mination of bodily actions, and therefore by the regulation of the rights and powers of men; for, it was concerned with external actions and behaviour alone. The power of ecclesiastics was the same as any other power in the state by which the bodies of the subjects were controlled. Since there was no other source of such power but the ruler, Constans concluded that ecclesiastical power was granted by the civil power to be exercised by its delegates— the ministers—for a certain purpose—the regulation of the external religious conduct of its subjects.

The second half [1] of the *De Jure* was designed to meet the objection that there was some other source of ecclesiastical power. In turn, Constans denied that divine law, whether of revelation or of reason, and human custom had granted a power to the church independently of the ruler. So that in Constans the natural law theory in its absolutist form was used to reduce the church to the status of a part of civil society.

[1] Tit. v–Tit. xii.

CONCLUSION

THE two controversies, begun by Uytenbogaert and Vedelius, and waged more or less bitterly by a number and variety of thinkers, were virtually discussions of the Calvinist two-kingdom theory. To the orthodox party, controversy meant a far deeper analysis of the essential differences between the two kingdoms and of the relation which governed them. The doctrine of collegialism indicated the necessity and capacity for development out of the earlier and unsatisfactory theory of the Contra-Remonstrants (in itself a clericalist advance upon the Genevan establishment). The Calvinists did not agree even among themselves upon the character of the two-kingdom theory, and each school had its variants. The Calvinist two-kingdom theory was not one, generally accepted, consistent, logical, and derived from Calvin's teaching alone; but was a changing and evolving theory, dependent upon circumstances, and of very different forms.

It was equally true of the critics of Calvinism that the two kingdoms constituted the core of their theories which largely depended upon the validity of their criticisms of the Calvinist versions. In some cases there was a religious and theological character which seemed of the original Calvinist stock: Uytenbogaert, Episcopius and, in some ways, Du Moulin developed theories which were not fundamentally different from the orthodox. In other cases, there was a humanistic character tempered by a religious influence which later passed into straightforward secularism: Grotius and Vossius were firm believers in a revealed religion and religious order, which distinguished both writers from Constans and Spinoza, whose secularism culminated in absolutism. Even in these latter, the two kingdoms were recognised in a simple form.

The two-kingdom theories were therefore, accepted by all, and in their Calvinist forms by nearly all. It is true that the consequences were in some cases rejected by Calvinists and the theory itself even rejected as contrary to Calvinist teaching. But it was by no means clear what was the Calvinist theory, while behind all the theorists was an acute consciousness of the importance of its varied principles. The elements in all these two-kingdom theories were of Calvinist inspiration and generally acceptable to the orthodox convictions; it was the patterns into which these similar materials were cast which produced two-kingdom theories as a whole incompatible with the expectations of the Calvinist church. Such patterns were moulded by the high-state or high-church sympathies of the theorists, and the Calvinist legacy was broad enough to include both. These controversies, therefore, are most easily understood in their relation to the development of the Calvinist theories of the two kingdoms, since all of them not only contributed to that development but were of the same piece and dominated directly or indirectly by Calvinist principles. Together, these controversies reveal the varied forms of Calvinist thought and the difficulties and misunderstandings which arise from treating the Calvinist two-kingdom theory as if one and indivisible.

All these theories showed in common the belief in Scriptural revelation but not all were influenced in the same way. It was in consequence of this faith that the two-kingdom theory was so generally acceptable, for the conviction that there was only one true church and that it alone was the Kingdom of Christ was the justification of the two-kingdom theory. When the belief in the true church ceased to be generally held, the two-kingdom theory, and with it Calvinist argument, lost its significance. The growth of the principle of toleration undermined the condition of the theory and demanded a new theory in which the rights of churches as associations were guaranteed, instead of the prerogatives of that kingdom which was not of this world. The two-kingdom theory rested upon the existence in any territorial unity of two and only two organisations of life here and life hereafter. Toleration denied such an absolute revelation and forced Calvinism to modify its theories of the relation of church and state. Before the close of the seventeenth century, Calvinist two-kingdom theories were obsolete, and in the Netherlands the work of Episcopius had laid in the first half of the century the foundations of a new theory which recognised the rights of churches and not of the church alone. In consequence, the relations of churches and state were determined according to principles vastly different from the Calvinist theory of church and state, since its essential principles were no longer valid. Calvinist theory was peculiar to the period of the Reformation and Protestantism before toleration was admitted, and the two-kingdom theories were products of that period.

Scriptural revelation also inspired the general belief in one community united both for the worship of God and for the government of men. The intimate connection between religion and human life demanded the dedication of all human organisation to the divine order. In this, Calvinism was in harmony with the Renaissance ideal of a self-sufficient and autonomous realm which was the political ideal for two centuries. It is true that Calvinist theory held a religious conception of this ideal and believed in a dual administration, but the ideal of one society dominated the two-kingdom theory until collegialism limited the state to civil matters alone. This ideal of one society was never in practice true of the Netherlands: its economic, political and constitutional differences were too acute. But the ideal inspired not only the church but also the states, and it was the source of the difficult relations between the two orders. The humanistic rulers felt bound to limit the church's aspirations on behalf of the large numbers hostile to rigid Calvinism, while the orthodox rulers were determined to prevent theocracy and to check the rise of clericalism. The church, for its part, could only preserve its faith by dominating the state. Such problems found reflection in current controversy, and the inconsistencies in Contra-Remonstrant theory arose from this fundamental belief in the Holy Community or Christian society, which was the Calvinist counterpart of the ideal of the imperial kingdom of the Renaissance rulers. The ideal implied some degree of co-operation and correlation between the two administrations, without which there could be no genuine unity. Collegialism alone denied the necessity of some harmony between the two functions of society since it had abandoned the ideal of one community. The two-kingdom theory expounded by the Contra-Remonstrants was formulated in accordance with the fundamental belief in the one Christian society. In large measure, the modifications introduced by

Uytenbogaert and later by Vedelius were due to their emphasis upon the unity at the expense of the dual administration of society. It was only in the theory of Constans and Spinoza that the Christian humanism of Vossius and Grotius, to whom the unity of society was of divine command, disappeared in a purely secular theory. Even in Salmasius the unity of society was a religious ideal. In general therefore orthodox Calvinism and humanistic thought in the Netherlands agreed upon the ideal of one community harmonising the revelation of God and the organisation of men. Episcopius was forced to modify that ideal, the collegialists to deny it, and Du Moulin to adapt it. Collegialism alone swept it away in favour of an unlimited two-kingdom theory, but in doing so removed the only justification for the establishment of the Calvinist church.

Apart from its exposition in collegialism, the two-kingdom theory involved a theory of adjustment between the two kingdoms, and such a theory depended upon the definition of the state, its function and power, and the definition of the true church and its mission. The connection presupposed between them could only be workable provided that the nature of each was so defined that each could interlock with the other without damage to either. The nature of both was to remain distinct and unique, although both were organised over the same area and included the same persons. Both worked in different ways for the same end, and, moreover, were to work together. Such conditions imposed a nicety of adjustment which was only possible when each respected the province of the other. The practical problem was one of co-ordination when there was no superior authority with the function of co-ordinating. The theoretical problem was ostensibly one of definition, but so great was the agreement upon the actual definitions that the problem was really the meaning attached to words and the logic of argument. The only logical form of the Dutch Calvinist two-kingdom theory was collegialism and its logic destroyed the Calvinist heritage. Consciously or unconsciously Dutch Calvinism was marred by equivocation—none of its apologists were prepared to acknowledge the fundamental impulses underlying their theoretical constructions. None of them was honest enough to admit that for them the two-kingdom

theory was legitimate only if the ruler endorsed the will of the
ministers. Formally denied but in fact the basis of argument, they
were all entangled in the task of masking this inconsistency of
theory and this discrepancy of word and meaning. Bound to their
Calvinist heritage, yet they would not be bound by it and chose
the meaner path of pretending to fidelity while deviating from
the principles they had accepted. They denied themselves all
vestige of sovereignty but sought to dominate the sovereign: thus
trying to make the most of both kingdoms they showed their
selfishness and ambition. Even collegialism was not an unequivocal doctrine: it taught in effect that the church was free of the
ruler but the Christian ruler was bound to serve the church. It
set aside political interference as a tyranny but demanded political
aid to render its own tyranny more effective. These results were,
indeed, natural: on the one hand because the ideal of Calvinism
remained an inspiration even in the Dutch church, and the help
of the ruler if used according to the discretion of the church was
not to be despised; on the other because the church would be in
fact limited in its development if these theories were in operation.
But though natural to men, this disingenuousness was not proper
in the legates of Christ.

Despite this Jesuitical reasoning, the Calvinist thinkers did not
differ radically in their conception of the state from the more
Erastian theorists. Both sides defined the state in terms of
sovereignty, and not according to the origin of the state or the
seat of sovereignty. It was generally accepted that there was some
ruler, whether a person or a collective body, but not being interested in the problems of political organisation as such no
thinker attempted to analyse the relation between the people and
the ruler. It was admitted that the ruler's power was in certain
polities bounded by his contract with the people, but usually the
organisation as distinct from the abstract nature of sovereignty
was neglected. Triglandius alone touched upon the origins of the
state but he only summarised current thought.

The nature of sovereignty was not in dispute. Whether it was
defined as the imperium, the architectonic or supreme power,
the meaning was the same and the common characteristic was a
superiority of power over all parts of the state in virtue of which

the state existed as a whole. The necessity of some such political supremacy was recognised as essential to the state, and was interpreted as the unifying agency of one will capable of adjusting the organisation of the state according to its own discretion. Sovereignty was the superiority of this will over all other wills so that no part might act independently to the detriment of the whole. It was the means of organisation. All these thinkers believed in law and order and disliked political chaos and constitutional conflict. To achieve these objects of all government, they accepted the superiority of some will which was supreme within its sphere because the nature of political life required some body entrusted with that discretion necessary for political decisions. This supremacy only existed when there was no human superior, and sovereignty was that power in political society which was not subject to any human will.

Sovereignty was more than a supreme will; it was the supreme or highest or architectonic power. The distinction between power and authority and the emphasis upon force was a recognition of the importance of coercion in the organisation of the state. Unless might was to be right and unless force was to govern human relations entirely, there must be a supreme will charged with the power to coerce. All force in the state must be concentrated at an official focus and used according to the discretion of the ruler. In the interests of law and order, compulsion must not be in the hands of the subjects but the peculiar prerogative of the ruler, when it became the instrument of legal action. Political society rested upon force but could only exist and progress when force was organised and used according to a known will. The compulsion which underlay the state was morally justified only when it was a public and official responsibility for the welfare of the state. To the Calvinist, the essential feature of the state was the divine disposition of coercion by which the organ of sovereignty became the instrument of God's Will. Throughout the state and in all its forms and actions there was manifested this supremacy of force which was an attribute of the office of the ruler and necessary to its existence. The function of the ruler was to compel; the nature of the state was to organise under one will all the force at the disposal of the individual parts. That supreme will was necessarily free from human control, since it was God's Will that all men should be subject to His lieutenant on earth. The Dutch Calvinists had no doctrine of constitutional limitations. The state being the organisation of force, sovereignty being the complete use of that force, and the will of the sovereign being supreme under God in all political matters, the Dutch Calvinists accepted that will as the basis of political society.

The same idea was present in Erastian theories. The distinction between power and authority was not artificial or vain, but an attempt to differentiate the two ways in which the will might be subordinated to the will of another in accordance with the moral order. Power was authority with the sanction of force and since compulsion had to be morally justified, i.e. shown to be the consequence of allegiance, it was regarded as a monopoly of one will in the interest of the whole political society. Power was sovereignty and of right belonged to the ruler alone: it existed, where the ruler's will was supreme. Compulsion by any other body was mere force and unjust, without any relation to morality, and therefore a usurpation. Authority, by contra-distinction, was a willing and spontaneous subordination of one will to another. It was gained by conviction and persuasion, and was a voluntary relation of a somewhat transient character. Authority was the attribute of any function, whereas power was the right use of force by the one uncontrolled will in the state. Therefore, no part of the state could use any form of compulsion without the ruler's assent—all coercion flowed from him. Salmasius alone held that the ruler's power was not merely physical force but capable of influencing the minds of his subjects, but even he admitted that force was the characteristic distinguishing the ruler's power and the expert's authority.

This supreme power was also the architectonic: its monopoly of force was given for the purpose of co-ordinating the different functional groups in the state, of keeping each to the limits of its own function and to see that each performed its legitimate function properly. It was a political power to adjust the relations of the functions to themselves and to the state and not a power to undertake the function itself. Authority was peculiar to a specific function and limited to that function; the architectonic power alone ranged over all functions and linked them in an associated body. The means of such association was the law, and for that reason there was in any state only one system of law. In no state could there be more than one system because law was the decision of the sovereign ratified by his power. The sovereign was the source of all positive human law since his was that compulsion which law embodied. The functional bodies could regulate their activities by rules agreed upon after common deliberation, but there was no right to force men to observe these rules except in virtue of a power delegated by the sovereign. Law was a matter of command which had to be obeyed. The sovereign as the final directive will in the regulation of public order had the ultimate judgment which was necessarily independent of the judgment of any other body in the state.

The supreme and architectonic power was not absolute or a mere tyranny where the ruler's will was arbitrary and beyond the law. To the Calvinists, the divine law determined the office of the ruler. To the high-state theorists, both divine and natural law limited the right to command, and when there was no right to command, the duty of obedience ceased. The ruler could not undertake any function other than his own—to govern the public organisation of political society. His sphere was limited to that area in which compulsion was possible—to the area of external action. His power operated through law and was justified by the enforcement of law. The Calvinists, and particularly Voetius, insisted that the ruler was not limited to the public order alone but could interfere in private matters. Private churches were not free from that regulation of sovereignty which was rightly applicable to the public church. The more the Calvinists denied the action of the sovereign in ecclesiastical matters, the more they tended to exalt the activity of the sovereign in civil matters, as if by compensation. But these limitations upon sovereignty were in practice dependent upon the sense of justice which governed the ruler's will. His power must not be defied even if it was abused, and the subject must submit to any punishment for disobedience, however justified he might be by divine law to disobey. No man might resist: he must rely upon his gifts of persuasion to convince the ruler of the error of his ways.

Although there was a general agreement upon the nature of sovereignty, there were divergent conceptions of its purpose because of different estimations of the place of the state in human life. The Calvinists themselves were divided into those who exalted the state as the instrument of God in order to secure religious orthodoxy and who regarded the state as a moral agency to compel external conformity to the Calvinist ideal, and those who treated the state as the means of realising a civil and political good. Their opponents were equally divided into those whose liberal and Christian humanism endued the state with a moral character as the means of human progress, and those whose thought centred around the natural law alone and whose secular theory left the state as the highest human association. There was a fundamental difference between each ideal of the state and this determined the purpose of sovereignty in the life of the organised community.

The conception of the church, of the nature of its function and the authority at its disposal varied considerably, but there was much greater divergence between the later than the earlier controversialists. The Contra-Remonstrants and the Arminians were in agreement upon the theological conception of the church. Erastians like Grotius and Du Moulin qualified but did not deny its essential form. Collegialism introduced a new conception and Salmasius was not slow to reply by an equally radical thesis which found its logical conclusion in the secular theory of Constans.

The theological conception rested upon the authority of Scriptural revelation. The character of the church and its function were indicated precisely in the Bible, and the church had no power of itself to alter what God Himself had prescribed. Moreover, apart from the forms, the church was not the true church in which Christ ruled unless His Spirit was present in the church and governed its activity. The church was the community organised for the worship of God according to the methods ordained by God and provided by Christ. It included all who accepted the articles of faith and made confession of their membership. It was the means by which the grace of God might be preserved and by which all believers might participate in the spirit of Christ. The church in its perfect form was organised to facilitate the proper performance of the sacred function of the ministers, who, as the legates of Christ, were the means by which His Spirit continued the work of salvation in the preaching of the word, in the sacraments and in the discipline by which the gates of heaven were opened or shut. That sacred function was of the ministry alone because to it was communicated Christ's Spirit. Thus, the church was a community organised to worship God through the function of the ministry and was ruled by Christ whom the ministers served. The church was a divine body because its human organisation was only that revealed by Christ as necessary to the communication of His Spirit to the faithful and was without that human discretion which other communities possessed. It had no inherent capacity to deviate from the absolute form imposed by Christ, nor to use any human power to fulfil His purpose. The divine charter of the church given in the Bible defined its activities and forbade any independent action upon human initiative. God's law was sufficient and absolute, and in so far as the church followed its own will it ceased to be the true church. The conviction that the order of the church was immutable removed the necessity of providing any authority to reorganise or adapt its constitution. The only authority in the church was Christ's and that spiritual power with which He endowed His ministers. That spiritual power wrought upon the souls of men to convert them to the true way, to hold them in the faith, and to cast them out of the church if persistent sinners against Christ's Law, but the ministers' power extended no further than to apply that law and do what it ordained. The discipline of the church, if in accord with the Will of Christ, was the working of His spirit upon the soul, and if not, it was no more than the persuasion of men. In either case it was not coercion because its object was the quickening of the soul and not the forced obedience of the body. Spiritual penalties were of different character from corporal, and neither to the church nor to the minister belonged that force which was proper to the ruler alone. So that the church had no imperium, no law-making power, and no jurisdiction save spiritual censure. The ministers were the servants of Christ and the church, to declare His Law and to utter His Sentence against sinners. They were the interpreters of that Law so far as the sacred function was concerned, but they had no judgment independent of Christ. Theirs was the ultimate judgment in the visible church in all matters touching that Law and defined by it, but only in so far as they expressed the judgment of Christ.

The qualifications made by Junius and Walaeus limited the independent activity of the church and the independent office of the ministry to the fulfilment of Christ's Law and only so far as the Spirit of Christ was in the church. The use God made of normal human means in the ordering of the ecclesiastical community, emphasised by Acronius, was embodied in His Law. Uytenbogaert was as convinced as his opponents that the ministry had its peculiar function and that the Law of God governed the activity of the church, but he denied that either the church or the ministry in a Christian community were by divine right solely responsible to God for the preservation of the true church and the essence of the Christian religion. He agreed that the church had no sovereignty and none of its prerogatives. Vedelius distinguished in the church the divine and spiritual function, and the ecclesiastical forms: in the first the ministry alone was responsible to God, in the last, the church as a whole was answerable.

The Erastians, like Grotius and Du Moulin, admitted the divinely ordained function ordered by the church in accordance with the divine law, and consequently recognised the spiritual power of the ministry; but they differentiated between the church as a natural association and its supernatural function. As a natural association, the church used a human judgment and human methods of government in all matters in which Christ had not clearly expressed His Will. In cases of dispute in the church, the divine law was not adequate and the decisions made by the majority involved a temporal mode of government which was the outcome of human organisation. Persuasion and conviction were the spiritual power of the ministers but the Law of Christ defined the divine function and not every necessity of church government. In so far as the church determined matters affecting its interests which had not been divinely determined, and decided by common deliberation the rules which should be observed for the common good and used penalties other than the spiritual censures, the church was not the divine community but a body held together by agreement under the law of nature.

The conception of the church held by the theorists of collegialism emphasised the contractual basis and the spontaneous character of its organisation, in consequence of which the church was empowered to determine all things concerning the sacred function of the ministry and the interests of the church. The divine mandate no longer circumscribed the sphere of the ministry but left to it that discretion and judgment needed in the organisation of the visible community. Christ's Spirit guided the church and His ministers in those ecclesiastical matters not defined in the Word, so that the church was no longer confined by God's Laws but was completely autonomous. Although it lacked that force characteristic of sovereignty, the church had full freedom to make rules which were enforced by the penalties upon which it agreed. Its independence was only qualified by its lack of those ultimate temporal means of coercion vested in the ruler.

Salmasius denied that the church was divine or that the sacred function and the holy rites were only efficacious in the hands of the ordained ministry. There was nothing of divine right to the church which was merely a human association for certain specific purposes. The visible church was no more holy and no more spiritual than the state. It was the invisible church which was the Kingdom of Christ, and the Holy Ghost which was of that Kingdom worked among and in men independently of human organisation. The final stage in the argument was the theory of Constans in which the church was a department of the state and external religion a matter for the ruler to regulate.

The relations between the church and the state turned upon the solutions given to certain problems involved in the conception of the church. First, in the Christian community was the true church alone to be permitted? Episcopius was the only one of these controversialists to question this principle. High-church and high-state thinkers alike believed in one true church which ought to be the national and only church; but in asserting this a number of subsidiary problems had to be met. Was the true church clearly defined in the Word? Again, was the ruler, who was the only means of preventing all other churches, to act upon his own judgment, and according to his convictions? If the church was corrupt, was it the ruler's duty to restore it to the purity of the Apostolic church and prevent further degeneration? When there was only one church, were not its penalties more than spiritual censure since they were followed by civil punishment? Was the ruler to sanction the majority decision of the church or to safeguard the minority, or to follow his own judgment according to the teaching of the Word? Moreover, since the church was to include all Christians, and therefore in a Christian community all members of the state, ought not the ruler to take care that no consciences were offended in matters which did not impugn the true faith and the Word of God?

Secondly, there was the dual nature of the church as a supernatural community inspired by the Spirit of Christ and ruled by the Law of God, and as a natural association, guided by human wisdom and using human means and methods of government. In its first capacity the church was unique and alone competent to act; according to the theologians by divine right, according to Grotius and Du Moulin as an expert body organised according to the social principle of the specialisation of function. In the second capacity, the church was like any other natural association because it used those means which were not spiritual but common to all groups of men. Collegialism alone held that the church in both capacities was autonomous; the other theories admitted in varying degrees and upon different principles the control of the ruler. In general the distinction was between those who held that the ruler who was a member of the church had a special and divine office to order by his sovereign power the organisation of the church as a human association, and those who held that by natural law the ruler had a certain final power over all human associations.

Closely related to this problem, were the proper distinctions which ought to be made between internal and external, spiritual and temporal, and ecclesiastical and civil. In collegialism internal, spiritual and ecclesiastical were identified and contrasted with the external, temporal and civil, in order to separate the visible church in every aspect from the state. To Constans the internal was that which each individual conscience held as holy, and the spiritual was those moral and religious influences which guided the conscience: so that the ecclesiastical was external and temporal, and in origin civil. Between these two extremes, there were a great number of variations, depending upon the degree to which the invisible church could be embodied in an earthly form. Salmasius believed that the Kingdom of Christ was the invisible church which was far different from the imperfect visible church; but he admitted that the external and ecclesiastical possessed a relatively though not absolutely spiritual character in so far as they were the instruments of the internal, i.e. the Holy Ghost. He did not, however, limit the operation of the Holy Ghost to the external and ecclesiastical order since the Spirit was wherever the mind of man was open to it. Vedelius also distinguished the ecclesiastical from the spiritual, the externally internal from the internal. The ecclesiastical, while not civil, was no more than the external order necessary for the means of grace in a Christian community. The Arminian thinkers separated the sacred function as internal and spiritual from the government of the church as ecclesiastical, external and temporal. Among the Contra-Remonstrants alone was there a confusion of thought and a failure to apply consistently the principles the theory adopted. They rejected the division of society into two, the spiritual and the temporal, because they denied that spiritual and temporal were wholly distinct, and because they held that the unity of society demanded that each should act in its own peculiar way upon the whole social structure. They identified the internal and spiritual with God's Grace and its works, and external and temporal with worldly force. But in the development of their theory, the Contra-Remonstrants interpreted the distinction between grace and force as the ecclesiastical and civil. They hesitated between the teaching of Calvin and example of Geneva in which the distinction between the external aspect of the church and the external order of social life was not sharply drawn, and the teaching of collegialism in which the church and all its interests were separated from the state. Their ultimate differentiation of internal and external depended upon an arbitrary division of the social order by revelation, instead of holding to their original doctrine that internal and external were the result of Grace and Force. Spiritual and temporal ceased to be the internal and external aspects of the one society and became the ecclesiastical and civil compartments in the one society.

The third problem was the nature of the church *sub cruce* and under the Christian magistrate. Early, these controversialists distinguished between the condition of the church where the ruler was hostile or indifferent and where it had to undertake its own organisation and government, and the nature of the church within the corpus christianum. Usually it was admitted that the ideal was the Christian society because the church no longer had to rely upon its own improvised and imperfect resources, but was then granted the fullness of the divine promise. Voetius, indeed, argued that since the church *sub cruce* had governed itself and created its own organisation, the Christian ruler had no right to interfere in its own administration but only to use his power to provide greater facilities and opportunities for the church to become more perfect. The opposite view held that the church *sub cruce* was only tolerated by the ruler and when he took it under his protection, its organisation was his duty: it had in either case no rights of self-government apart from his consent. The government of the church *sub cruce* was a matter of confederated discipline or constitutive rule under the law of nature, in common with all human groups, and such rights of government only continued until the ruler assumed his true responsibilities toward the church. In between these two views was the theological conception of the church in the Christian community, by which the church gained a divinely ordained protector in the Christian ruler. The church included the Christian ruler as an officer of God who was absent in the church *sub cruce* which on that account was imperfect. Of these theories only that of Voetius contemplated with equanimity the alternative of the church *sub cruce*.

The fourth problem was the conception of the Christian magistrate. Collegialism distinguished the magistrate and his office from the Christian and the member of the church. He had a political discretion independent of the church; but his conduct and faith were regulated by its judgment. Grotius and Uytenbogaert held that the power of the Christian ruler was that of the office and that his religion added nothing to his power. It was a power inherent in his office and, therefore, proper to all rulers,

Christian or otherwise. In this, both agreed with the argument of Voetius, but whereas his theory left to the ruler no part in church matters, they held, that all rulers had by natural law the power to regulate the human organisation of the church. The faith of the ruler did not add to his power but enabled him to use it according to the Will of God: the heathen ruler either knew not how to use this power or abused it. The theological conception was of a divinely ordained office with the duty of protecting the church and of enforcing the divine moral law. The ruler was the principal member of the church. Whatever he could contribute to the help of the church was to be done by him alone, and if he failed, no other body, not even the church itself, could assume the power to do it instead. Vedelius in particular stressed that the power of the Christian ruler was very different from that of the unorthodox, and that his orthodoxy added a new power in church matters to his original power in civil society.

Finally, there was the problem of the public and private church, or, from another point of view, of its compulsory and voluntary characters. The Arminians and particularly Episcopius insisted that since the church was a public organisation organised nationally through the ruler's sanction and active aid, all that was public was properly belonging to and derived from the ruler, and therefore ought to be recognised as directly or indirectly under his control, so far as he claimed this right. Episcopius made a most effective use of this point. He limited the degree of state control to the proportion of state establishment. The private or voluntary church was autonomous but subject in ordinary matters of civil law on account of its character as part of the state. The church as a voluntary association ought to be free to deter-mine its own forms and purposes so long as these did not conflict with the safety and welfare of the state and the system of law and order which protected the rights of all. But it was only in Episcopius that the private church was recognised as a voluntary society, and free. To the others, the public church was alone to be recognised and therefore possessed an involuntary character. It was the paradox of collegialism to found the autonomy of the public church upon its spontaneous, contractual and voluntary character; when it denounced the very condition of voluntariness, the right to secede and organise a new community. Dutch Calvinism failed to make a valid distinction between the church as a voluntary society and as the state organised ecclesiastically.

The two kingdoms, therefore, were interpreted in different forms. Some thinkers limited the spiritual kingdom to the inward working of the individual conscience and denied that it could ever find a collective expression. Others contrasted the visible and invisible church and denied that the Kingdom of Christ could be contained within the limits of one form of human organisation. A third school defined that Kingdom as the visible church which was in but not of the Kingdom of God, and therefore totally distinct. A fourth saw His Kingdom in the means of Grace by which salvation was granted to men. Finally, the Contra-Remonstrants limited Christ's Kingdom to the church of His own revelation as the organ of His Spirit, but at the same time held that the church as a national organisation grounded on the ruler's power was of the Kingdom of God.

The two kingdoms were generally interpreted as the special kingdom of Christ, which might be the individual conscience, the invisible church, the mission of grace or the visible church; and the general kingdom of God which was either the theological conception of the community ruled by God's Law or the natural law conception of the state, enhanced in some cases by a divine right.

The issue between the Contra-Remonstrants and the Arminians was not of the separation of the church and state, since both accepted the ideal of their interdependence; but whether the ruler alone was responsible to God for the religious order in his kingdom or whether the ministers were not indeed guided by the Law of God and the Spirit of Christ, and thus independent of the ruler. Both admitted that the Christian revelation was beyond human control. Both admitted that the ruler was bound to use his sovereign power to establish the true church alone in his kingdom, and that he was alone responsible to God for the use of coercive powers in the church. Both also admitted that the ruler could not usurp the function and ministry of the church. To both, the ruler's office was divinely ordained, not only for civil matters, but for the ordering of the church itself. The problem was whether the ministers could have any independent judgment in church matters or only that spiritual power without any discretion which their ordination conferred upon them as the legates of Christ. Arminian theory was both logical and intelligible, while it was by no means an absolutist ideal; but Contra-Remonstrant theory was inconsistent and unintelligible. It either admitted too much to the Arminians to be logical or admitted too little of what it really claimed on behalf of the church to be intelligible.

The issue in the second controversy was much clearer and the arguments more logical. Was the church completely independent of the state in all matters affecting its own administration, and upon what grounds could this claim be substantiated? Collegialism argued that the church was organised on a voluntary basis by a contract between its members. Its critics denied that the church as an association of the members of the state was independent of the ruler's authority. In both cases the argument had passed beyond the Calvinist belief in a specific revelation regulating both church and state which Vedelius had attempted to recast.

Two doctrines emerged from these controversies with some significance for the future. The first was the theory of toleration formulated by Episcopius which not only defended freedom of thought upon the ground that the ruler's power was incapable of convincing men of the Truth, and, therefore, that persecution was morally unjustifiable, but also demanded freedom to worship God in common and in private according to one's convictions, as a civil right. The second was the conception of the state held by the later Calvinists as a human organisation for strictly material ends. It was limited to its political and civil purpose. Principles of utility and expediency were necessarily admitted to be the determinants of its policy.

The common characteristic of these controversies was the gradual eclipse of the theological conceptions of the state by theories resting upon natural law, although the two elements were by no means exclusive of each other. In Grotius and particularly in Du Moulin, both ideas were apparent, while in Salmasius the natural law theory was predominant and in Constans exclusive. The theory of collegialism represented the triumph of natural law in Calvinist speculation. The problem ceased to be one of the sect-church and the corpus christianum and became instead the problem of sovereignty in relation to the church as an association. In proportion as the supernatural ideal waned, the conception of both state and church as associations formed according to the law of nature grew stronger. The fundamental issue in dispute had been the supernatural and natural character of the church; the one immutable, the other determined by human reason; the one of revelation, the other of organisation according to immediate needs of time and place. In so far as controversy revealed the weakness of theories resting upon revelation, the debate shifted to the authority by which the church was organised and governed. To those theorists who emphasised the unique character of sovereignty, the church as a natural association derived its authority from agreement according to the law of nature, but since that agreement was governed by the agreement creating political society, the authority of the church was subject to the sovereignty of the state; and in so far as the church could compel or govern by the threat or implied use of coercion, its power was delegated by the sovereign. The extreme Calvinists saw no safeguard for the spiritual mission of the church unless it was as an association autonomous, and the theory of collegialism resorted to the contract which natural law embodied to free the church entirely from the state. The emphasis upon sovereignty qualified the contractual origin of the church but did not reject it; only in the theory of Constans was the church reduced to a department of state and denied any independent origin.

This decline in the influence of the theological theories was due to the evident failure of Scriptural theology to meet the vicissitudes of social life. The tradition of Calvin was doctrinaire and fantastic; and its influence tended to distort the nature and function of the state, turning it away from the sphere of natural life and public welfare to the application of the divine sovereignty and the enforcement of the moral law. Thus, the relations of church and state were falsified from the beginning. But the course of the Dutch controversies and the policy of the Dutch church revealed the inherent desire of the church for autonomy, which resisted the logical development of Calvin's theory and tended to define the nature and purpose of the state more in terms of human life than of religious ideals. The separation of church and state made by the later Calvinists was not only the culmination of this movement but a reaction from the political principles of the Reformation. In the high-state thinkers there survived much of the Reformers' thought, particularly of the nature of sovereignty and law, but the state was understood to be not so much God's community, as a human association according to the law of nature with the unique power of sovereignty by which all other associations might be regulated. The ideal was not one of clerical orthodoxy but of freeing the Christian revelation by controlling the church. Nevertheless, the development of the ideal justified de Lagarde's criticism that the teaching of Luther and Zwingli gave to the state a spiritual function which would survive when the gospel ideal was neglected. These controversies, therefore, illustrate the development of biblical theories into natural law theories, both by reaction on the part of Calvinism and by adaptation on the part of its critics.

APPENDIX

BRITAIN AND THE DUTCH
CONTROVERSIES

IT is interesting to note that there was some connection between
these Dutch controversialists and Scottish and English
writers. It would have been more surprising if there had not
been a certain mutual exchange of ideas considering the number
of contacts between the two countries.[1]

Baillie's *Journals and Letters*[2] illustrate the channels of communication and Scottish interest in the works of Voetius and
Apollonius, particularly after the Westminster Assembly had
shown the strength of the Independents and the lawyers. Through
Spang, Baillie was in touch with both, and with many other
prominent divines. In that way, Baillie obtained[3] official letters
from the Synod of Zeeland and the Classis of Walcheren to the
Westminster Assembly in favour of the Calvinist church government; but failed to obtain any satisfactory replies from the
Theological Faculties of Leiden and Utrecht. He had to be
content with the book of Apollonius against the Independents.

Moreover, Spang[4] sent to Baillie various Dutch works for the
benefit of the College, and "a new peace of that Erastianism"
against Larenus, which was evidently one of the pamphlets in
defence of the *Grallae*. Baillie[5] asked Spang to send copies of
Revius, Cabeljavius and Maccovius, the first two being critics and
the third a champion of Vedelius. He asked[6] at another time for
Voetius' *Theses de Episcopis et Presbyteris*, since the Westminster
Assembly was in a "pitifull labyrinth" about the office of ruling
elders. He sent[7] his own *Dissuasive* to Apollonius, Voetius and
Spanheim.

[1] Cf. "Scotland and the Synod of Dort", by Prof. G. D. Henderson in
vol. XXIV (New Series), *Nederlandsch Archief voor Kerkgeschiedenis*.
[2] Edited D. Lang (Edinburgh, 1841), 3 vols.
[3] *Ib.* II, 165, 174, 180.
[4] *Ib.* III, 70; cf. II, 72.
[5] *Ib.* II, 371.
[6] *Ib.* II, 111, 115.
[7] *Ib.* II, 327.

It is also clear that Baillie was by no means in agreement with the Dutch divines. Not only were the Dutch professors loth to commit themselves to support him in his exposition of Presbyterian principles, but Baillie[1] had to urge Spang to warn Dr Stewart "to keep his colleagues silent, if they be not willing to declare flatlie against all the branches of Independencie, as Apollonius and Spanheim has done, and for the rooting out of all kinde of Episcopacie, according to our Covenant". He expressed considerable (though private) dissatisfaction with Voetius' *Theses of Presbyteries and Synods*: "in the manner, I think he is obscure, with a multitude of needless distractions and long involved discourses; in the matter, he sticks so to Parker's grounds of mutuall association and *ecclesia prima* that I wish he had written nothing in this purpose; but this to you onlie."[2] He explained the consequence of this congregational principle of Voetius as detrimental to Scottish tradition. "Many besides the Independents, by Voetius' writes, are brought to give the rights of both these actions (e.g. ordination and excommunication) to the congregational presbytery, much against our mind and practice."[3]

In two works of George Gillespie, a knowledge of these Dutch writers was admitted. *Aaron's Rod Blossoming*[4] gave as the chief critics of Erastus and his disciples the names and works of Walaeus, Triglandius, Revius, Apollonius, Cabeliavius, Voetius in his *Politica Ecclesiastica* together with Acronius "who were champions against that unhappy error revived in the Low-Countries by Utenbogard a Proselyte of the Arminians". In one passage,[5] Gillespie acknowledged his debt to Rivetus. The second of his books—*A Treatise of Miscellany Questions*—begins[6] with an indirect reference to the *Grallae*. "That which hath long lurked in the hearts of many Atheists, is now professed and argued for, by that fierce furious *Erastiane*, whose book was published the last year at Franeker." Finally, another of Gillespie's books—*CXI Propositions concerning the Ministerie and Government of the Church*—was delegated by the General Assembly to Baillie and Gillespie[7] "at Voetius' motion", although it was left to Gillespie

---

[1] *Journals and Letters*, II, 288.   [2] *Ib.* II, 65.
[3] *Ib.* II, 205; cf. II, 240.   [4] 1646 edit. 167.   [5] 263 (misprinted 262).
[6] Cf. also ch. 3.   [7] Letters etc. *op. cit.* III, 20.

to complete this task. In the *Politica Ecclesiastica*,[1] the letter of Gillespie accompanying the *Propositions* and the official report of the Theological Faculty of Utrecht, were both given.

Finally, Samuel Rutherford made many references to Dutch writers. According to Baillie, he was offered, by the influence of Voetius, the opportunity "to be Professor of Divinity and the Hebrew tonge in the new University of Harderwick".[2] His reputation rested not upon his English works but upon the "Latin treatise against the Jesuites and Arminians". His *Pretended Liberty of Conscience* was an attack upon the Independents, and upon the writings of Episcopius in defence of the Remonstrants.[3] In *The Divine Right of Church Government and Excommunication*,[4] Rutherford revealed a great attachment to the works of Triglandius, while mentioning the works of other Dutch Calvinists and of the chief Erastians.

Among English writers, there was little reference to the Dutch authorities. The fact that the *De Imperio* and the *Grallae* were each published in translation, and that many of the Dutch writings were in the libraries of contemporary English clerics, suggests that there was some interest in Dutch problems.

Baxter made frequent reference to the *De Imperio*, and in the *Difference between the Power of Magistrates and Church Pastors* he was outspoken in his praise of Grotius, "Grotius de Imperio summarum potestatum circa sacra hath said so much and so well of all this controversie, that it is a shame to us all that we need any more......—and to any one to cloud that which he hath clearly and judiciously stated".[5]

Stillingfleet's *Irenicum* was in the same tradition as the *De Imperio*, and testified to the greatness of its thought and the extent of its influence. But he also made some reference[6] to Vedelius as a suggestive, if somewhat extreme, thinker.

Finally[7] Philip Nye, one of the five Holland Ministers, and a leader of the Independents at the Westminster Assembly, appealed to the disputes of Voetius in defence of the Independent theory of church government.

[1] I, 246.   [2] Letters etc. *op. cit.* III, 82.
[3] 125; cf. 321.   [4] 560.
[5] 33: Article 31.   [6] 47: for reference to Grotius, *passim.*
[7] *The Lawfulness of the Oath of Supremacy* (London, 1683), 40, 41, 63.

BIBLIOGRAPHY

ACRONIUS, R. *Nootwendich Vertooch....* Delf, 1610.

ALLEN, J. W. *History of Political Thought in the Sixteenth Century.* London, 1928.

APOLLONIUS, G. *Jus Majestatis circa sacra....* Medioburgi Zelandorum, 1642–3.

BLOK, P. J. *History of the People of the Netherlands.* (4 vols.) New York, 1898.

BONNARD, A. *Thomas Éraste et la discipline ecclésiastique.* Lausanne, 1894.

BRANDT, G. *The History of the Reformation...in and about the Low Countries,* translated by John Chamberlayne. (4 vols.) London, 1720.

BUCER, G. *Diss. de Gubernatione Ecclesiae....* Middelburgi Zelandorum, 1618.

BURIGNY, J. L. DE. *Vie de Grotius.* Paris, 1752.

CALDER, F. *Memoirs of Simon Episcopius.* London, 1835.

COHEN, G. *Les Écrivains français en Hollande dans la première moitié du XVIIe siècle.* Paris, 1920.

CONSTANS, L. A. *De Jure Ecclesiasticorum, Liber Singularis.* Alethopoli, 1665.

CRAMER, J. A. *De theol. faculteit te Utrecht ten tijd v. Voetius.* Utrecht, 1932.

DUKER, A. C. *Gisbertus Voetius.* Leiden, 1897–1915.

EEKHOF, A. *De theologische faculteit te Leiden in de 17e Eeuw.* Utrecht, 1921.

EPISCOPIUS, S. *Opera Theologica.* Tom. 1 (editio secunda). London, 1678.

—— *Pars Altera* (editio prima). Roterod. 1665.

FIGGIS, J. N. *Studies of Political Thought from Gerson to Grotius.* Cambridge, 1916.

GLASIUS, B. *Godgeleerd Nederland, Biographisch woordenboek.* 1852–56.

GOMARUS, F. *Waerschouwinghe over de Vermaninghe aen R. Donteclock....* Leyden, 1609.

GROTIUS, H. *Ordinum Hollandiae...Pietas Vindicata.* 1613.

—— *Apologeticus eorum qui Hollandiae...praefuerunt.* Parisiis, 1622.

—— *De Imperio summarum potestatum circa sacra.* 1647.

—— *H. Grotius of the authority of the highest powers about sacred things; or, the right of the state in the church......*Put into English by C. B[arksdale], M.A. London, 1651.

HAAR, H. W., TER. *Jacobus Trigland.* 's Gravenhage, 1891.

HAENTJENS, A. H. *Simon Episcopius.* Leiden, 1899.

HARRISON, A. W. *The Beginnings of Arminianism.* London, 1926.

HONDERS, H. J. *Andreas Rivetus.* Hague, 1930.

HOOIJER, C. *Oude Kerkordeningen der Nederlandsche Hervormde gemeenten 1563–1638.* Zalt-Bommel, 1865.

ITTERZON, G. P. VAN. *Franciscus Gomarus.* Hague, 1930.

JUNIUS, F. *Verclaringhe van twee vraghen....De eerste, Van de over-een-cominghe ende het onderscheyt der Politijcke ende Kerckelijcke bedieninghe. De tweede van het Recht des Magistraets in de sichtbare Kercke.* Amsterdam, 1610.

KNAPPERT, L. *Geschiedenis der Nederlandsche Hervormde Kerk.* Amsterdam, 1911–12.

KNIGHT, W. S. M. *The Life and Works of Hugo Grotius.* London, 1925.

KNIPSCHEER. *Henricus Leo.* Huis ter Heide, 1929.

KUYPER, A., Jr. *Johannes Maccovius.* Leiden, 1899.

LAGARDE, G. DE. *Recherches sur l'esprit politique de la réforme.* Paris, 1926.

LEIDEN, The Theological Faculty of. *Synopsis purioris Theologiae.* Ed. 3, 1642.

—— *Censure...vande Professoren der Theologie...over de belijdenisse ...van't gevoelen der...Remonstranten, door A. Walaeum...in de Nederduytsche Sprake uytgegeven.* Leyden, 1627.

MARONIER, J. H. *Jacobus Arminius.* Amsterdam, 1905.

MEYJES, P. *J. Revius.* Amsterdam, 1895.

MOULIN, LOUIS DU. *Paraenesis ad aedificatores imperii in imperio....* London, 1656.

—— *Corollarium ad Paraenesim....* London, 1657.

—— *Of the Right of Churches, and of the Magistrates Power over them.* London, 1658.

—— *Papa Ultrajectinus* (under the pseudonym Ludiomaeus Colvinus). London, 1668.

Nederlandsch Archief voor Kerkgeschiedenis onder redactie van Dr A. Eekhof en Dr J. Lindeboom. Vol. XXIV, New Series.

Nieuw Nederlandisch Biografisch Woordenboek.

PAQUOT, J. N. *Mémoires pour servir à l'Histoire littéraire des dix-sept Provinces des Pays-Bas.* Louvain, 1763.

REITSMA, J. *Geschiedenis van de Hervorming en de Hervormde Kerk der Nederlanden.* 4th edit. Utrecht, 1933.

REVIUS, J. *Examen Dissertationis D. Nicolai...Vedelii.* Amsterdam, 1642.

RIVETUS, A. Operum tom. primum, Roterod. 1651–60. *Praelectiones Pleniores in Cap. xx. Exodi in quibus ita explicatur Decalogus....*

ROGGE, H. C. *Johannes Uytenbogaert in zijn gevoelen aangaande de Magt der Overheden in Kerkelijke zaken, tegenover zijne bestrijders;* in *Nieuwe Jaarboeken voorwetenschappelijke Theologie.* Vols. I, II. Utrecht, 1858–63.

—— *Johannes Wtenbogaert en zijn Tijd.* Amsterdam, 1874–76.

SALMASIUS. *Grallae, seu vere puerilis cothurnus sapientiae*...Franeker 1646; translated as, *The supreame power of Christian states vindicated against the insolent pretences of Guillielmus Apollonii, or a translation of a book...intituled, Grallae....* London [1647], Brit. Mus. Thomason Tracts.

SEPP, CHR. *Het Godgeleerd Onderwijs in Nederland gedurende de 16e en 17e eeuw.* Leiden, 1873–74.

TIDEMAN, J. *De Stichting der Remonstrantsche Broederschap.* 1619–34. Amsterdam, 1871, 72.

TRIGLANDIUS, J. *Antwoorde op Dry Vraghen.* Amsterdam, 1615.

—— *Verdedigingh van de Leere end' Eere der Ghereformeerde Kerken ende Leeraren....* Amsterdam, 1616.

—— *Christelijcke ende Vriendelijcke Vermaninge....* Amsterdam, 1628.

—— *Dissertatio Theologica de civili et ecclesiastica potestate et utriusque ad se invicem tum Subordinatione, tum Coordinatione.* Amsterdam, 1642.

TROELTSCH, E. *The Social Teaching of the Christian Churches.* Transl. Olive Wyon, London, 1931.

UYTENBOGAERT, J. *Tractaet van't Ampt ende Authoriteyt eener hooger Christelijcker Overheydt in Kerckelycke Saecken....* 3rd edit. Rotterdam, 1647.

VEDELIUS, N. *De Episcopatu Constantini Magni....* Delf, 1661.

VISSER, J. TH. DE. *Kerk en Staat.* Leiden, 1926.

VOETIUS, G. *Selectt. Disputt. Theol. in Acad. Ultraj....* Ultraj. 1636–44.

—— *Politica Ecclesiastica.* Amsterdam, 1663–76.

VOSSIUS, G. J. *Dissertatio Epistolica de jure magistratus in rebus ecclesiasticis.* Amsterdam, 1669.

WALAEUS, A. *De Munere Ministrorum Ecclesiae et inspectione magistr. circa illud;* in *Opera omnia.* Lugduni Batavorum, 1647, 48.

WIJMINGA, P. J. *Festus Hommius.* Leiden, 1899.

WIJNGAARDEN, J. D. DE LIND VAN. *Antonius Walaeus.* Leiden, 1891.

INDEX

PRINTED BY W. LEWIS, M.A., AT THE UNIVERSITY PRESS, CAMBRIDGE

DATE DUE

MAY 20 76			